MG Sports Cars

MG Sports Cars

Compiled by Peter Garnier
from the archives of
Autocar

St. Martin's Press
New York

First published in the United States of America in 1979

Originally published in Great Britain by
The Hamlyn Publishing Group Limited
London · New York · Sydney · Toronto
Astronaut House, Feltham, Middlesex, England

This edition published by
St. Martin's Press/New York

Library of Congress Cataloging in Publication Data

Main entry under title:

MG sports cars.

   Includes index.
   1. M.G. automobile. I. Garnier, Peter.
II. The Autocar.
TL215.M2M16   629.22'22   78-65889
ISBN 0-312-50156-0

Printed in Great Britain

CONTENTS

SAFETY FAST
Britain's best-loved sports cars, described through the pages of *Autocar*

Thousands of words have been written by hundreds of authors in an attempt to define the sports car. Apart from one or two unsporting vehicles forced by insensitive management to wear the octagonal badge, one of the simplest ways to explain 'sports car' is to point at any two-seater MG. Few MGs have been anything other than sports cars first and foremost; that marque, more than any other in the British Leyland empire, will always be associated with sports cars.

MG cars occupy a unique position in motoring; they have not always been the fastest, the most technically advanced or the most glamorous of cars, even if some outstanding feats of racing and record-breaking were achieved by MGs before the Second World War. Yet, out of a somewhat prosaic beginning came a series of cars which were the ultimate ambition of many a young man pining for something more dashing than the family car which was so often his four-wheeled destiny. There has nearly always been an MG cheap enough for him to achieve his ambition and even to give him a taste of competitive motoring if he fancied it.

William Morris began his remarkable career repairing and then building bicycles and (later) motor bikes. Disused stables in Longwall Street, Oxford, provided his workshops. By 1911, he had turned his attention to motor cars, selling various makes from the same premises, now rebuilt and called The Morris Garage. Further expansion and new premises made the title plural—The Morris Garages—and the first Morris was actually assembled there.

Morris himself became engrossed in production of his new Oxford car, undertaken at an old school in Cowley, and he put The Morris Garages under a manager. In 1922, this position was occupied by Cecil Kimber, an energetic man who, as well as running the firm, set about designing special bodywork for Morris chassis.

The name MG first appeared in 1923, when Kimber drove a re-bodied Morris Cowley, prepared by The Morris Garages, on the Land's End Trial, winning a 'Gold'. This car was the real prototype MG, rather than the famous, pointed-tail two-seater which appeared in 1925 and is now known as "Old Number One".

A year later, in 1924, Kimber took a new, 1.8 litre, six-cylinder Oxford and turned it into the MG Super Sports, with a lightly-tuned engine, improved handling and a handsome aluminium body. Backed by Morris reliability and service, the MG was a great success. When Morris went over to a flat radiator in place of the old 'bull-nose' for 1927, Kimber followed suit. By this time, he was calling his car the 14/40hp, because of its increased power compared with the standard Oxford's 14/28hp.

It was at the 1928 Motor Show that the first true production MG Six made its debut, with the 2.4 litre, 60 bhp, Morris ohc engine. Based on the Morris Six, Kimber designed for it a completely new cylinder block and head, a light body and a high axle ratio and called it the MG Mk1 18/80hp. The result pleased the customers in numbers large enough to warrant building an additional factory. Around 2,000 had been turned out by 1929, when what was now the MG Car Company moved to Abingdon—their home ever since.

During their first year at Abingdon, MG introduced the Midget, based on the 847cc Morris Minor. The chassis and engine were retained, with very little alteration other than lowering the suspension and improving the steering. The little fabric-bodied, pointed-tail, two-seater M-Type, with its engine tuned to provide 20 bhp, good acceleration and a top speed of 65 mph, was Britain's first really cheap and practical sports car.

MG went racing in 1930, their competition cars using superchargers and various other special parts, but retaining many components from the road cars. Development began with the Double-Twelve M-Type, named after the factory team of M-Types had won the team prize at the Brooklands Double Twelve Hours race in 1930. The following year, a special MG became the first 750cc car to exceed 100 mph, and the racing and record-breaking continued until interrupted by the Second World War, with competition innovations constantly finding their way onto the road cars to prove that racing does improve the breed.

It is difficult, in these days of commonplace 100 mph family saloons, to imagine what great fun these early MGs provided. Though their maximum speed was not much more than 70 mph, at least one was allowed to use it and they were essentially *drivers'* cars with their excellent driving position, their stubby, remote-control gear levers only a couple of inches from the driver's left hand, their extensive instrumentation and their well-placed controls. Somehow, they represented a piece of machinery, as distinct from mere transport; their styling, with a strap round the bonnet, wire stone-guards over the lamps,

Still bearing the Morris Oxford badge on its "bull-nose" radiator, this 1.8 litre tourer with special bodywork was effectively the first ever MG. It was subsequently re-named the MG Super Sports.

aero screens and suchlike, made them pure 'Le Mans'.

Looking back on the 1930s, one finds it difficult to recall an event in which MG sports cars were not prominent in one form or another. Although the Bugattis and the Alfa Romeos were there for those who could afford them, it was the ubiquitous MG that put many hundreds of ordinary enthusiasts into all forms of motor sport, very often bringing them success against far more expensive opposition. One saw on the roads every kind of MG, from the sporting saloons to out-and-out racing cars like the K3 Magnettes. They were, somehow, the very personification of the fun and competition of motoring.

This image has remained with the marque right into the 1970s, despite legislative attempts to deface the cars with unsightly bumpers and handling deficiencies imposed by ride-height regulations. A brief introduction such as this does not allow space for the whole story, but the staff of *Autocar* have described and tested MG sports cars throughout the company's life, while also covering much of the marque's competition and record-breaking activity. Something of the appeal of an MG can be sensed from the articles which follow, most of them road tests with some cutaway drawings by the late Max Millar, and some evocative photographs from the unrivalled historic files of *Autocar*. There is the original, M-Type Midget—"An Extraordinarily Fascinating Little Car: Comfort at Speed"—which obviously appealed to the magazine's staff in 1929, who also described it as "the infant phenomenon". Then comes the beautifully businesslike Montlhéry Midget of 1931, a supercharged 750 which returned an impressive 88 mph. And the famous J2 Midget of 1932 which, through no fault of the magazine or of their test driver, Sammy Davis, went much faster than it ought to have done—to the deserved embarrassment of its makers.

There are nostalgic memories of driving an MG during the Second World War on limited supplies of low-octane petrol, and the material continues right up to the latest MGB GT which, according to the *Autocar* report, "remains pleasant to drive, easy to service and maintain, with classically sporting lines and predictable handling".

Thanks to the sturdiness of the reputation of MG built up by the various people at Abingdon over the years, the MG is still the most popular British sports car and amongst the most popular in the World.

The name behind it all—Cecil Kimber. As sales manager of The Morris Garages in 1922, he started the whole MG cult, later directing the MG Car Company. He is seen here with his own, specially modified, supercharged, six-cylinder car, which was also used for experimental work by the factory.

More than 40 years after its creation, this J2 Midget (now supercharged) continues to give pleasure in the manner for which it was intended. Roy Newton—its owner—is seen making one of the very few clean climbs of Cutliffe Lane on the 1972 Land's End Trial.

A SIX-CYLINDER M.G.

Sports Car with Many Interesting Mechanical Features.

THE latest model M.G. is an entire departure from previous practice in a very interesting manner. The engine is the Morris six-cylinder of 69×110 mm., which has a capacity of 2,468 c.c. It has an overhead camshaft, which, by the way, is an interesting point for this type of engine, designed to be produced in considerable quantities, forced lubrication, and an immense crankshaft held by massive bearings in a cast-iron crank case, the whole being just about as stiff as can be imagined; stiffness in these parts is three-quarters of the secret of success of the modern six-cylinder engine.

The clutch, the gear box (with its central control), and the transmission as a unit are also Morris, but—and this is where the interest of the latest M.G. arises—these units are assembled in a new frame of M.G. design.

Now the M.G. is a sports car, and the difficulty hitherto has been to adapt for this special purpose units and details of a chassis designed originally for a totally different purpose. Obviously the high performance necessary for a sports car, as distinct from a touring model, involves a lot of detail alteration, and detail alteration is hampered considerably by the necessity of using already existing parts.

Accordingly, for next year the frame has been designed entirely for sports car work, and, as the illustrations show, the side members are not only massive in themselves, but are very rigidly tied together by cross-members, of which one, near the centre of the frame, is a four-sided box girder—probably the stiffest type known.

Either side of the box girder

SPECIFICATION.

ENGINE : 17.7 h.p., six cylinders, 69 × 110 mm. (2,468 c.c.). Tax £18. Overhead valves and camshaft, detachable head, coil ignition.

TRANSMISSION : Three-speed and reverse gear box in unit with the engine.

SUSPENSION : Half-elliptic springs.

BRAKES : On all four wheels.

WHEELS : Wire detachable. Tyres 28× 4.95 in.

WHEELBASE : 9 ft. 6 in. Track, 4 ft.

WEIGHT : 24 cwt. 2 qr.

PRICE (provisional) : £425, Four-seater.

The chassis, showing the box girder construction.

2½-Litre Model with Special Box Girder Frame.

the frame is extended by wide webs, and there are additional webs also on either side of the front cross-member just below the radiator, while the forward cross tube between the dumbiron is splined at each end into bosses. Thus the frame has been made rigid, and by its rigidity prevents movement between the components, the other method of dealing with the same problem being to allow the frame to whip, but to isolate the power unit so that the effect of such whip is not apparent.

Then the brake mechanism is also of new design, and every care has been taken to prevent lost motion and to make the brake pedal feel as though it were directly attached to the cams without whip or delay. To do this the two brake cross tubes are of large diameter, and all the levers in the brake actuation are triangular, instead of being the usual comparatively thin stamping, which in itself is liable to whip.

Of compensation there is none, the designers believing that the most effective form of brakes has the minimum number of parts, and an independent adjustment for each pair of shoes, as well as a single adjustment below the floorboards to take up all four sets of shoes simultaneously. Servo shoes—that is, shoes which tend to put themselves on further when applied to the brake drum, are used for the front axle, the axle beam being really stiff and strong. Extra shoes in the rear drums are operated by a lever on the right-hand side of the driver; this lever stays in position only if the trigger is depressed, an idea that has come from racing practice, and possesses great advantages.

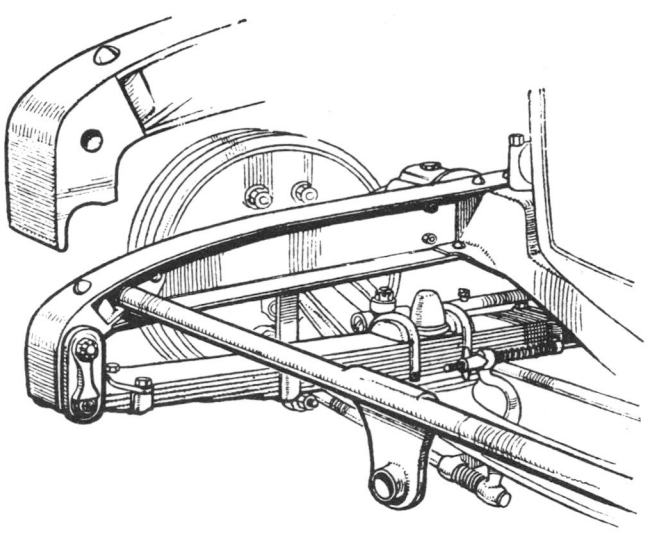

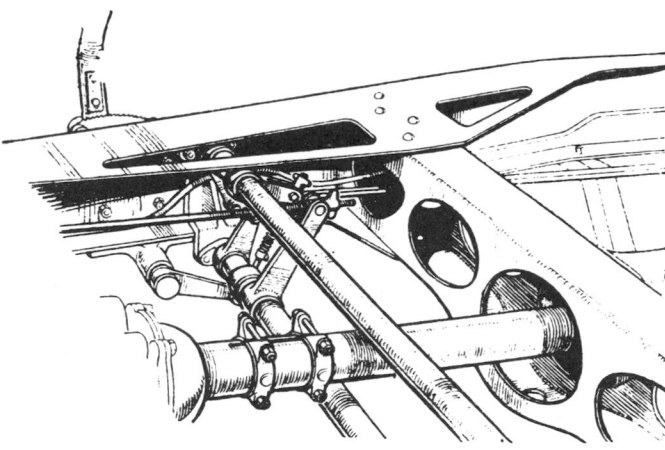

Brake cross-shafts and box section cross-members of the frame.

The method of steadying the spring shackle on the dumbirons.

Marles steering gear is standard, the steering gear box being held on the frame by two bronze blocks, of which the upper is rigid and the lower can be adjusted by two bolts, so as to grip the steering gear effectively at the frame end, the upper end being secured by a bracket from the dashboard a little below the spring-spoked steering wheel. Castor action for the steering, which is an important point in a sports car, is obtained by canting the front axle through the medium of adjustable wedges.

The springs are wide, and in front are canted to slope from the front dumb irons towards the rear, another interesting feature being that the dumbirons act as guides to the side plates of the shackle, the shackle being in front of the spring, thus assisting greatly in preventing side sway. The shackle in front brings the centre of movement of the front axle, which is the rear anchorage of the front spring, nearer to the drop arm, and therefore reduces the automatic movement of the steering wheel as the tyres pass over inequalities in the road.

A new radiator of unusual design is mounted on trunnions in front of the frame, and between the rear cross-mem-

Auto-pulse fuel feed pump located under the rear seat.

bers is a big fuel tank with two vent pipes and its filler on the right-hand side, free from interference from luggage, and at the same time out of the way of the exhaust pipe running along the left side

of the chassis. Above the tank is a tool box, and over that again on the finished car, either open or closed, is the fabric suitcase carrier.

Fuel is fed to the two S.U. carburetters by an electrically operated diaphragm pump combined with a glass bowl filter, and placed near the fuel tank itself, so as to deaden the clicking noise noticeable when the pump is operating. Both pump and filter can be reached after raising the rear seat cushion.

On the dashboard is a two-gallon spare fuel tank feeding by gravity when required, together with a tank for spare oil and the apparatus for upper cylinder lubrication, that feeds oil through the carburetters to the combustion space. In the latest engines the two carburetters are mounted on the left side, just above the exhaust branches.

There are two standard bodies, a fabric saloon and an open four-seater. The saloon has adjustable front seats, a one-piece windscreen that opens entirely, and an armrest between the two rear seats, sufficient leg room for the rear passengers being provided by sinking wells in the floorboards, which pass slightly underneath the front seats.

The new car is a great improvement on the old one, is beautifully sprung, holds the road well, has very powerful brakes, and, by reason of the six-cylinder engine, is quiet and very smooth. At the moment the provisional price of the saloon is £525, and of the four-seater £425.

The new M.G. chassis is exceedingly handsome and clean in design.

"THE AUTOCAR" ROAD TESTS

No. 61.—M.G. MIDGET TWO-SEATER

An Extraordinarily Fascinating Little Car: Comfort at Speed.

NOT only has the M.G. Midget a fascinating appearance, but it goes so exceedingly well. Sixty to sixty-five miles an hour with it are not adventure but delight. It sits down on the road like a thoroughbred and at high speed feels more like a big car than a tiny one. Nor does it fuss when travelling quickly.

All cars seem to have a speed to which a sensitive driver settles down automatically. Some call it the "cruising speed," others the "kindest" speed. On the Midget this speed is 50 m.p.h. However, too much stress must not be laid upon the upper end of the performance scale, although for its size the car is decidedly fast, for there is plenty of flexibility, and on top gear it is possible to crawl along in traffic behind a slow-moving vehicle and get away quite smoothly again. In this respect the redoubtable S.U. carburetter and the battery ignition play their parts. Acceleration on top gear from very low speeds is notable for its smoothness more than for its rapidity, though the latter is pretty useful.

From 25 m.p.h. onwards on top gear acceleration is very brisk, while on second gear the little car fairly leaps away, as the figures in the table show. The gear change needs knowing. Changing is not difficult to accomplish after a little practice, but at first the shortness of the gear lever and the short travel of the clutch pedal are disconcerting. The clutch takes up the drive smoothly, and at the end of an hour one is accustomed to the process.

The speeds claimed by the makers for the various gears are, on first 20, second 40, and top 60 m.p.h. The claims are modest and the car will exceed these figures quite easily, though at 25 on bottom gear and at 45 m.p.h. on second there is a period of valve bounce. Although the exhaust has

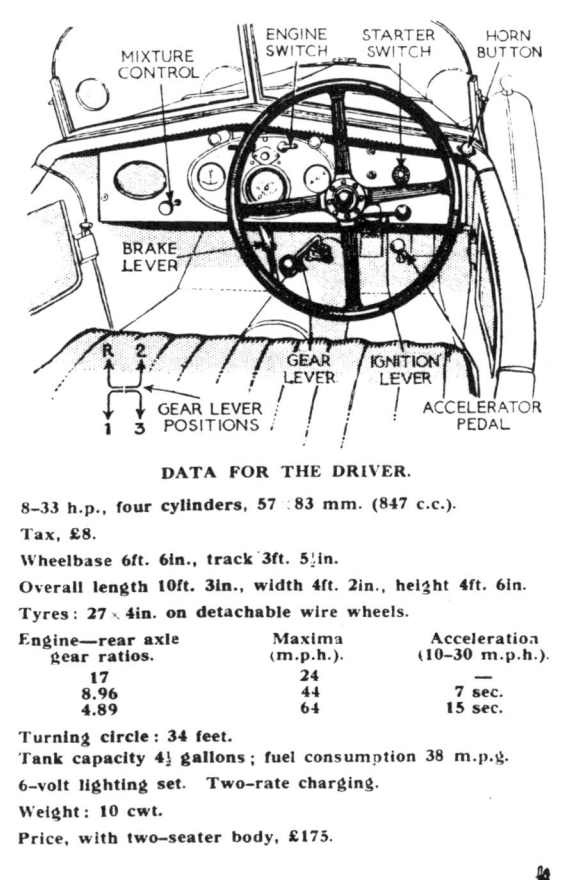

DATA FOR THE DRIVER.

8–33 h.p., four cylinders, 57 : 83 mm. (847 c.c.).

Tax, £8.

Wheelbase 6ft. 6in., track 3ft. 5½in.

Overall length 10ft. 3in., width 4ft. 2in., height 4ft. 6in.

Tyres: 27 × 4in. on detachable wire wheels.

Engine—rear axle gear ratios.	Maxima (m.p.h.).	Acceleration (10–30 m.p.h.).
17	24	—
8.96	44	7 sec.
4.89	64	15 sec.

Turning circle: 34 feet.

Tank capacity 4½ gallons; fuel consumption 38 m.p.g.

6–volt lighting set. Two–rate charging.

Weight: 10 cwt.

Price, with two–seater body, £175.

24 FEET *from* 25 M.P.H
7·2 FEET *from* 40 M.P.H

" THE AUTOCAR " ROAD TESTS

a fairly healthy crackle when the throttle is wide open, the car itself is not unduly noisy; there are no annoying mechanical sounds, and the indirect gears do not shout about their work.

When the car is bowling along at 20 or so in the streets of a town the wary policeman is more interested in the look of the car than in the noise it is making. In confined spaces the Midget is very easy to manœuvre, for the steering is light and quick, and one can twist and turn rapidly through traffic. At high speed on the open road the car can be steered comfortably with one hand. It is very steady even over poor surfaces, really remarkably so in view of its small size.

Where the Infant Shines.

It is perhaps on hills that this infant phenomenon really excels. It will shoot up a straight 1 in 10 grade on top gear. One particular hill of this kind was approached at 52 m.p.h. and crested at 33 m.p.h. on top. Another 1 in 10 gradient, with a sharp turn at the foot which quite precludes a rush being made, was very nearly climbed on top. Steeper hills of the type which reach a maximum of 1 in 6 served to show up a surprisingly vivid second gear. They were surmounted on second at speeds varying between 32 and 38 m.p.h. This car is most excellent at hill-climbing.

Petrol consumption on a car of this nature depends very largely upon the way in which it is handled and the speed at which it is driven. The makers claim that the consumption lies between 37 and 45 m.p.g., according to circumstances. Over a run of 60 miles, including one or two hills, and driving fairly fast, the consumption worked out at 38 m.p.g., which is an economical figure in view of the liveliness of the car.

Not the least satisfactory feature is the brakes. They are effective, do not require a lot of force on the pedal, and do not show any tendency to lock an odd wheel. Also they are smooth unless applied with extreme

Front view of the M.G. Midget.

Over the whole top of the tail is a hinged lid.

The driving compartment.

violence. Each brake has an adjustment for its cable, and these are fairly accessible. There is also a single main adjustment for all four brakes under the floor boards, beneath the driver's feet. This adjustment is not very accessible.

As regards other matters of accessibility: the battery is below the driver's legs and is quite easy to reach. The engine oil filler and dipstick are on the off side and, with the ignition coil, the make-and-break and the distributor, as well as a drain-cock at the base of the radiator, are quite accessible. The sparking plugs, which are at a slight downward angle, can easily be tackled with a spanner, except that nearest the dashboard, this one being screened by the coil. On the near side of the engine is a detachable oil filter; on this side also lies the electric starting motor, while the cut-out and junction boxes of the electrical system are attached to the forward side of the dash.

Smart and Up to Date.

Outwardly the car is smart and up to date, with its striking radiator, fat filler cap, detachable dumb-iron shield, cycle type wings, and side valances. Actually the wings are carried on the car, not on the axles, and are rigidly attached. The two doors are extra wide, and it is easy enough to enter or leave the car. The screen is a fixed V type.

Pneumatic upholstery is employed and the seat is adjustable; also the back squab is movable, not only fore and aft, but can be set as to angle as well. Just behind the seat is a compartment in which the hood stays are carried when out of use. Over the whole top of the tail is a hinged lid, and in the compartment beneath is stowed the spare wheel, whilst above it is fair space for luggage.

Altogether the M.G. Midget is an extraordinarily fascinating little car, both to look at and to handle on the road.

1930 M.G. PROGRAMME

New Four-speed Six-cylinder Chassis to Supplement Existing Range. Midget Sportsman's Coupé.

AMONG those to whom a high performance as regards acceleration and speed particularly appeals the M.G. range has become extremely popular. For 1930 a new model has been introduced, the 18-80 h.p. Mark II Six, which supplements the existing 18-80 h.p. Mark I Six, and the range is completed by the M.G. Midget, now available as an open two-seater and as an attractive sportsman's coupé.

For the new chassis the same engine as used in the Mark I model is employed, but the frame is stiffer throughout, a four-speed gear box is fitted, the front axle and steering are more robust, and very powerful brakes with 14in. diameter drums are standardised. These are the major differences between the two six-cylinder-engined chassis, but minor points of variance also exist, such as in the layout of the half-elliptic rear springs, the provision of central chassis lubrication, and the method of brake operation.

Exceptionally Smooth Running.

As regards details of the engine, the bore and stroke are 69 × 110 mm. (2,468 c.c.), the R.A.C. rating being 17.7 h.p. The cylinders and crank case form a single casting in iron of great strength and rigidity, and in this the robust and carefully balanced crankshaft is mounted in four large bearings. It is largely due to this construction that the engine has achieved an excellent reputation for its smooth, vibrationless running. In the detachable head are mounted the inclined valves, operated through rockers from the overhead camshaft, the latter being chain-driven from the crankshaft, with the drive so arranged that the head can be dismounted, complete with the valve gear, without disturbing the timing.

Two S.U. carburetters, each with its own float chamber, are fitted on the near side, each supplying three cylinders, and ignition is by coil, the distributor being driven by a vertical shaft on the off side at the front of the engine. The lower end of this shaft actuates the gear-type oil pump, which delivers oil under pressure to main and big-end bearings, to the camshaft and valve gear, and to the distribution gear. Also, on the off side and driven from the front of the engine is the 12-volt dynamo, while the water impeller is driven in tandem from the dynamo, being situated towards the rear of the cylinder block.

On the near side are the exhaust manifold, with its connection to the exhaust pipe at the front end, the water outlet to the radiator, the large oil filler, and the dipstick oil gauge for the sump. A new type breather is fitted to the aluminium valve gear cover, and leads oil fumes away from the vicinity of the dash and body.

With the engine the five-plate clutch, having cork inserts and running in oil, and the four-speed gear box form a compact unit. The gear box is especially interesting, as helical teeth are used for the constant-mesh and third-gear pinions, engagement being by dog clutches. Thus not only is a quiet third speed obtained, but the change from top to third, or from third to top, is very easy. Another point is that a central division in the gear box carries intermediate bearings for both main and lay shafts, so that the shafts are supported close to whatever gears are transmitting power. An extension rearwards from the lid of the box carries a short, stiff gear lever with a ball joint, a gear lock being incorporated. The ratios are 14.58, 8.5, 5.58, and 4.27 to 1.

A Well-braced Frame.

At the rear of the gear box is the spherical joint at the head of the torque tube, enclosing the split-ring type universal joint at the head of the propeller-shaft. The final drive is by spiral bevel, and the rear axle is of stronger construction than that formerly used.

While the main frame members are similar to those of the Mark I chassis, except for minor modifications to give additional strength, being upswept at front and rear, they are united by a

M.G. Six saloon, Mark II.

The two-seater 18-80 h.p. M.G. Six.

box girder section cross-member just behind the gear box and by stronger front and rear cross-members. Stiffer tie bars are also fitted between front and rear dumb irons. Incidentally, use is made of the large central cross-member to carry the two batteries, one on either side of the torque tube.

The half-elliptic front springs are shackled at their forward ends, the shackles being fed by the Tecalemit automatic chassis lubrication system, which also attends to the steering pivots and joints, and to the trunnion bearings of the half-elliptic rear

springs on the axle casing. The rear springs are wider than those of the Mark I chassis, and are mounted at the side of, and not beneath, the main frame, Silentbloc bushes being used for the shackles. There are thus no points needing attention with the grease gun, and there are only the engine, gear box, back axle, steering box, and chassis lubrication tank to be attended to at fairly long intervals of time.

For the front axle a straight H-section beam with stiffened, upswept ends is employed. Marles steering is used, the column being adjustable for rake and carrying an 18in. Bluemel spring-spoked wheel with throttle and ignition levers in a neat mounting above it.

One of the advantages of the brake gear of the new chassis is that it leaves the body builder full scope for fitting foot wells. It is also extremely simple, for there is only one cross-shaft, carried by stainless steel cones received between three bronze rollers, so that lubrication is not necessary, and there is no possibility of the shaft binding owing to frame flexion. On each end of this cross-shaft are double-ended levers to which the operating cables are connected.

The brake drums are ground internally and have ribbed aluminium bands shrunk on them. Orthodox two-shoe expanding brakes are used, with Halo linings, giving a total braking area of 208 sq. in. The brake lever is straight and is mounted on the frame, and it has the pawl and ratchet brought into engagement only when the knob is depressed, a reversal of normal practice and one which is favoured for sports and racing cars.

Petrol and Oil Supplies.

In the dash is mounted the auxiliary 2½-gallon fuel tank, which is fed by an Autovac from the 12-gallon main tank at the rear. A two-level tap for the auxiliary tank provides a reserve supply of 1 gallon. A Jaeger electrically operated gauge on the instrument board gives an indication of the state of the main tank, which has a 3¼in. diameter quickly detachable filler cap. A reserve oil supply of 1 gallon is also afforded by this tank, and the sump can be replenished merely by turning a tap.

The wiring has been made very neat, and a junction box on the dash carries the fuses and an inspection lamp. On the compact instrument panel are mounted clock, speedometer, revolution indicator, oil pressure gauge, and petrol gauge. Large Rotax head lamps are carried by stays, bracing radiator and wings. Rudge-Whitworth racing-type wire wheels are shod with 29in. × 5in. Dunlop Fort tyres, and the wheelbase and track are identical with those of the Mark I chassis—9ft. 6in. and 4ft. 4in. respectively. Accordingly, the coachwork is identical with that of the Mark I range, the complete 1930 programme being as follows:—

Mark I.—Chassis, £445; two-seater, £510; tourer, £515; sports salonette, fabric £550, coachbuilt £555; four-door saloon, fabric £560, coachbuilt £570.

Mark II.—Chassis, £550; two-seater, £625; tourer, £630; sports salonette, fabric £655, coachbuilt £660; four-door saloon, fabric £660, coachbuilt £670.

Midget.—Two-seater, £185; sportsman's coupé, £245.

In producing the 8-33 h.p. Midget sportsman's coupé the M.G. Car Co., whose address is now Pavlova Works, Abingdon-on-Thames, Berks, have aimed at providing a really comfortable and well-finished small car, as well as one capable of a high performance. It is possessed of good lines, but is also roomy, and has wide doors which assure ease of access, and a sliding sunshine roof in which are let lights, so that, even when the roof is closed, the occupants of the rear seat do not feel shut in.

The front bucket seats are adjustable and have pneumatic cushions, while the rear seat has both pneumatic cushion and squab. The doors are recessed to give additional elbow room and carry useful pockets. Triplex glass is fitted throughout as standard, and the rear luggage trunk has the spare wheel mounted on the hinged lid. The oval instrument panel is sunk into the facia board, which provides a very useful locker at each end.

A sectioned drawing of the Mark II Six saloon appears in the photogravure pages.

Amy Johnson, whose solo flight to Australia in 1929 in her D.H. 60G Gipsy Moth "Jason" made world news (as did her many other flights, and later those with her husband Jim Mollison), is presented with an M.G. Six Mark I saloon by Sir William Morris, later Lord Nuffield. The radiator mascot is a model of the Gipsy Moth, and alongside Amy Johnson is her mother.

THE 1930
M.G. SIX
MARK II.

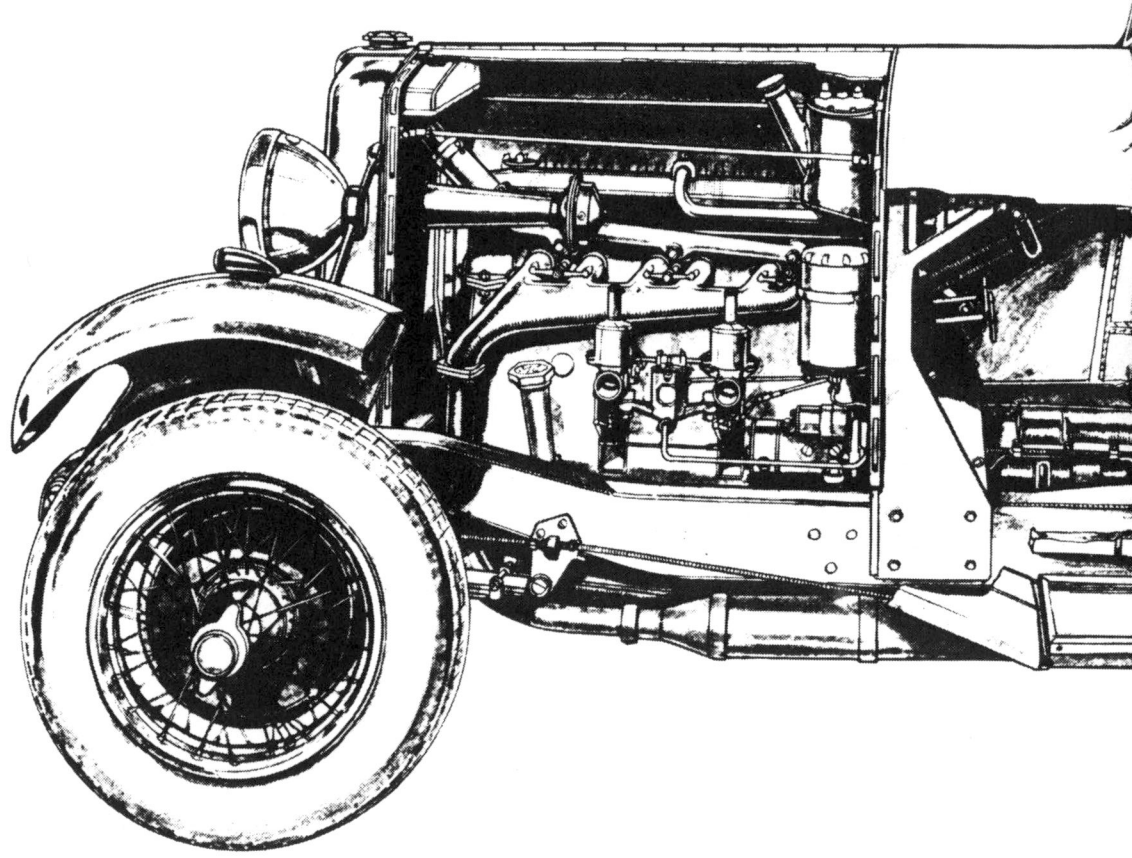

An addition to the range of an increasingly popular Sports Car. Its features include a strong and very rigid frame, a high-efficiency engine and four-speed gear box with constant mesh helical gears for third speed.

MAX MILLAR

The Autocar, January 24th, 1930.

RACING AND THE M.G.

THE AUTOCAR is informed that there is no truth in the rumour that Sir William Morris has authorised the M.G. Car Co. to enter for races during the coming season. However, there are private entries for the " Double-Twelve-Hour." L. G. Callingham and H. D. Parker are driving an M.G. Six Mark II, and a privately organised team of three Midgets, probably under the leadership of C. J. Randall, will run in the same race.

INEXPENSIVE SPEED.

THE directors of the M.G. Car Co. in general, and Mr. Cecil Kimber in particular, are to be congratulated warmly on the fine plant, at the Pavlova Works, Abingdon-on-Thames, for production in considerable numbers of M.G. sports cars, which was formally opened on Monday last. At a very largely attended lunch Sir William Morris, Bart., made a characteristic and vigorous speech on the outlook for the motor industry and for M.G. sports cars in particular. He emphasised that very shortly enthusiasts would be able to obtain, in either the three- or the four-speed types, high-

efficiency cars moderate in running cost, distinctly attractive in price, and with an efficiency comparable to that of any rivals. Sir William paid warm tribute to the keenness and loyalty of the staff and workmen engaged in the production of the cars, and uttered a powerful plea for a common-sense attitude on the part of the Government towards the British motor industry.

The works themselves are admirable—new, large and airy, and already the M.G. Midget and the Mark I and Mark II Sixes are coming through in routine production on assembly lines. It is obvious that M.G. products will be well to the fore in the sporting events of 1930 and onwards.

Fun-cars in the making, and a few dreams about to come true—the late F. Gordon Crosby's impression of the M.G. factory at Abingdon, with an M-type Midget coming off the line to the right, and what might be a six-cylinder chassis on test on the rolling-road dynamometer.

THE M.G. MARK III

Designed to Conform with International Racing Regulations and Turned Out Prepared for Racing.

BY reason of a certain silken swiftness of running and an appearance indubitably elegant, the M.G. Six Mark II has gained many ardent admirers. As a result, a demand arose for a model with which to race, and hence the 18-100 h.p. M.G. Six Sports Mark III Road Racing Model made its début.

Some twenty-five of the new cars form the first batch, and are on sale in the perfectly ordinary way at a price of £895 complete, and ready for racing without need of further preparation. Only one style of coachwork will be supplied, a four-seater body conforming to existing International Racing Regulations.

Bore and Stroke.

In actual size, namely, 69 mm. bore and 110 mm. stroke, giving a capacity of 2,468 c.c., the six-cylinder engine is the same as that of the Mark I and II models, this being for manufacturing reasons, but in other respects the differences are considerable. The crankshaft, which is carried in four bearings in a particularly rigid monoblock crank case, is bored out in the crank pins and has the webs fined down so as to reduce the load on the bearings. Connecting rods which are machined all over are employed in conjunction with a special piston of the waisted type, and all reciprocating parts are balanced individually, whilst the crankshaft is balanced statically and dynamically.

Within the water jackets the cylinder barrels are specially ribbed to prevent distortion; moreover, the water circulation is maintained by a centrifugal pump instead

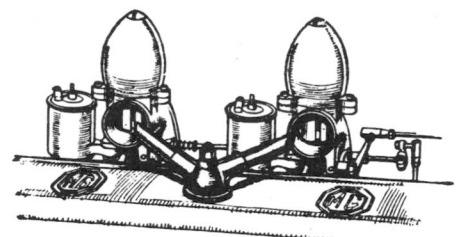

Breather pipes are taken to both the carburetter intakes.

On the M.G. Mark III the axle ends and steering arms are polished to facilitate inspection for flaws.

above the engine, and work on the down-draught principle. It is noticeable that the down-draught pipes are not arranged in bends, but in a series of angles.

On the opposite side of the cylinder head the exhausts are arranged to issue in three pairs to a triple pipe which blends into a Brooklands-type expansion chamber, having at each end a breather joint that allows for expansion and contraction. On this engine the overhead valves are operated by an overhead camshaft, which is driven by chain and spur gears from the front. A new type of camshaft is used, giving considerably more over-lap, whilst the valve springs are compounded.

Dry-sump lubrication is adopted. As compared with the normal M.G. engine it is noticeable that the vertical shaft which normally drives the pump has been moved from the right side of the engine at the front to the centre, and the drive for the verticle spindle passes from the chain gear to the extra stout spindle of a special high-duty dynamo.

Water and Oil Pumps.

Beyond a skew gear which drives the vertical shaft is mounted the water pump. At the base of the vertical spindle is a special twin pump. The upper of the two gear pumps draws oil from the sump and delivers it to an oil tank carried between the front dumb irons, flexible pipes being used for the purpose. The lower pump draws its supply from this tank, and delivers it under pressure to the engine bearings. There is a filter on the main suction pipe. There are no separate

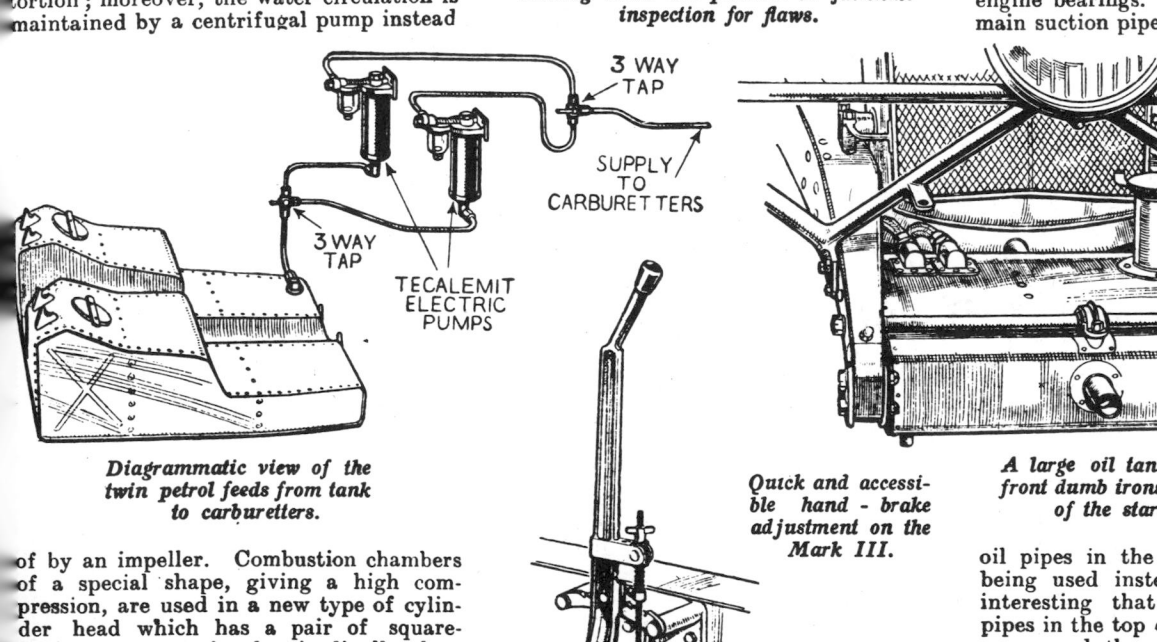

Diagrammatic view of the twin petrol feeds from tank to carburetters.

Quick and accessible hand-brake adjustment on the Mark III.

A large oil tank is located between the front dumb irons, through which the axis of the starting handle passes.

of by an impeller. Combustion chambers of a special shape, giving a high compression, are used in a new type of cylinder head which has a pair of square-section ports running longitudinally along one face of it for the gas intake, these ports being internally machined. Mixture is fed to these two separate ports from a pair of S.U. carburetters of an exclusive design, which are carried high

oil pipes in the engine, cast-in galleries being used instead. It is particularly interesting that there are two breather pipes in the top of the cover for the valve gear, and these permit oil mist to be drawn in through the carburetters to give top-cylinder lubrication. The oil pressure is set for 90 lb.

A double-ignition system is used, there being two sparking plugs in each cylinder.

The hand brake, with its quick adjustment, and the four wheel brake adjusting handle project through the body.

At the top of the vertical shaft of the oil pumps is mounted an electrically synchronised dual distributor, so arranged that the sparks of the two plugs occur simultaneously. Battery ignition is employed and the twin coils are neatly mounted saddle-wise over the dynamo.

Engine and four-speed gear box unit are carried in the frame from a cross-member in the front and from bearer arms extending from a new type of cast-iron banjo casing around the flywheel and clutch. Rubber pads are used in the engine mounting to give a small degree of flexibility.

For the purpose of racing, which demands quick gear changing, a new type of clutch has been designed. It is a single-plate design with highly compressed cork inserts. The clutch is toggle-operated, and has a compressed-graphite thrust race for the pedal fork.

The frame has channel-section side members which are up-swept at front and rear. Aft of the engine and gear box unit comes the keystone of the design. It consists of two very wide and deep channel-section cross members which are jointed together in the centre by a large-diameter tubular member, and through the centre of this the forward end of the propeller-shaft casing passes. Cradles formed by the cross-member on each side of the big tube are utilised to carry the batteries.

The top flanges of the frame are very wide between the spring anchorages, and again from the engine rear bearer arm right back to the front anchorages of the rear springs. Between the main double cross-member and the rear axle there is suspended, mainly below frame level, a 28-gallon petrol tank. In plan view this follows the shape of the frame, but the upper portion is shaped suitably to give a tunnel for the propeller-shaft case, and to allow room for the feet of rear-seat passengers. The tank is very firmly supported from three points, but at the same time is free from frame distortion. It is carried low and between the axles so as to give a good distribution of weight with as little variation as possible, whether the tank is full or nearly empty.

Half-elliptic springs are used both back and front, but the front springs are pinned at their rear ends and shackled at the front in boxes which prevent side play. The spring pin and shackle bearings are automatically lubricated from a central lubrication system, which will be described later. For the half-elliptic rear springs Silentbloc bushes, which need no lubrication, are employed. Large double Hartford shock absorbers are fitted to the front axle, whilst the rear axle has two pairs of double Hartfords, the units of each pair being set at right-angles to one

another. Also, the axle has check straps and rubber buffers, so that the spring travel is suitably limited.

Practical simplicity is a feature of the four wheel brake gear. From the pedal a tie-rod runs back to a lever mounted on a very stout cross tube carried in bearings in brackets hanging below frame level. These bearings are large in diameter and narrow, so that any twisting of the frame is not likely to cause binding of the cross-shaft. At each end of

The M.G. Mark III viewed from the rear.

the cross-shaft is a double lever, one arm pointing up, the other down.

From the upper lever on each side a rod runs forward to terminate in a thimble connection to the end of a stranded steel cable. The cable passes through a slide attached to a frame bracket, and then through a flexible cable covering, passing on to an anchorage on the hub bracket. The cable terminates in a steel slide which embraces the end of the lever, and is adjustable by means of a wing nut pin and a lock nut. From the lower lever on each side a cable runs back to a bracket by the front anchorage of the rear spring, and then passes through a flexible casing to a rear hub in the same way as at the front.

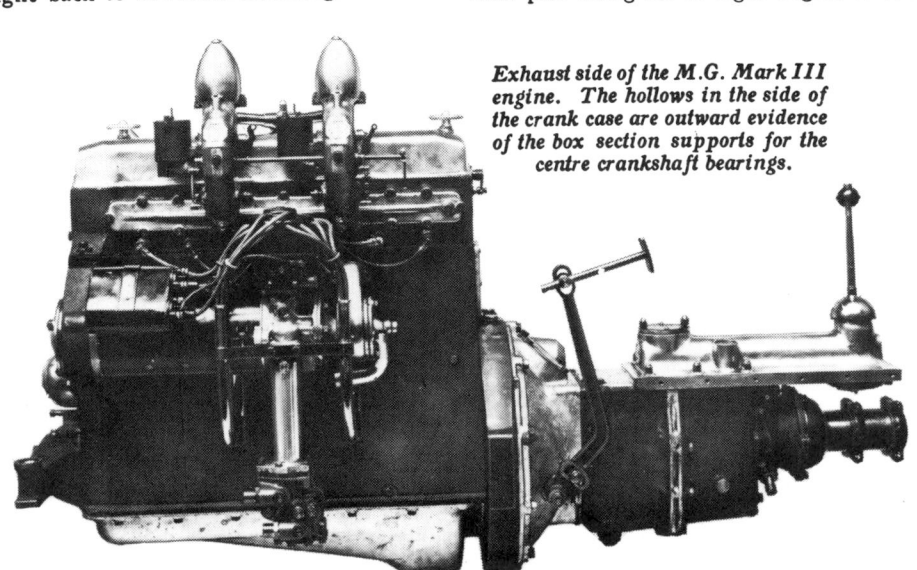

Exhaust side of the M.G. Mark III engine. The hollows in the side of the crank case are outward evidence of the box section supports for the centre crankshaft bearings.

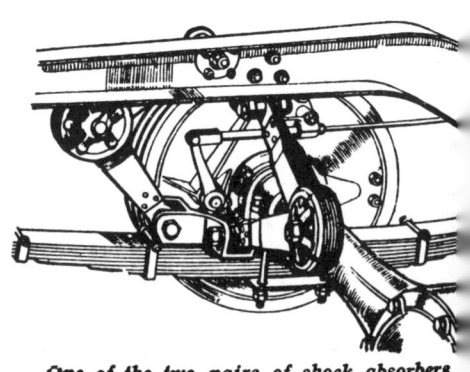

One of the two pairs of shock absorbers fitted to the rear axle.

There is a very ingenious method of taking up the main adjustment, which is situated on the end of the tie-rod that couples the cross-shaft lever to the brake pedal. A V-ended thimble screws on to the end of a tie-rod, and this thimble is attached to a flexible cable which is swept round at right angles and passes out through the frame to an adjustable wheel. When the wheel is turned the cable twists with it, and thereby rotates the sleeve on its screw thread.

Deep-valances cover the frames and help to increase the sturdy appearance of the car.

...wed from the front the most striking feature of the M.G. is the powerful third head lamp.

Outside the body, and well forward, is a long hand-brake lever with the customary racing-type ratchet, and this lever operates all four brakes independently of the pedal by means of a trip lever attachment to the cross-shaft. Adjustment at this point is made by means of a large set pin. The brake drums are of very large diameter, with wide shoes, and the drums are also heavily ribbed so that they should stand up to prolonged hard work. Incidentally, the brake cam spindles are cadmium plated, and work in roller bearings which are packed with grease.

Reverting now to the fuel system. First, the big tank has two filling caps, one on each side of the floor of the car.

These caps are very large and of the quick-action variety, and the idea is that both caps would be removed when filling so that a large quantity of fuel can be poured in at one orifice whilst the other makes a large vent for the escape of air. At the left-hand forward corner of the tank is the delivery stand-pipe. This is sheltered by a tube attached to a cap screwed in from the bottom; the tube has various large holes in it and is covered with fine-mesh gauze.

There are two separate fuel-delivery systems. From the stand-pipe and its union a flexible petrol-resisting tube goes forward to a two-way tap, and from each of the tap leads a pipe runs forward to a separate electrically operated pump. From each pump a pipe runs up to a two-way tap concealed under the dash. From this tap a flexible pipe then runs forward to the two carburetters. The two electric Tecalemit petrol pumps are controlled by separate switches. Thus, a leak in one pipe will not affect the other.

Another interesting feature is the automatic central chassis lubrication. It is a Tecalemit design, wherein a glass-bodied container attached to the front of the dashboard carries in its head a special

form of automatic vibratory pump, the inertia of a bob-weight being used to build up oil pressure at between 60lb. and 90lb.

The car carries three head lamps, besides side and tail lamps. All electrical circuits throughout the vehicle are wired separately, and each line of wiring has its own separate fuse, a large fuse box being carried on the engine side of the dash. The idea of this is to localise faults as far as possible.

Very strong support is given to the three-head-lamp system and to the front wings, there being a double triangulated structure of streamline section steel tubing right across the front of the car.

All the vital points in the steering, by the way, are filed and polished to make sure that no hidden flaws exist.

The intention is to turn the car out absolutely run-in, with the bearings free, the brakes bedded in, all nuts split-pinned and wired, with racing tyres on racing rims, and, in fact, everything tuned up to the degree where there is no need for further work on the machine. It is hoped to guarantee a speed of 100 m.p.h.

The instruments include speedometer, rev counter, stop clock, oil gauge, ammeter, radiator and oil thermometers.

The body is a simple and sturdy metal-panelled four-seater, with a single shallow door on the near side, and it has a considerable portion of the off side cut away. The car carries a windscreen which can be folded flat forward, and there is, of course, a regulation hood.

Two down-draught carburetters are fitted to the Mark III M.G. Six. Note the arrangement of the dynamo drive and vertical spindle drive with double ignition distributor at the top.

HAND ADJUSTMENT

BRAKE PEDAL ROD

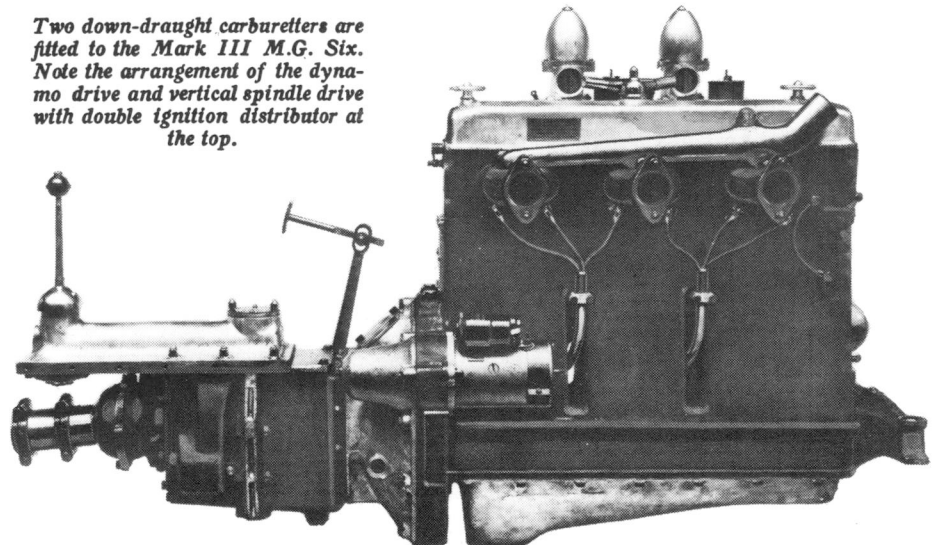

An ingenious hand adjustment is provided for the foot brake.

**OUTLINE OF
SPECIFICATION.**

Bore 69 mm.   Stroke 110 mm.
Capacity 2468 c.c.
R.A.C. Rating 17·7 h.p.   Tax £18.
Wheelbase, 9ft. 6in. ; Track 4 feet.

THE · M.G. MARK III.

A standardised sports car designed to comply with
International road racing regulations.

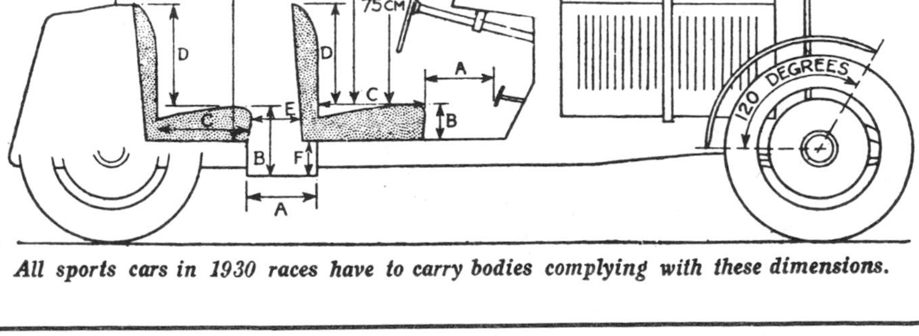

All sports cars in 1930 races have to carry bodies complying with these dimensions.

October 17th, 1930.

M.G. (16)
Country of Origin: Great Britain.

M.G. CAR CO., LTD.,
PAVLOVA WORKS,
ABINGDON-ON-THAMES.

8-33 h.p., 4-cyls., 57×83 mm. (847 c.c.), tax £8. coil ignition, thermo cooling, single disc cl., 3-sp. unit gear box, spiral bevel, ½-E. front and rear springs, 27×4.00in. tyres on wire wheels, four wheel brakes. Prices: 2-seater touring car, £185; 2-seater coupé, £245.

SUCCESSFULLY and definitely built as sports cars, the M.G. range has become famous for speed, refinement and beauty of line. To the Midget no special alterations have been made, but the sportsman's coupé now has a panelled body and cleaner roof lines. Just as the two-seater is an ideal type of small specialised speed car, so the coupé is an extraordinarily smart and cleverly arranged little town carriage, with a remarkable amount of room inside, despite the compactness.

18-80 h.p., 6-cyls., 69×110 mm. (2,468 c.c.), tax £18, pump cooling, multi-plate cl., 29×5in. tyres, four wheel vacuum servo brakes. Prices: Chassis £445; 4-seater touring car, £525; 4-seater saloon, £565.

Other details as in 8-33 h.p.

Remarkable for the fact that its six-cylinder engine is marvellously smooth running for all its power and flexibility, the M.G. Six is a much-appreciated car. There are two types, Mark I and Mark II, the latter having a four-speed gear box and other refinements. An example of the Mark I chassis shows individuality of design and sturdy build. There is also a two-door four-seater close-coupled light saloon with deep footwells in the rear compartment, and a new edition, a speed model with a four-seater open body. The Mark II sports saloon de luxe is another new type of coachwork, very smart and up to date, with close-fitting wings, novel, curved running boards, and Pytchley sliding roof; the price is £699. Tasteful paintwork and upholstery are another feature of this exhibit.

A really sporting appearance is imparted by the lines of the M.G. Six Mark I Speed Model

Two-door, four-seater close-coupled M.G. Six Saloon

An M.G. Six Mark III with special sports coachwork by Carbodies

INTO BATTLE 1933

*M.C.C. EXETER TRIAL 1931: H. S. Linfield's M.G. Speed Model, with its crew of four, completes an observed section. Then a staff member of **The Autocar**, Linfield was later to become editor of the journal. This is the same car that had been the subject of a Road Test report in the issue of 14 November 1930 (see opposite page)*

"THE AUTOCAR" ROAD TESTS

M.G. SIX SPEED MODEL.

Fascinating Car with an Excellent Performance, which Handles Very Well Indeed.

The illustration above indicates the size of the M.G. Six Speed Model compared with a 40-50 h.p. Rolls-Royce.

UNTIL recently the buyer wanting a real four-seater sports type car of medium size has been limited in scope by the fact that the majority of sports machines are, by their nature, relatively expensive. The M.G. speed model, which is a new type on the latest Mark I six-cylinder chassis, admirably fills this need, and, into the bargain, is a remarkably fascinating motor car to handle and own.

It is a very big asset that the engine is exceedingly smooth, devoid of all fierceness sometimes associated with this kind of car in the ordinary driver's mind, and in fact, the vehicle is capable of being driven for the greater part of a day's running on top gear alone. In a sense, this extreme smoothness is deceptive, for, although the engine can be throttled down so as to run without jerk at 5 m.p.h. on top, there is in reserve that extra liveliness of performance which is the very essence of a sports model.

Without using the indirects at all, except, of course, in starting from rest, the acceleration is very good, and a cruising speed which can be as high as 60 m.p.h. is quickly reached, and maintained, if the driver

wishes, for as long as road conditions permit. On the other hand, second gear of the three-speed box is a relatively close ratio and exceedingly useful, in that a speedometer reading of 61 can be obtained on it. Obviously, therefore, the man who buys this type of car, who, as a rule, finds gear changing an art instead of an annoyance, can very materially improve the performance by judicious use of second, the change itself handling exceptionally well.

On a long run the M.G. is most satisfying, the high cruising speed—in almost complete silence, only the rush of air and the sound of the tyres on the road surface showing that the machine is travelling fast—and the performance on second gear already referred to, being just what are wanted. As illustrating the ability of the car to maintain a good speed, it was taken through an officially observed trial on Brooklands, in which, driven continuously for one hour, it covered 69.75 miles in the sixty minutes. The maximum is, obviously, excellent, and 80 is attainable on the road in conditions not unduly favourable to the car. The car handles most satisfactorily,

too; the control is light, and the brake action, with the vacuum servo now added, extremely good. The hand brake lever outside the body is of racing type, and the brake itself will hold the car on a steep gradient.

Steering is light, positive, and does not transmit road shock to the steering wheel itself—which has a thin rim and spring spokes —though it is possible that even more definite caster action than is provided at present, with consequent automatic sense of direction, would help a car of these speed capabilities, and is not difficult, by the way, to introduce. The suspension is exactly right, it being possible, of course, to set the big double-acting friction shock-absorbers so as to make the springing comparatively hard at low speeds, but giving the car an extraordinary stability that is essential for fast corner work.

A most interesting point is that the back seat is really comfortable, the occupants experiencing no direct shock, a thing not altogether common with a sports four-seater. The way in which the car can be taken round corners absolutely accurately, with not the slightest sway, contributes not a little to the success of the machine. It is interesting that the car is quiet, which is a very big point indeed, with just the right note in the exhaust to distinguish it from that of an ordinary touring car; while, in passing, the obvious possibilities of the car for competition work are worth mentioning.

The driving position is excellent, the bucket front seats holding one, as it were, in just the right position, the driver's seat being adjustable; the other front seat swings forward so as to make access to the back compartment more convenient, there being one door at each side of the car. The upholstery is very good indeed and comfortable; while as to detail, the instruments are grouped, panelled, and well lighted by two neat lamps giving a green-tinted light, among the dials being a rev. counter, fuel tank gauge, trip-type

speedometer, engine thermometer, and a clock. At either side of the instruments is a deep cubby hole, there are three pockets in the sides of the body, and the single panel windscreen, which has an electric wiper with dual arms, folds right down flat on the scuttle—a feature really worth having.

The engine is extremely neat, with all the sparking plugs very accessible indeed; the overhead-valve gear is easily reached when the cover secured by two hand wheels is removed; while the ignition distributor and coil, and the junction box for the electrical connections, are also well placed. On the other side of the engine, the carburetter, which is a dual type with a single float chamber, is also very accessible indeed, fuel feed being by an electric pump; and the oil filler is big, combining in its cap the dipstick.

The head lamps, by the way, are powerful, the dimming device is controlled by a convenient switch on the steering column, and with all the lights on there is a surplus of 3 amperes at normal speeds.

The chassis is well laid out for maintenance, the floorboards being held down by locks which are operated by an ordinary carriage key, which arrangement allows them to be removed with unusual ease. In the scuttle are separate spare tanks holding respectively a gallon of oil and two gallons of fuel.

Racing-type wire wheels give the right touch, and the hood is very neat, held securely when furled, and has a good cover. An interesting point was that during a particularly heavy rainstorm, with the hood up but none of the side curtains erected, practically no water at all came inside the car.

The appearance of the car as a whole is obviously just right for the type of machine; the general finish, too, is excellent.

The M.G. speed model is an exceedingly pleasant car to drive—in short, an enthusiast's delight — and should have a bright future.

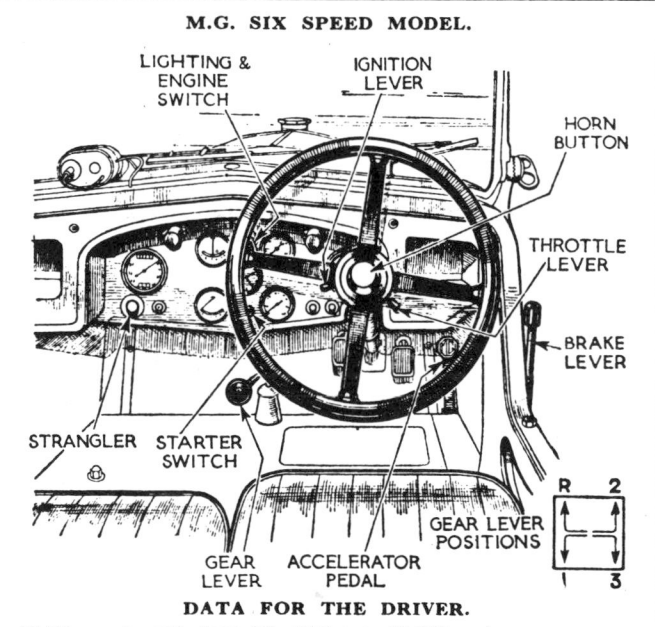

M.G. SIX SPEED MODEL.

LIGHTING & ENGINE SWITCH

IGNITION LEVER

HORN BUTTON

THROTTLE LEVER

BRAKE LEVER

STRANGLER   STARTER SWITCH

GEAR LEVER POSITIONS

GEAR LEVER   ACCELERATOR PEDAL

DATA FOR THE DRIVER.
17.7 h.p., six cylinders, 69 × 110 mm. (2,468 c.c.)
Tax £18.
Wheelbase 9ft. 6in., track 4ft.
Overall length 13ft. 9in., width 5ft. 1in., height 5ft. 2½in.
Tyres: 29 × 5in. on detachable wire wheels.

Engine—rear axle gear ratios.	Acceleration from steady 10 to 30 m.p.h.	Timed speed over ¼ mile.
13.2 to 1	—	
6.58 to 1	7⅗ sec.	79.64 m.p.h.
4.25 to 1	11 sec.	

Turning circle: 43ft.
Tank capacity 12 gallons; fuel consumption 18-20 m.p.g.
12-volt lighting set cuts in at 12 m.p.h., 12 amps. at 30 m.p.h.
Weight: 22 cwt. 3 qr.
Price, with speed model four-seater body, £525.

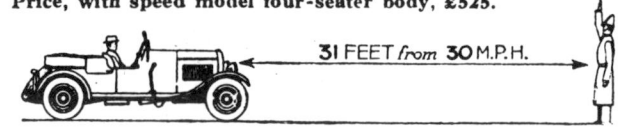

31 FEET *from* 30 M.P.H.

The colour of speed

Above: Twenty-four years apart—the little M-type Midget, which started it all 'way back in 1929, seen through the screen of the infinitely more refined TF, still unmistakably MG

Below: Stark, functional and more typically MG Midget than any other body style—the sports-racing J4, of which only nine were produced, with its supercharged 746 c.c. 4-cylinder engine.

Overleaf:- TF Midget (October 1953 to October 1955)—last of the true Midgets and by far the most stylish and civilised with its faired-in headlamps and gracefully curved radiator

Responsible for starting the MG sports car cult in the States—the TC Midget (1945 to 1949) which endeared itself to hundreds of American servicemen stationed in Europe, and accompanied many of them back across the Atlantic when the war was over. In the background, the latest MG BGT-V8

The M.G. Magna close-coupled coupé.

THE 12-70 h.p. M.G. MAGNA

Further Details of a High - performance Small Six of the Most Interesting Character

FOLLOWING the preliminary announcement which appeared in last week's issue of *The Autocar*, it is now possible to give a detailed description of the new M.G. Magna 12-70 h.p. small six-cylinder car. It is a design which must inevitably fascinate those enthusiasts to whom a sporting performance is the true zest of motoring, in whom there is an æsthetic ability to appreciate beauty of line, and by whom refinement of running is admired and enjoyed.

To look first at the low-built and utterly workmanlike chassis of the Magna, and then at the finished clean-cut car, is to experience a feeling of insular gratification that this job is British. Emanating as it does from a firm whose 750 c.c. Montlhéry Midgets have handsomely won this year the three most important international races held on British and Irish soil, the Magna is definitely something more than a mere new model: it is a car of latent possibilities.

Simple and Light

Possibly the outstanding feature is the simple directness of the design. The car is light, because it is devoid of complication. The frame, for example, follows the principles adopted for the successful Montlhéry Midgets; that is to say, the channel section side-members are arched over the front axle, and thereafter drop low down and parallel with the ground, and pass some five or six inches below the rear axle. Steel tubes form all the cross-members, and the springs, which are of the half-elliptic type and almost flat, are attached with the ordinary spring eyes at the front, and rollers at their rear ends in place of shackles, so that the possibility of side-play due to wear is brought down to a minimum, a point which considerably affects lateral stability. Hartford shock-absorbers are fitted back and front. At the extreme rear of the frame is a cradle in which a long, narrow battery is supported.

One of the reasons why the chassis looks so clean is that the brake-operating mechanism is so simple. In a heavily ribbed drum on the hub of each wheel is an expanding shoe brake provided with an individual adjustment. The brakes are operated by means of flexible steel cables, which pass through armoured casings, and the cables run to the centre

of the car, where they pass over grooved pulleys on the ends of a cross-shaft. The mechanism is so arranged that the pedal operates all four brakes, while the centrally placed lever separately operates four brakes. By the base of the central lever is a fly nut master adjustment within easy reach of the driver's hand, whilst below the floorboards is another master adjustment for the pedal. One of the points about the brake mechanism is the fact that it is unaffected either by steering movements or spring movements of the axle. Care is taken to make sure that the cables do not rust, and that they can move freely in their casings, by providing a proper system of lubrication, and a grease gun applied to one of the nipples grouped in sets just in front of the dashboard pillars forces grease through the cable casings. Rudge-Whitworth detachable hub wire wheels are fitted.

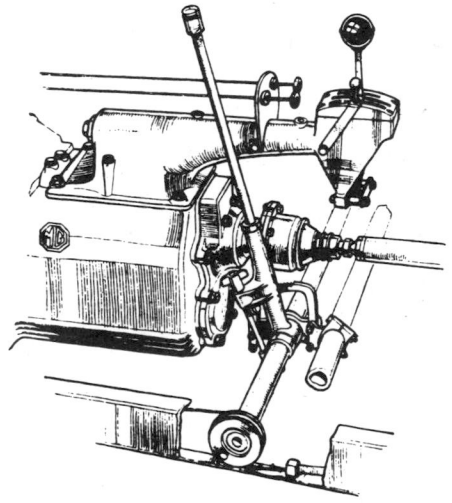

Layout of gear and brake mechanism on the Magna chassis. Note the position of the strangler and throttle controls.

Sitting fairly well back in the front of the frame is the engine and gear box unit. It is mounted with a three-point form of suspension, and an extension of the centre bracket at the forward end is arranged to carry the radiator, so that this component is unaffected by torsional movements of the frame. Naturally, the greatest interest attaches to the engine. This is a six-cylinder design, 57 by 83 mm. (1,250 c.c.). The cylinder block and the greater part of the crankcase are formed in one casting, in which an exceptionally stiff crankshaft is carried in four main bearings. From the front end of the crankshaft a spiral-bevel gear conveys the drive through a vertical shaft, and via the spindle of a vertically mounted dynamo, to a second gear above the cylinder block, and through this agency an overhead camshaft is driven. The camshaft actuates the overhead valves through light fingers having adjustable fulcrum points.

Lubrication

At the front of the engine is a gear pump which draws its supply of oil from a large aluminium sump with cooling fins containing $1\frac{3}{4}$ gallons of oil, and delivers it through an easily detachable filter to the main bearings, the big ends, and upwards to the camshaft and rockers. On the left side of the engine is a special induction pipe, fed by a pair of S.U. carburetters, and on the same side a large separate exhaust manifold is coupled up to an exhaust pipe situated by the front of the engine, and thus out of the way of the floorboards.

Aluminium pistons with three rings are employed in conjunction with steel connecting rods, and it may be mentioned that the crankshaft, reciprocating parts, valves, and so forth of this engine are specially prepared with a view to giving a sustained high performance.

Between the engine and the gear box is a large-diameter single-plate clutch. Four speeds are provided by the gear box, and the three top ratios are fairly close, the overall ratios being: First 19.6, second 9.79, third 6.65, and fourth 4.89. These close ratios give every possible opportunity for obtaining the best advantage from the gear box for acceleration, hill-climbing, and fast cornering. On the top of the box is a

The 847 c.c. M.G. Midget with Montlhéry-type frame and four-seater body.

cast aluminium tunnel which proceeds backwards to a point convenient to the driver's left hand, and here there is mounted a short and comfortable little gear lever working in a normal gate. A plate just in front of the gear lever carries a mixture control, and a control for throttle setting.

Drive from the gear box passes to a three-quarter floating spiral-bevel-driven rear axle through an open propeller-shaft of not excessive length, and having a Hardy Spicer metal universal joint at each end. One particularly interesting point about the design is the way in which the front driving compartment is insulated from heat and smell from the engine by using the circular casing around the flywheel as a bulkhead to carry a large rubber sealing ring which, in turn, fills up the circular hole at the point where the dashboard crosses the engine and gear box unit. Mention has been made of a grouped lubricating system. Under the bonnet in front of the dashboard on each side is a group of three nipples, through which all the bearings of the chassis can be lubricated, with the exception of the front spring parts, and the joints on the front axle and steering gear which have their own individual grease gun connections. For the steering a worm and wheel gear is used. The drag link from the gear passes transversely across the car, as the column is considerably raked so as to give a comfortable position for the steering wheel, which is a 16in. celluloid-covered spring-spoke type. The water cooling system of the engine is of the thermo-syphon system, and the effectiveness of the radiator is increased by a belt-driven fan. The radiator itself is of a special design, in shape somewhat similar to the well-known Midget,

but deeper from back to front, and provided with a sloping front, in which a stoneguard is incorporated.

Accessibility in the design has been very carefully studied, and to that end the bonnet is very long and is arranged so that when opened it discloses both sides of the bulkhead, dashboard, and

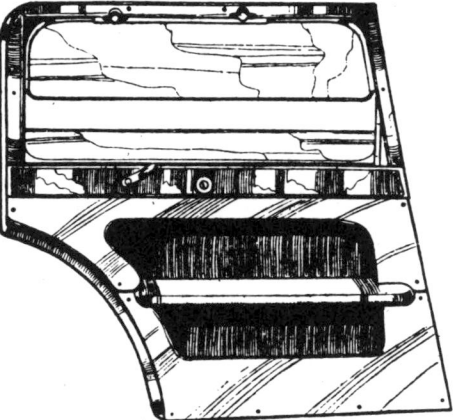

Window mechanism and arm-rest on the door of the Magna coupé.

also the back of the instrument board, besides the pedals and part of the gear box. There is room, therefore, not only to get at the engine, but many of the other important parts of the chassis as well.

Before turning to the coachwork, the following details of the chassis will be of interest. The Treasury rating of the engine is 12.08 h.p., and the tax £12; the track of the car is 3ft. 6in. and the wheelbase 7ft. 10in.; the wheels are shod with 27in. by 4in. tyres, and the chassis weighs approximately 9¼ cwt. The over-

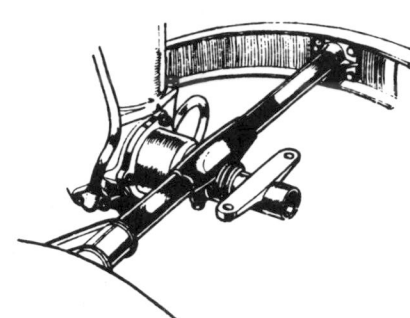

Redesigned front engine mounting and radiator support on the Midget Occasional Four.

all width is 4ft. 2in. and the overall length 10ft. 6¼in., whilst the overall height of the close-coupled saloon is only 4ft. 5in. One other chassis point demands mention: the petrol tank contains six gallons, and is carried at the rear of the frame, and is provided with a conveniently placed two-way tap which retains two gallons in reserve.

Now as regards coachwork. There are two bodies available; the first is a sports four-seater, priced at £250. This is a low-built, two-door, close-coupled design with plenty of room in the front seats, but with rear seats intended for occasional use. Alternatively the rear compartment can be used for the con-

(Right) The chassis of the Midget Occasional Four and (left) that of the Magna compared.

veyance of a good deal of luggage. This is a metal-panelled body of very attractive lines, and has at the front a single-panel windscreen which can, when desired, be folded flat forwards out of the way. Packed flat and partially in a recess at the back of the body, is a hood which will cover the whole of the interior of the car. All-weather side-panels are included in the equipment. Leather upholstery is used, and the front seats are of the adjustable bucket type. Being low-built, the body has no running boards, whilst the wings are of the close-fitting, deep-sided type.

In appearance the closed edition of the Magna is particularly striking. The body is a close-coupled coupé with a sliding roof, and has been christened the Foursome. It has two wide doors to give access to the interior, and the pneumatically upholstered back seats are reached when the backs of the front seats are tilted forwards. Wells in the rear floorboards give increased room. Although the car as a whole cannot be described as a large one, every possible inch has been utilised in the width of the body, which swells out nearly to the full width of the rear wheels. Additional elbow room is given to the front seats by recesses in the doors in which are arm-rests, whilst below each arm-rest is a deep pocket for occasional packages.

Pleated leather upholstery of extra fine finish helps to render the interior very attractive, and another feature is that in the sliding portion of the roof is a series of celluloid windows which not only allow vision upwards, but also make the interior of the car bright. The price of this model is £289. For both cars the stock finish is ebony black with apple green, tudor brown, deep red, or Cearulean blue or suède grey leather upholstery. Other colours that can be obtained if desired at an extra charge of £2 10s. are biscuit, British racing green, russet brown, nile blue or rich red and white. Any other colours

The dropped frame from the rear showing the method of attachment of the rear springs.

than these may be had at an extra charge of £4 10s., whilst a deviation from the five leathers that have been standardised costs an additional five guineas.

The Midget Occasional Four

Finally a few notes may be added to the information already published about the 8-33 h.p. M.G. Midget Occasional Four. This is a new addition to the Midget range, and has an open four-seater body very similar to that of the

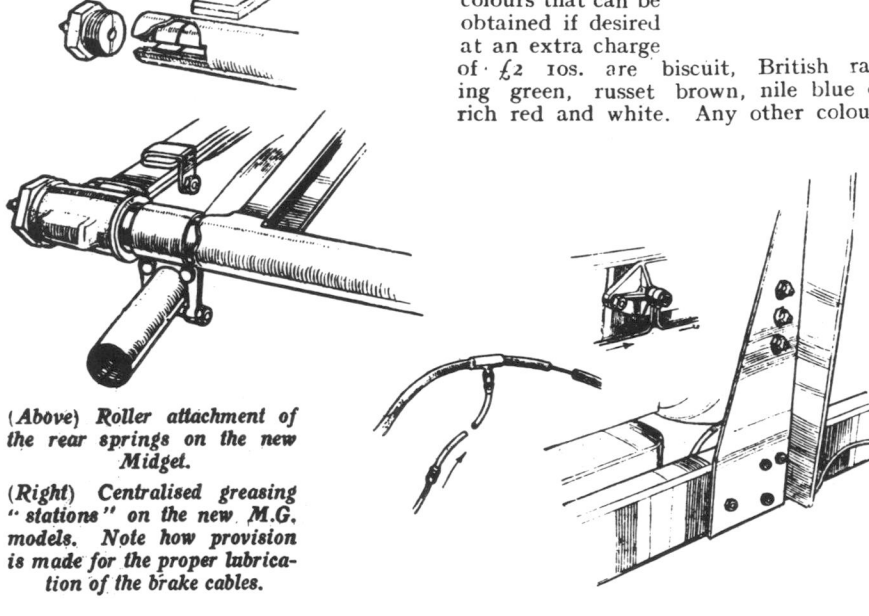

(Above) Roller attachment of the rear springs on the new Midget.

(Right) Centralised greasing "stations" on the new M.G. models. Note how provision is made for the proper lubrication of the brake cables.

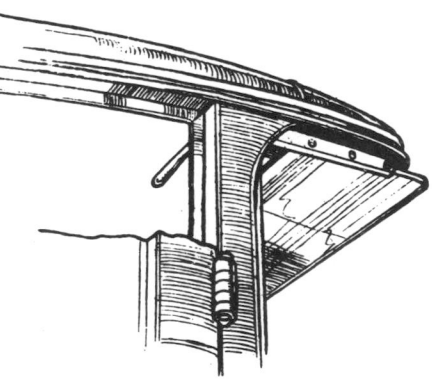

The sun visor on the Magna coupé can be conveniently operated from the interior of the car.

Magna. The chassis is also of the underslung frame type, with flat springs and slides instead of shackles. Most of the detail can be seen in the accompanying illustrations.

Special points of the model are that the gear lever is mounted at the end of a rearwardly projecting bracket on the top of the gear box, a grouped nipple system of chassis lubrication is provided, and the use of a long bonnet makes it possible to secure immediate access to the scuttle as well.

It is possible, additionally, to obtain this model with a four-speed box instead of three speeds. The chassis is very similar to the Montlhéry type, but the engine is the normal four-cylinder 847 c.c. type. This car has the petrol tank situated at the back, and Rudge-Whitworth racing type wire wheels are fitted. It is priced at £210.

The M.G. Magna has twin carburetters.

THE M.G. MAGNA.

A NEW SMALL SIX-CYLINDER SPORTS CAR.

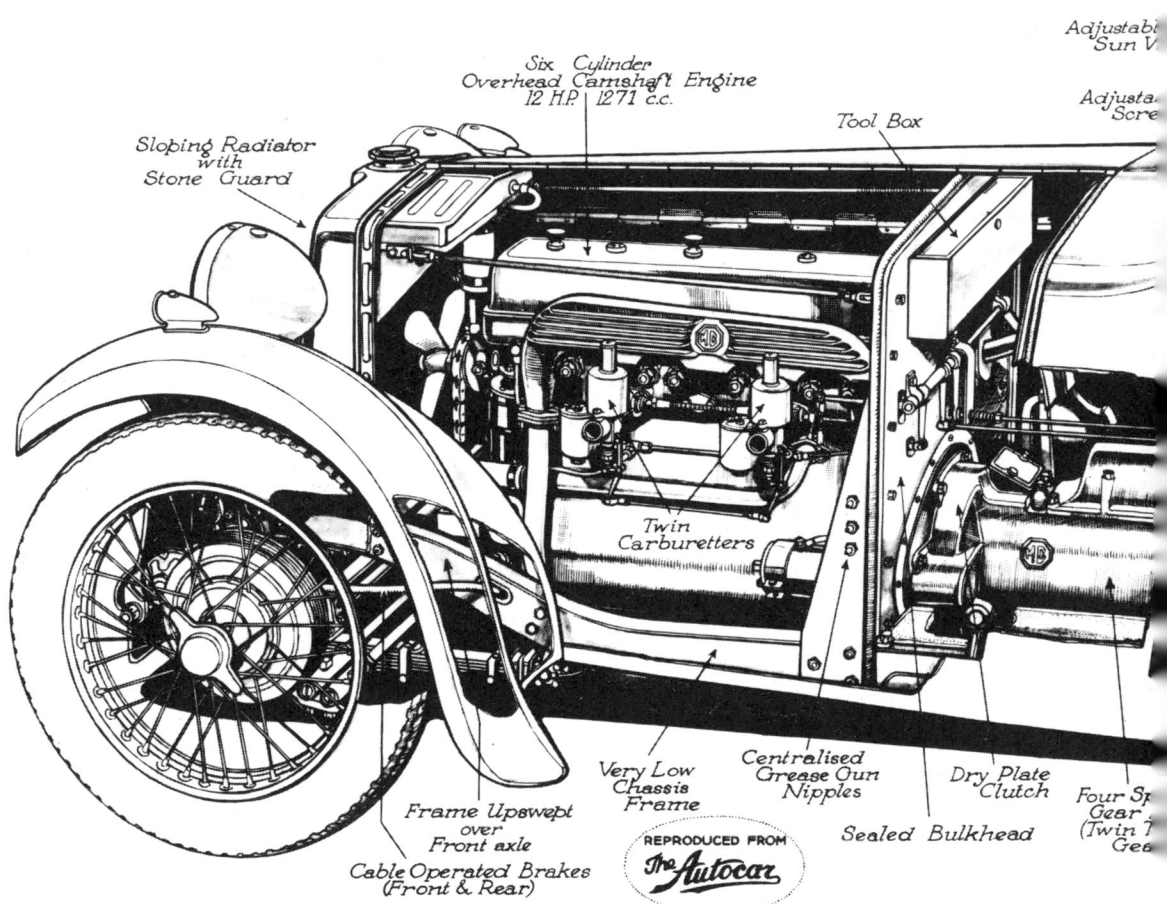

Adjustable Sun V...

Adjusta... Scre...

Six Cylinder
Overhead Camshaft Engine
12 H.P. 1271 c.c.

Tool Box

Sloping Radiator
with
Stone Guard

Twin
Carburetters

Very Low
Chassis
Frame

Centralised
Grease Gun
Nipples

Dry Plate
Clutch

Four Sp...
Gear...
(Twin...
Gea...

Frame Upswept
over
Front axle

Sealed Bulkhead

Cable Operated Brakes
(Front & Rear)

SALIENT FEATURES.

1271 c.c., o.h. camshaft engine, four-speed gear box with silent third. Frame underslung at rear. The engine is entirely separated from the passenger accommodation by an aluminium bulkhead and undershield.

Tax £12.   Wheelbase, 7 ft. 8 in.   Track, 3 ft. 6 in.
Overall length, 10 ft. 4½ in.   Overall width, 4 ft. 2 in.

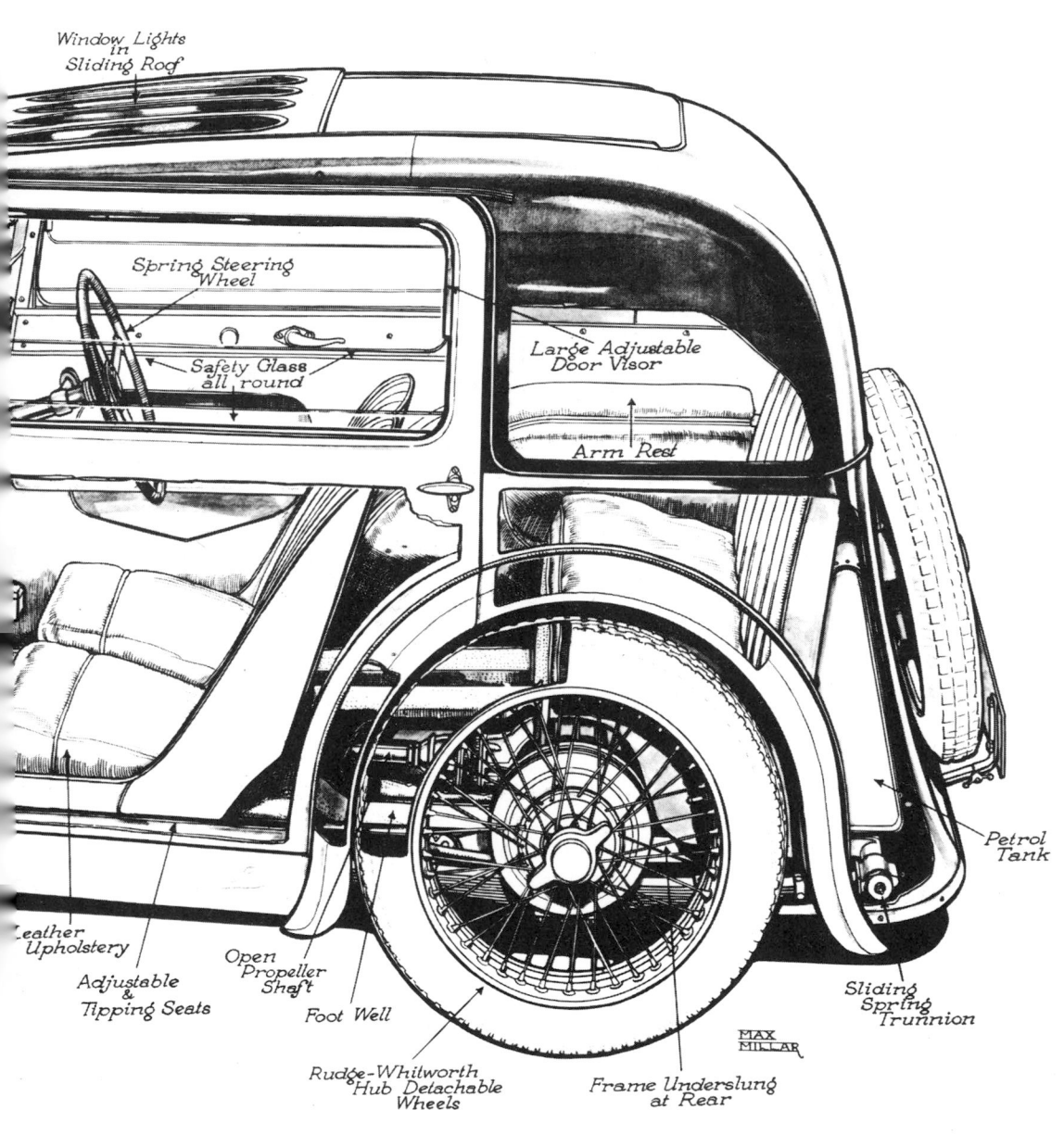

Window Lights in Sliding Roof

Spring Steering Wheel

Large Adjustable Door Visor

Safety Glass all round

Arm Rest

Leather Upholstery

Adjustable & Tipping Seats

Open Propeller Shaft

Foot Well

Rudge-Whitworth Hub Detachable Wheels

Frame Underslung at Rear

Sliding Spring Trunnion

Petrol Tank

MAX MILLAR

This little car is based on the design of the racing
M.G. Midget, which has been so successful this
year at Brooklands and in the two big Irish events.

**Published *The Autocar,*
20 November 1931**

"THE AUTOCAR" ROAD TESTS

The illustration above represents the size, in feet, of the Montlhéry M.G. Midget two-seater

No. 678 (Post-War Series).—MONTLHERY M.G. MIDGET TWO-SEATER

WHATEVER one's experience of cars may be, there is a new thrill in handling the Montlhéry Mark II M.G. Midget, especially the supercharged model. It is not a question of how extremely well this small car goes, but, by contrast, how extraordinarily good is this car among cars as a whole. Apart altogether from the personal interest, great as that is, there exists as a background the fact that this particular model has become famous in about the shortest possible time on record, and has to its credit the winning of the three classic British races in 1931—two of them without being supercharged—as well as averaging over 92 m.p.h. for 500 miles in the last big race of the year. Few cars have achieved success so rapidly.

The point of the machine is that it is produced to be a competition car, and to that end is complete with every imaginable specialised fitting, and each machine is built individually and with an amount of painstaking hand workmanship of which the price of the complete car is a reflection.

The dimensions of the two-seater body conform to the international regulations, and one glance round the machine suffices to show that nothing need be added to enable one to take the car at once into a race. The instrument board has every conceivable gauge, the brakes can be adjusted while the car is moving, the back shock absorbers also; clip fillers are used for the radiator, fuel tank, and oil tank, the rear fuel tank is really usefully big, the bonnet has not to be lifted for oil replenishment since the tank in the scuttle supplies the engine as required, the wire mesh screen folds flat, there is a stone guard for the radiator, the wire wheels are of racing type, and the hand brake has a racing pawl mechanism.

It is extraordinarily interesting, first of all to test the car on Brooklands track for maximum speed and other data, and then to take it on the road for a long run. This impresses one forcibly with the fact that so many of the features at present regarded as racing practice are actually the best and most efficient for everyday work. For instance, nothing could be better than the big fuel tank, with its touring range of over 350 miles, the quick-acting filler caps, and the method of brake and shock absorber adjustment.

In spite of the fact that this is a proper competition car, there is nothing which makes the machine unsuitable for touring. The car, in fact, constitutes a concrete instance of the value of the developments that are encouraged by modern racing. The exhaust note means that one has to be careful in going through towns, but no trouble need be experienced with the authorities. One would not expect the slow running on top or even third gear to be good; but, in fact, no one interested in a car of this nature would want to make it run slowly on the higher ratios.

With touring plugs in the engine, all the speed that can be ordinarily used on the road is obtainable, and there was no suggestion of any plug oiling up, racing plugs being used only for the fast work on the track. As to the timed speed figure for the half-mile, it is obviously outside everyday requirements, yet is by no means a

limit for the car as a type. It may be mentioned that the actual machine tested was one that ran unsupercharged in the Double-Twelve, and was a practice car for the Tourist Trophy, being an early example, used a good deal by all sorts of people. Something close on 90 m.p.h. is an amazing speed for a 750 c.c. car that is also a practical vehicle on the road; and for all its power the engine is remarkably smooth.

Apart altogether from the maximum, the car has

"THE AUTOCAR" ROAD TESTS

fascination beyond the measure of cold words, for it handles beautifully, is as steady as the proverbial rock, is comfortably sprung as well, possesses a gear change that is a delight in consistency, meaning that the same treatment produces similar results each time, has brakes which recorded the shortest stopping distance during the past twelve months, steers literally to an inch, almost irrespective of road surface, and has terrific acceleration.

Acceleration figures have not been taken for top and third gears for the reason already indicated, and that on second from 10 m.p.h. gives but the slightest impression of the capabilities. It is over the middle range of speed, say from 20 to 50, or 30 to 60, that the car literally shoots away, of course using the indirects, and in the circumstances something rather unusual may be introduced as conveying an idea of what the car can do. From a standing start, going through the gears, it is possible to reach 60 m.p.h. in 20⅘.sec. A normal limit for the engine is 5,500 r.p.m., and at that the equivalent road speeds on the indirects are 20 on first, 40 on second, and 60 m.p.h. on third. Far higher revs are possible, and during the test the engine held 5,750 r.p.m. on top gear, going actually to 6,200 when entering the timed section.

The car is compact, meaning that it can be slipped in and out of traffic with the greatest of ease, but the impression gained from the solid, steady feel is of a machine far bigger than the actual dimensions. The performance is a combination of opposing qualities. With the car once under way at a steady pace it is possible to climb most main-road hills on top gear, even accelerating up them, so considerable is the power developed; but the real joy of the machine lies in employing the indirects to the proper extent, and on a long run one finds one is maintaining in this way a steady speed, whether the road happens to be level, downhill, or ascending, all of which helps in giving a good average.

Of mechanical noise there is remarkably little, and except at quite low speeds the blower can scarcely be heard at all, while the exhaust possesses a remarkably satisfactory crackle to delight the ear of the enthusiast. Perhaps the most striking thing of all is that the car feels safe, so absolutely steady is it under all conditions, taking corners with very little diminution in speed, answering at once to the wheel, and never deflecting from the straight even when the brakes are applied hard. As another aspect of this machine—one able to win races, as has been amply demonstrated, and a practical touring car as well—there is the further point that it is perfectly capable of shining in a reliability trial, since first gear is low and there is sufficient power to take the car up the fiercest gradients. Further, the engine runs very cool.

The equipment has already been mentioned—in fact, it is this which appeals, next to the performance. The instrument panel is entirely free from unnecessary decoration, and carries a most imposing array of dials and push-and-pull switches. Both ignition and fuel supply systems are duplicated. In view of the way in which the car can be used, it should be worth providing a speedometer and lighting for the instruments.

The bucket type seats give support exactly as they should, that for the driver being adjustable; accessibly behind the passenger's seat is the battery; behind the driver's seat is space for oddments and small baggage, whilst in the tail, where the spare wheel is carried, there is additional space. There is a hood of the type fitted to the larger-engined Midgets, which, with its supports, is also stored in the tail.

Starting from cold is easy when the carburetter has been flooded; the fuel used is an 80-20 per cent. mixture of benzole and petrol. Unsupercharged, the machine costs £490.

Using a much misused word, the Montlhéry Mark II M.G. Midget is unique —and is a development that is essentially British.

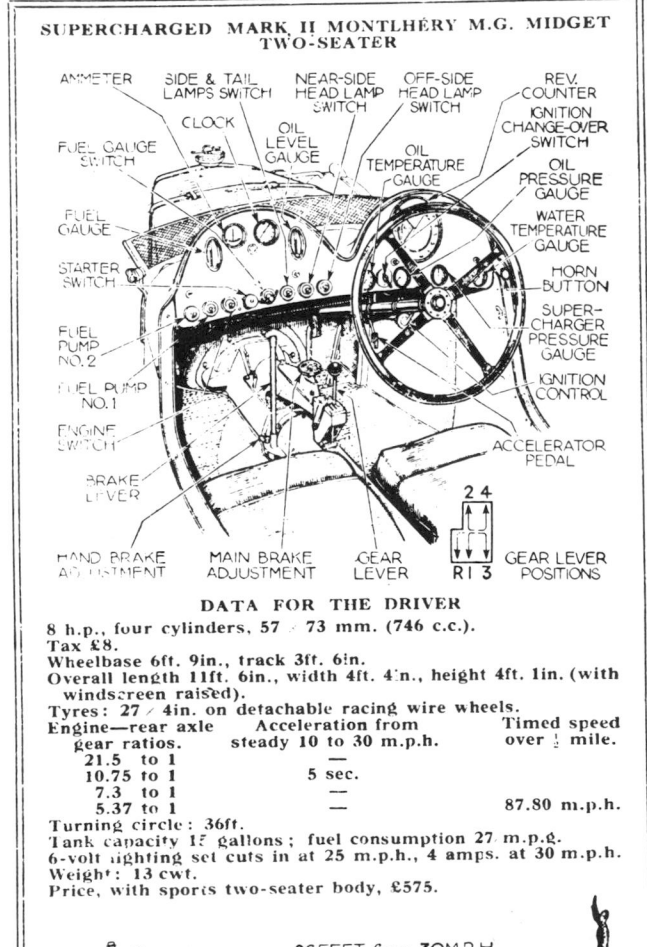

SUPERCHARGED MARK II MONTLHÉRY M.G. MIDGET TWO-SEATER

DATA FOR THE DRIVER

8 h.p., four cylinders, 57 × 73 mm. (746 c.c.).
Tax £8.
Wheelbase 6ft. 9in., track 3ft. 6in.
Overall length 11ft. 6in., width 4ft. 4in., height 4ft. 1in. (with windscreen raised).
Tyres: 27 × 4in. on detachable racing wire wheels.

Engine—rear axle gear ratios.	Acceleration from steady 10 to 30 m.p.h.	Timed speed over ¼ mile.
21.5 to 1	—	
10.75 to 1	5 sec.	
7.3 to 1	—	
5.37 to 1	—	87.80 m.p.h.

Turning circle: 36ft.
Tank capacity 15 gallons; fuel consumption 27 m.p.g.
6-volt lighting set cuts in at 25 m.p.h., 4 amps. at 30 m.p.h.
Weight: 13 cwt.
Price, with sports two-seater body, £575.

26 FEET from 30 M.P.H.

USED CARS ON THE ROAD

No. 51. M.G. Six Mark I Saloon   No. WL7125

PERFORMANCE DATA

Price, new	-	- - £545	Timed speed over measured	
Second-hand -	-	- £225	mile - - 69.77 m.p.h.	
Acceleration -	10-30 m.p.h.		Brake test figure from	
Second gear -	-	6¼ sec.	30 m.p.h. - - - 42ft.	
Top gear - -	-	11 sec.	Speedometer records	
Fuel consumption	19¼ m.p.g.			35,000 miles.
Oil consumption	400 m.p.g.		First registered	1929.

IT is a real pleasure to test a car like the M.G. Six saloon, submitted by University Motors, Ltd., Brick Street, W.1, which demonstrates how little effect 35,000 miles need have on a well-made car. Barring the oil consumption, which, even so, was no heavier than on many cars of a lesser mileage, and which was partially accounted for by really hard driving, there were no signs of mechanical wear. The engine was smooth and quiet, free from any mechanical knocks and noises. It started readily from cold in the morning, and required little warming up.

Once warm, its performance was excellent. The car could be driven at a walking pace on top gear without snatch, and then, by due manipulation of the sensitive ignition control,

accelerated to a speedometer reading of 73 m.p.h., which was not more than 3 m.p.h. optimistic. This corresponded to about 3,600 r.p.m. Above this speed—and 4,000 r.p.m. could be reached on the gears—the engine became more noisy, and valve bounce set in. The timed speed was taken over a full mile against a distinct breeze.

The ignition control needed handling with discretion, if "pinking" was to be avoided, but otherwise the engine was as docile as any touring design.

The gears were reasonably quiet, and 50 m.p.h. was a comfortable maximum on second. On the first ratio Brooklands test hill was surmounted from a standing start at 23 m.p.h. Road-holding was, perhaps, not up to the high standard otherwise set by the car.

The suspension was a little bumpy and could probably be improved by adjustment of the shock absorbers. If really fast cornering was attempted, the car tended to "judder" outwards—not to skid.

Externally, the condition of paint and fabric was good, except for naking on the off-side rear mudguard. Internally also there were no faults to find, all the instruments working well, the roof light and rear blind being in good order, and the leather upholstery not in the least shabby. The dynamo charged at eight amperes—sufficient to supply all the lights.

The head lamps were quite adequate, though not superlative, but the pneumatic-type dipper was out of action.

The seats were comfortable, and the driving position was good. A certain amount of resonance was noted, but one soon became accustomed to the low booming noise.

The brakes were adequate, and, though requiring a fair pressure, did not pull the steering to either side. In the course of the brake test the front off-side cable broke, but this has now been renewed. Even with the cable broken, the car was under perfect control, though naturally there was a pull to the right.

The M.G. was definitely a good car—gentle, yet with a sporting performance. It was sound, reliable, and smart, and no faults beyond those mentioned could be detected.

INTO BATTLE 1931

FEBRUARY 1931 - the first-ever meeting of the newly-formed M.G. Car Club, a half-day trial in the High Wycombe Oxford area in which 60 members entered their cars. Here, Viscount Curzon, son of Earl Howe, sets off on the standing start acceleration test up Waterwork Hill, near Tring.

MONTE CARLO RALLY 1931: Norman Black's Speed Model, which led the John o'Groats starters, put up fourth fastest time in the Acceleration and Brake Test (15·8 sec to Donald Healey's Invicta 15·0 sec, outright winner of the Rally, and finished 16th in the Over 1,100 c.c. Division - winning the Barclay's Bank Cup. Of 149 starters, 62 finished, 25 of them British.

The Autocar Road Tests

The illustration above indicates the size, in feet, of the M.G. Six Mark II saloon

No. 681 $\left(\begin{smallmatrix}Post\text{-}War\\Series\end{smallmatrix}\right)$—M.G. SIX MARK II SALOON

AS from time to time acquaintance is renewed with the M.G. Six, the feature which impresses itself most vividly upon the mind is the amazing smoothness of the engine. This is a car which has many admirable qualities; it has power, it has performance, it handles very well indeed, it appeals at once to the enthusiast, yet is suitable for a driver who prefers to run for a great part of the time on top gear.

It is not too much to say that this particular engine is one of the smoothest and least obtrusive in existence, irrespective of price of car. This in itself, desirable as it is, would not be so attractive if the rest of the car did not make the driver feel that it is a machine responsive at once to all the controls, which amply repays intelligent handling, and is the kind of car for which the possessor soon comes to feel real pride of ownership. Moreover, it is one on which high average speeds are maintained without sense of effort.

Why one car should produce this effect, yet another, perfectly good in its way, remain to the discriminating motorist as chiefly a means of conveyance, is elusive.

But to start with, the M.G. has steering which is accurate and gives just the right amount of caster action. Further, the car can be cornered fast without sway or roll, and feels safe at speed. As might be expected, the springing has necessarily to be on the hard side, which is noticeable at low speeds, but even as far as back-seat passengers are concerned there is no suggestion of direct discomfort. Friction shock absorbers are employed, and with these set fairly tight the road-holding is all that can be desired, the springing smoothing itself out, as it

were, as the speed increases. The general stability for what is a comfortable saloon car is very good indeed.

Then the car could not be what it is if the brakes were not entirely adequate to the speed. They have proper progressiveness, so that light pressure produces the amount of slowing required in ordinary circumstances, whilst fairly heavy pressure on the pedal is needed to effect an emergency stop. At no time is it easy to lock wheels, nor is there any deviation from the straight. The hand lever is of racing type, which is actually the best type of hand brake for any car.

Of the several excellent features appealing to a driver who takes any interest at all in driving for its own sake, the gear change, with the short, stiff lever coming to hand at exactly the right point, is, again, one of the most delightful in existence. The movement of the lever from gear to gear is comparatively short; third speed is a silent ratio, and, incidentally, has been found to be quieter on other cars of this model previously driven. The change is perfectly straightforward, very quick for anything bar a machine of racing type, and changing from top to third is especially easy, the ratios being quite close. The clutch takes up its work smoothly, and the pedal action is light.

Top is a well-chosen ratio, though there is every reason, from the interest point of view, why third should be employed frequently to good effect. On the indirects, speedometer readings of 20 on first, 36 on second, and 65 on third are possible without forcing the engine to the point where it becomes even slightly harsh.

As to the limit on top, the great merit of this remarkable engine is that it

remains smooth almost to the very maximum, and is entirely happy to cruise at a speedometer reading as high as 65. During the timed speed test the speedometer went to a reading of 84 m.p.h. and the rev counter recorded 3,750 r.p.m. The speed, as an average over a measured distance, is excellent for a saloon of this engine capacity.

In studying the car from the point of view of maintenance and convenience, the feature which emerges strongly is that, much more than most, the M.G. has been laid out by practical motorists whose aim has been to make the owner's task as easy as possible, with full appreciation of the kind of difficulty that usually arises. For instance, in detail, the floorboards are arranged in sections, each section being held by locks operated by an ordinary carriage key, so that the floorboards are very easily removed.

Again, the luggage container at the back, which is built very neatly into the body, is capacious in itself, but should an unusual amount of luggage be carried, the lid hinges down, and is already provided with straps so that extra suitcases can be attached to it. Under the bonnet, too, on the cover for the overhead valve gear, is a metal plate inscribed with all manner of information. That alone may be a small thing, but it goes to show something of the attitude of those responsible.

The four-door saloon body has plenty of leg room, there being wells in the floor for the back-seat occupants; and though there are only two windows at either side a point upon which passengers comment is the unusual sense of light and spaciousness in the interior, as well as upon the lack of any drumming effect. The ventilator in the roof, which is provided with glass, helps materially in making the interior light, yet does not detract from the appearance of the car outwardly.

The upholstery is very good, being of durable leather; the bucket-type front seats are immediately adjustable, their backs sloping rearwards rather more than is usual for this type of seat, whilst at the rear there are arm-rests at either side and a central folding arm-rest, as well as neatly recessed companions.

Glass of the safety type is fitted to all the windows, including that at the back; the blind for the latter is controlled from the driving seat, there being a proper catch to hold it in the raised position. A blind is provided for each of the side windows; the screen opens fully and has an electric wiper with two blades, the mechanism being mounted very sensibly on the near side, out of the driver's line of vision. The instrument panel carries an engine thermometer as well as an electric fuel gauge, a clock, and a revolution counter, the dials being very nicely balanced and beautifully lighted at night by two direct lamps with green-tinted bulbs. On either side of the instruments are cubby holes with lids; and, in addition, there is a pocket in each of the rear doors, and a roof net.

The engine is very neat indeed; each of the sparking plugs is easily accessible, the coil also, there being the advantage that it is in a protected position. Carried in the scuttle, with their filler caps accessible under the bonnet, are containers for a spare gallon of oil and a gallon of fuel.

The engine starts remarkably easily, it being unnecessary during warm weather even to employ the mixture control when starting from cold. A special type of automatic chassis lubrication is fitted, the container for the oil being under the bonnet. This is operated by the movement of the car itself actuating an oscillating weight, and so a small plunger pump, with no other mechanism.

The head lamps give a very good beam indeed the charging rate of the dynamo is sufficiently high to provide a surplus of current with all lights on.

This is a car with a definite personality, most fascinating to drive.

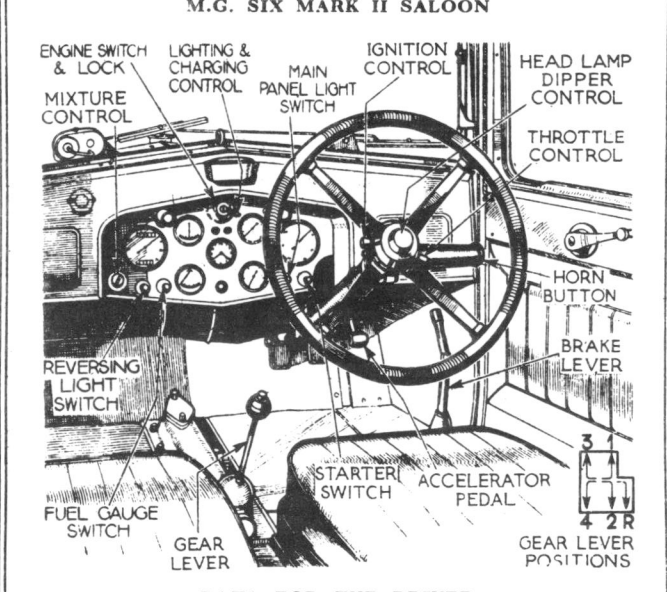

M.G. SIX MARK II SALOON

ENGINE SWITCH & LOCK — MIXTURE CONTROL — LIGHTING & CHARGING CONTROL — MAIN PANEL LIGHT SWITCH — IGNITION CONTROL — HEAD LAMP DIPPER CONTROL — THROTTLE CONTROL — HORN BUTTON — BRAKE LEVER — REVERSING LIGHT SWITCH — FUEL GAUGE SWITCH — GEAR LEVER — STARTER SWITCH — ACCELERATOR PEDAL — GEAR LEVER POSITIONS

DATA FOR THE DRIVER

17.7 h.p., six cylinders, 69 × 110 mm. (2,468 c.c.).
Tax £18.
Wheelbase 9ft. 6in., track 4ft. 4in.
Overall length 13ft. 1in., width 5ft. 5in., height 5ft. 7in.
Tyres: 29 × 5in. on detachable wire wheels.

Engine—rear axle gear ratios.	Acceleration from steady 10 to 30 m.p.h.	Timed speed over ¼ mile.
14.58 to 1	—	
8.5 to 1	6¼ sec.	
5.58 to 1	9 sec.	
4.27 to 1	12¼ sec.	74.38 m.p.h.

Turning circle: 38ft.
Tank capacity 12 gallons, fuel consumption 20 m.p.g.
12-volt lighting set cuts in at 13 m.p.h., 12 amps. at 30 m.p.h.
Weight: 29 cwt.
Price, with four-door saloon body, £670.

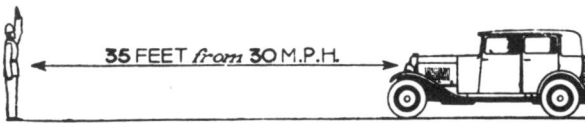

35 FEET *from* 30 M.P.H.

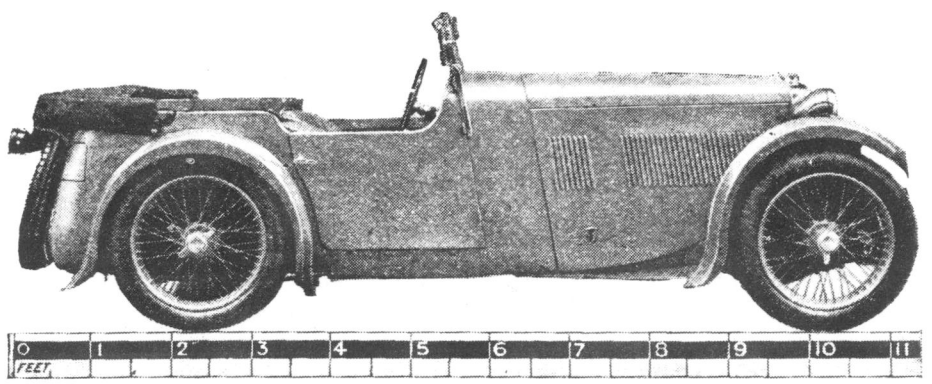

No. 692 (Post-War Series).—M.G. MAGNA FOUR-SEATER

THERE are some few cars, not necessarily of any one type, destined to be a success from the commencement. The new model which has inspired this remark is the M.G. Magna. This is definitely a car of the moment, and there are two sharp divisions at present—those who have tried the Magna, and those who have not. The former may almost be said to be equivalent to wanting to own one.

The Magna should be to the economical six-cylinder sports car class what the Midget has come to be in the smaller four-cylinder world. For £250 what one gets is this: A six-cylinder machine, noticeably but not freakishly low built, with a four-speed gear box, obviously laid out with sports car ideals in mind, yet giving the things that practically every driver wants, or would appreciate if he knew.

Add to this a trim little four-seater body—it being the open car that has been tested—with an imposing length of bonnet and scuttle, yet a perfectly clear view forward, and not the slightest suggestion of unwieldiness. In fact, one of the most marked points is the extreme ease with which the car can be handled on crowded roads, and the lack of effort associated with manœuvring it.

The strongest first impression is that the machine feels solid and rigid in the right way, suggesting a strong chassis properly built, and can be taken round curves and corners just as one pleases, the position of the steering wheel and other controls, coupled with this stability, making for confidence and accuracy right from the beginning, as nothing else can.

The Magna can maintain well above a genuine 70 miles an hour, as the timed speed in the accompanying table shows. That is excellent when one is in a hurry or feels like speed, for there is no particular sense of effort even at the limit; but the great charm of the car lies not at all in this maximum, good though it is to have in reserve. It is utterly fascinating to drive the car even in traffic, with its bright acceleration, or to cruise for mile on end at never more than 50 or 55, a speed which is reached very quickly, the engine running smoothly and quietly with just a pleasing but subdued note from the exhaust, simply because the "feel" of the car is exactly right—thoroughly satisfactory to an unusually enthusiastic driver, or subtly removing some of the doubts and difficulties of a possibly less experienced or less interested driver.

Five miles an hour is feasible on top gear without jerk or snatch, and hills are taken in the car's stride. But for those who like to use it there is what is probably the most delightful gear box fitted to a car of moderate price: four speeds with three close ratios, meaning that 60 can be reached on third and 40 on second, with a low first that will take the machine, fully loaded, up a hill of the trials order with power in hand, controlled by a short, stiff lever working in a visible gate, and with a really easily operated catch to guard reverse. The positions of the lever for the various ratios are different from what is normal, but that is a thing to which one is quickly accustomed; third and second gears run quite quietly, first being noisier by comparison, though it

---

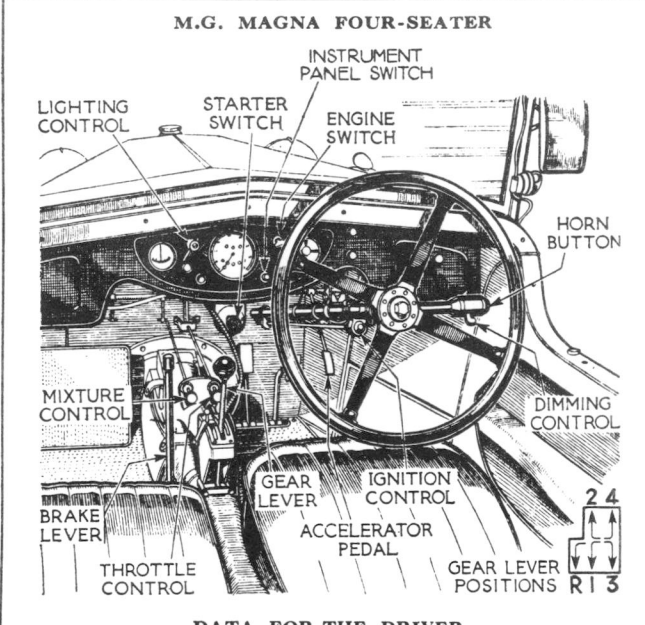

M.G. MAGNA FOUR-SEATER

LIGHTING CONTROL — STARTER SWITCH — INSTRUMENT PANEL SWITCH — ENGINE SWITCH — HORN BUTTON — MIXTURE CONTROL — DIMMING CONTROL — BRAKE LEVER — GEAR LEVER — IGNITION CONTROL — ACCELERATOR PEDAL — THROTTLE CONTROL — GEAR LEVER POSITIONS

DATA FOR THE DRIVER

12–70 h.p., six cylinders, 57 × 83 mm. (1,270 c.c.).
Tax £12.
Wheelbase 7ft. 10in., track 3ft. 6in.
Overall length 11ft. 6½in., width 4ft. 2in., height 4ft. 6in.
Tyres: 4 × 19in. on detachable wire wheels.

Engine—rear axle gear ratios.	Acceleration from steady 10 to 30 m.p.h.	Timed speed over ¼ mile.
19.2 to 1		
9.56 to 1	6 sec.	
6.3 to 1	8¼ sec.	
4.78 to 1	11⅘ sec.	72.58 m.p.h.

Turning circle: 35ft.
Tank capacity 6 gallons, fuel consumption 26 m.p.g.
12-volt lighting set cuts in at 15 m.p.h., 8 amps. at 30 m.p.h.
Weight: 19 cwt. 1 qr.
Price, with sports four-seater body, £250.

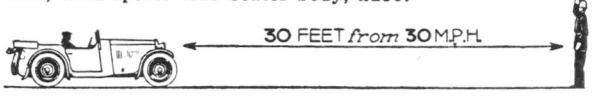

30 FEET from 30 M.P.H

Chassis described in "The Autocar" of September 11th, 1931.

M.G. MAGNA FOUR-SEATER

is seldom used for more than a few yards. The steering is very light, but not to the point of being indefinite, and the spring-spoked wheel has a nice thin rim, whilst the clutch works lightly, too, and takes up the drive smoothly. The brakes have plenty of power and, what is more, do not make the car swerve when they are put on hard. The hand-brake lever is of what is termed racing type, and is excellent in every way, besides having at its base an adjustment that can be taken up by hand.

As has been mentioned, the car holds the road very well indeed, helped by big double-acting friction shock absorbers front and rear, so that it might be expected that at quite low speeds, with the shock absorbers tight, the effect would be hard. That, however, is largely a question of adjustment to taste. Even the back seat is comfortable by sports car standards; there is good leg room for one tall passenger, and reasonable space for two normal people.

The separate front seats have pneumatic cushions and backs, the latter sloping rearward rather more than is usual in the interests of firm support for driving, though this is a point that comes rather to be liked. Each seat is quite easily adjustable, but a more rapid action might be preferable; the hood goes up easily and there are good side screens to make the interior snug, whilst a tonneau cover normally fits over the back seats. The front seats tilt forward to give access to the back compartment, the two doors being wide.

In each door is a wide pocket, above which is a small arm-rest on each side. The grouped instruments —speedometer, ammeter, and oil feed indicating dial, in place of a normal pressure gauge—are brightly lit indirectly. A fuel gauge and an engine thermometer would be welcomed. The single-panel screen folds flat on the scuttle, if wished, and has a twin-blade suction wiper, which works at as much as 50 m.p.h.

A great thing is the instantaneous starting of the engine at all times. The accessibility of the engine, the tools—carried in a locker beneath the bonnet—the clutch housing and gear box, as well as the interior of the driving compartment for cleaning-out purposes, is excellent, because what is usually the scuttle is included in the hinged portion of the bonnet, and therefore opens up.

With its polished valve cover, and nicely red-painted cylinder block, the engine looks pleasing, and, on the practical side, the sparking plugs are eminently accessible, also the coil, distributor, and the electrical fuse box. Even with the fan belt removed the engine does not run hot. Also beneath the bonnet are two groups of lubricators, facing outwards ideally, which feed oil from the usual pressure gun through pipe lines to most of the chassis bearings, leaving very few to be dealt with individually.

An unusual point is the concealment of the filler for the fuel tank by a hinged lid in the side of the body tail; this is undeniably neat, but not too convenient.

The head lamp beam is good, and either the dimming switch or the horn button can be operated without removing the right hand from the wheel.

AN UNUSUAL BODY ON AN M.G.

November 20th, 1931.

THE M.G. Six Mark II, illustrated here, has a body by the Carlton Carriage Co., built to the special requirements of University Motors, Ltd. It is unusual in that the cant rails, from the rear pillars of the doors forward, fold inwards, and the canopy can then be rolled back and secured, thus converting the body into a modified coupé de ville. The hood can also be folded down to form a fully open car. In the tail is space for a considerable quantity of luggage. The chassis is a standard Mark II with four speeds, and the price of the complete car is £750.

December 25th, 1931.

The Earl Howe and the M.G. Magna he has just had delivered. It is finished in the Earl's racing colours.

PUTTING IN THE PEP

The Inner Meanings of " Faster than Most " and " Safety Fast "

O N a nasty bleak morning early in 1931—February 16th, to be exact—Mr. G. E. T. Eyston, as is now well known, drove a British motor car with an engine of less than 750 c.c. at 103.13 m.p.h. over five kilometres. He kept up the remarkable speed of over 100 m.p.h. for ten miles, over which distance he averaged 101.86 m.p.h. He was attacking International Class H records at Montlhéry track, near Paris.

Eyston did more than annex the record on that occasion; he was the first man to attain a speed of over 100 m.p.h. with an engine of less than 750 c.c. He achieved this with an M.G. Midget.

The whole effort—car, driver and organisation — was purely British: This record had been the goal of designers and makers of what the public love to call baby cars for a long time. Whatever may be done in the future it must never be forgotten that this achievement, perhaps one of the most remarkable in the latter-day history of motoring, was accomplished by the Midget. Since then, on October 17th, 1931, Eldridge covered five kilometres on a 750 c.c. Midget at 110.28 m.p.h., a speed exactly equal to that of Kaye Don on the water with Miss England II.

M.G. cars hail from about as unlikely a spot to house a motor car factory as any I can imagine. I always regard Oxford as an unlikely spot wherein to find motor cars being pro-

By

MAURICE SAMPSON
Illustrated by F. GORDON-CROSBY

duced; but, as all the world knows now, that always surprising person, Sir William Morris, and his associates, manage to turn out quite a number from the ancient city of learning. But if Oxford is unlikely as a motor car centre, how shall we regard Abingdon-on-Thames? Yet, tucked neatly away in this little Berkshire town of just over 7,000 inhabitants, is a modern, beautifully equipped, and marvellously clean factory, from which at least one hundred or more sports cars can be produced weekly.

The history of what is now known as the M.G. Car Co., Ltd., is interesting because it shows how a single individual with a single mind fired with great enthusiasm, and backed by a sympathetic and encouraging director, can from nothing, as it were, step right into the forefront of motor car constructors who matter.

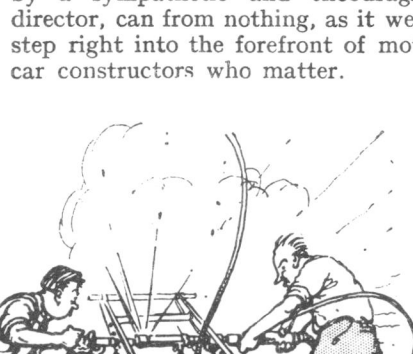

Magna frames.

About seven years ago there was no such thing as an M.G. car, but soon afterwards it was very much alive, and this is how it came about. In Oxford, in addition to his great and growing establishment at Cowley, Mr. (now Sir William) Morris owned one or two garages. These were, and still are, known simply and appropriately as the Morris Garages. The bright, shining light in charge of them was one Cecil Kimber, who had already spent many years enthusiastically making fast motor bicycles faster and doing the same to cars when he got the chance. He prevailed upon his employer to let him get to work on the round-nosed Morris-Oxfords of the period, and he put the 'fluence on them to such purpose that they outdistanced every other Morris-Oxford on the road.

The first year's production of these hand-made cars—and do not forget they were produced only in the intervals of running busy garages, and more or less with the aid of the necessarily limited tool equipment available, Cowley merely supplying the chassis—amounted, I believe, to six in all. But those six were seeds that took root to some purpose, and next year things began to get busy. Then came the time when the round-nosed radiator of the Morris models gave way to the present rectangular type, and more ambitious plans were conceived.

The result was that only the essentials, such as the engine and its components, the gear box, and the back axle, and main frame, were obtained from Cowley. These were then " specialised," and the M.G. car began to take on an entity of its own. They began to be recognised in trials and became a usual mount for the sporting driver.

So things continued in a steadily growing volume until a little over two years ago, when an opportunity came

to purchase a very excellent modern factory, and a transfer of activities was made from Oxford to Abingdon, half a dozen miles along the Thames.

A new company was formed, Cecil Kimber placed in command, still, of course, with the sympathetic backing of Sir William, and a completely new line of cars evolved. There are three types of M.G. cars made at Abingdon —the six-cylinder of 17.7 nominal h.p., the Midget of 8 nominal h.p., and the Magna. The last was one of the greatest popular attractions at Olympia.

Safety Fast.

Their designer and maker has hit upon what I think are two of the cleverest and most apposite of slogans yet used in the motor industry. He boldly labels his cars "Faster than Most," and adopts the motto of "Safety Fast." I do not think a truer and more concise description could possibly be found. The M.G. Six, although not the fastest two-and-a-half litre, or thereabouts, sports car in the world, is certainly faster than most.

Appearances DO Count

What sort of an establishment do we find at the prettily named Pavlova works at Abingdon? Although assembly lines in the most modern style are used, every car is essentially hand-made. Indeed, so completely is hand-work carried out that almost the first thing I saw was two men busily filing and finishing the dumb-irons of an unpainted chassis frame of an M.G. Six, and apparently imparting such a gloss that one might have thought they were trying to convert the dumb-irons into mirrors.

"Why that?" I asked. "It seems a funny way to spend money."

"Yes," said C. K., "but it makes the cellulose look nice and smooth at the front of the car, and I believe in appearance as much as in performance." Incidentally, the works have their own frame-building department, wherein the very rigid frame of the Magna is the biggest centre of interest.

This little incident is typical of the whole establishment, and, indeed, it

PUTTING IN THE PEP
(continued)

is typical of the designer, for not only does he conceive his working mission in life to be to provide ever better, and more efficient, speedy cars, but to do something worth doing towards making motor cars more beautiful and artistic objects than most of them are at present. "C. K." will unite with any Royal Academician in allowing that the average motor car is not yet a thing of beauty. You may arrange it so that, viewed sideways, it is very attractive, but seen from the front, or from the back, or from a three-quarter angle, ten to one something has gone wrong. So he spends hours plotting and planning and devising new lines which in due course may be incorporated in the finished article for which he is responsible.

A Chassis to Fit the Seats

Hitherto the bodymaker has been handicapped by the chassis maker. The chassis maker presents his structure and expects the bodymaker to render the whole symmetrical, and very often this is desperately difficult. After all, the only constant thing in a car is the seats. We all take up much the same space unless we happen to be very outsize or small size, but on the average we all require about the same head-room, leg-room, and elbow-room.

So I was not at all surprised to find some little experimental work proceeding whereby a set of seats had been arranged and drawings were

Midgets.

being made to design a chassis to go under the seats, thus reversing the principle of designing the seats to go over the chassis, and I thought how coachbuilders would, if such a millennium, from their point of view, came to pass, bless the name of Cecil Kimber, and raise statues to him in such places where they make motor car bodies.

Now it is a desperately difficult thing to make a fast car at all, and it is even more difficult when it has to be made more or less conventional. Yet the M.G. people have done it. Let us step right into the Pavlova works and see how it is brought about.

The first impression is one of spaciousness. No one is cramped; everyone has ample elbow room. The concrete floors are spotlessly clean. There

Faster Than Most.

are lines of Midgets, Magnas, and M.G. Sixes moving slowly from nothing to complete cars.

In a sense it seems incongruous that assembly lines are used for cars built so slowly and meticulously. But the lines ensure orderliness; they keep everything and everybody in their places, as it were. Now and again, from a high-up overhead gallery, a chain lowers an engine or a gear box to its appointed place.

Time Means Money

I need not follow the chassis bolt by bolt, so to speak. It is at length finished. Not to-day, perhaps, or even to-morrow. Time is expensive in a motor car factory, especially in one where the labour is necessarily very skilled. That is why the Magnas and the others are not cheap. They are never likely to be. They are made with two main objects in view: to run far and fast and to look attractive. It may be that a car here and there is a "special"; it has to embody certain little details to its future owner's desires. It will take an extra long time to get this one out of the works. Never mind! It is not a matter for worry or grumble; rather of pride. Here will be an M.G. which will go a bit faster than its fellows, or look just a little more *soigné*.

It is in touches like this that a sports car is judged. Sports cars are made for those who want "something different." As a pronounced and unrepentant individualist, I rejoice that there are such cars and people with the means and inclination to buy them. Many firms do not like people who have special ideas for their cars. Quite reasonably, from their viewpoint, they call the ideas fads, and discourage them. Their business is to make a lot of one sort. Probably very good cars, but each a twin of the last. It is because of this "like each other" method of production that we get such good cheap cars to-day. But a man who sets out to make and sell sports cars resembles some world-famous dressmaker; he must create exclusive models.

So if you say you want an M.G. differing in appearance and details and even faster than the one that insufferable young sportsman who lives down your road owns, you can have it—if you can pay for it and do not mind a little delay in delivery.

This is one of the reasons why people making sports cars are always enthusiasts. They have to be, they are for ever meeting enthusiasts. If I hadn't my own work to do I'd rather make sports cars for sporting men and women than do anything else. The whole atmosphere at Abingdon is keen, alert and enthusiastic. It is the sports car atmosphere. I noticed just the same air at Molsheim when I was there, and, I doubt not, would find it at a certain place in Milan, if I went there.

Of International Importance

Sports cars are really and truly international affairs. The keen amateurs of France and Italy and England, and of many other countries, know and appreciate and respect the sports cars and their makers of countries other than their own. Believing this, I believe in motor car racing. It is not only good for cars; it is good for humanity, which is more important.

Forgive this jump off the assembly line; we will go back there.

Behind the line, in a near-by bay, but visible through the narrow steel pillars, is a line of bodies, and as, at last, the chassis is complete and finally tested, its appropriate body steps forward to meet it.

Properly joined up, the complete M.G. car, no matter of what sort, goes

Black magic.

through three kinds of tests on machines I have not seen in operation under one roof before. Let me explain.

One of the difficulties confronting manufacturers of extra fast and necessarily rather costly cars is the matter of thoroughly testing them on the road. As I have just indicated, every M.G. chassis is properly tested, and every complete M.G. car is also taken on the road, and it is taken out to discover any lurking rattles or noises from chassis or body before delivery.

Safe Testing

There are several very potent reasons why road testing alone is not advisable for cars of the M.G. types. First of all it is far better, however experienced the tester, to have tests conducted under the eye of the principal factory officials. This cannot be the case when the car is miles out in the country. It is also difficult to ensure that highly finished coachwork does not acquire some small blemish however carefully washed after road tests at speed.

More serious still, there is the possibility of accident to be avoided. No

manufacturer wants any of his employees to run any unnecessary risks, and it is evident that risks are involved in testing a fast car on the road if the test is to be a real test and is to do anything more than discover and rectify a rattle.

The Testing Apparatus

So at the Pavlova works three extremely clever and interesting mechanical installations are employed to obviate these drawbacks. These are respectively the Bendix-Cowdray brake tester, the Comparator, or high-speed tester, and a machine for checking any misalignment of the front wheels and indicating, while the adjustment is being made, the exact moment when accuracy is achieved.

The brake-testing apparatus consists of four sets of two small rollers, each of which receives a wheel of the car. Once the car is on the rollers the front axle is anchored to the machine by a chain; driving each of the four sets of rollers are electric motors, and connected to each of the roller sets is a torque resistance indicator. If the brakes are applied, the amount of braking resistance on each wheel is indicated on four dials, and each individual wheel can have the brakes adjusted so that resistance shown on the dials is equal; or, if desired, a greater resistance is shown on the front than on the back dials. While all this is taking place the head lamps are focused on a screen set at the correct height and distance from them.

On the wash.

Thus time is saved and accuracy in brake setting ensured without the car leaving the shop.

The brakes having been adjusted, the car is taken to the wheel tracking machine, which consists of two strips of steel let into a hollow platform and arranged on ball bearings so that they can be moved inwardly or outwardly, the motion being parallel. This motion is transmitted to a large dial on a pedestal, and all that is necessary is for the tester to drive the car over the two strips of steel, and if the alignment is correct the plates are not moved either inwards or outwards. If the wheels are "in-toed" the plates are forced outwards and the dials record the degree of "in-toe"; and conversely if "out-toe" is present. Adjustment of the track rod can then be made with the car on the machine, the dials registering all the time the exact position of the wheels. Compared with the old-fashioned trammels, the time saved and the accuracy attained are remarkable.

The Comparator

Our M.G. now having its tracking correct and its brakes perfectly adjusted, is taken to the Comparator, a device mainly composed of two sets of large-diameter rollers upon which the rear wheels of the car rest. When the engine has been started and top gear engaged the wheels drive the rollers. These are coupled to a brake fan, the size and resistance of the fan being adjustable so that the speeds obtained on this device are comparable with the speeds obtainable on the road, the resistance of the fan representing the resistance of the air.

PUTTING IN THE PEP
(continued)

Every Midget must show a genuine speed of 60 m.p.h. on this device, and if it fails the necessary engine adjustments and carburetter timing are made until the desired figure is reached.

The "once over."

Thus, without risk to anyone and with no possibility of damage to the car, high-speed tests are carried out in the privacy of the works.

Every engine, of course, has undergone long and strenuous bench tests before it has ever reached the chassis, and it can be said without possibility of contradiction that an M.G. car is a thoroughly tested machine the instant it is in its owner's hands.

Perhaps one of the most interesting corners in the works is that railed off and screened from prying eyes and de-

> *AUTHOR'S NOTE.*
> *Since writing the foregoing, George Eyston has run a 750 c.c. Midget for 10 miles at Montlhéry at 114·46 m.p.h. For 5 km. he averaged 114·77 m.p.h. Some Pep!*

voted to experimental work. Here the cars destined to compete in races are got ready, new ideas are tried out, and much experimental designing work is engaged in.

Adjoining this experimental department is the drawing office, and nothing more clearly conveys the amount of work involved in the production of sports cars than the fact that over 3,000 drawings have been made relative to the putting into production of the last two models.

I have deliberately tried to convey the atmosphere of these works rather than detail the processes of construction overmuch. A sports car must be made and manufactured—the two terms are *not* synonymous if you think about it—just like any other car.

By the way, what *is* a sports car? It used to be one which was fast and/or noisy and/or uncomfortable. But the M.G. is only fast; it fails dismally in the other characteristics. It is quiet and it is comfortable. Therefore it cannot, according to some people, be a sports car. But it is; most emphatically Yes!

What is a Sports Car?

My own idea of a sports car is a car which, once tried, makes ordinary cars feel ordinary when previously they felt remarkable. Certainly the M.G. models go a long way on this errand, and I take off my hat to them. What is more, I rehearse the "Come by" signal when I see the radiator of one in my driving mirror. Yes, although my own very good car is no slug. 114 m.p.h. (see author's note) with a 750 c.c. engine! Some of our quiet, old-fashioned English towns do produce rather wonderful things sometimes.

INTO BATTLE 1932

INTER-CENTRE RALLY. L. F. Robson's M.G. Magna skidding a corner at Ledbury during th J.C.C. Inter-Centre Rally. Liverpool Centre were the winners.

The new Abbey coupé on the M.G. Magna chassis.

SWEET AND LOW

WITH the ever-increasing number of standard type cars on the road the demand for special bodies increases in like proportion. Among the several firms meeting the needs of this market are Abbey Coachworks, Ltd., of Minerva Road, Chase Estate, North Acton, and their most recent design is a coupé on an M.G. Magna chassis, which particularly lends itself to special designs in coachwork on account of its low frame, long bonnet, and attractive radiator. These features provide the coachbuilder with plenty of scope for producing something really smart and out of the ordinary in the way of either open or closed bodywork.

Ample Comfort

This two-seater all-panelled coupé is of interesting design and is certainly striking. The unusual treatment of the wings and tail is the most outstanding feature of the body, coupled with a total height of only 4ft. 1½in., notwithstanding which there is ample headroom for even a tall passenger, while the width of the body is such that ample elbow room is provided for both passenger and driver. It will be seen, therefore, that comfort and practicability have not been sacrificed for appearance. Behind the two adjustable bucket seats, the squabs of

A Smart and Roomy New Special Coupé on the M.G. Magna Chassis, with Overall Height of Only Four Feet One and a Half Inches

The figure is admittedly tall and slightly over-emphasises the extremely low overall height of the car.

which fold forward, is space for two or three large suitcases.

At first sight it might appear that the narrowness of the single panel screen, which, incidentally, opens out fully,

restricts the driver's view, but such is not the case. The view from within the car is remarkable when one thinks of the dimensions from ground to roof. Tandem electric screenwipers are fitted, and wipe nearly the whole area of the glass, which makes for increased safety and comfort of mind in wet weather. The eight-gallon rear fuel tank is provided with a special quick-action cap, and is handily placed for refueling from a pump or can.

Easy to Enter

Ease of entry and exit is assisted by the wide doors opening from their forward edges. Winding windows are provided, that at the rear being in two halves. Tools are housed in a locker beneath the bonnet, which is standard practice on the Magna, and in every other respect the chassis is unaltered. The performance of the car is too well known to need any reference. It is sufficient to say that that performance, coupled with coachwork such as is illustrated on this page, is all that can be desired in the way of distinctiveness.

The price of the complete car is £345, so it cannot be considered a cheap car. On the other hand, it is good value in view of the general excellence of the workmanship and the high grade of finish.

The style of the panelling, which is well carried out, together with the unusual treatment of the wings and tail, are seen in these two "three-quarter" views of the little car.

Published *The Autocar,*
5 August 1932

THE AUTOCAR ROAD TESTS

No. 739
(Post-War Series)

M.G. MIDGET TWO-SEATER

7′2″
10′4″

THERE is every reason to suppose that the new M.G. Midget will be a great success. The latest car, described in detail elsewhere in this issue, is a direct and logical development from the experience gained by the firm in competition work of all kinds, yet its appeal is not based solely on performance, tremendous though that is for the engine size and the price of the complete car. Comfort has been studied so carefully that it is a remarkably pleasant car to ride in, quite apart from what it is able to do.

It would naturally be expected from the mechanical modifications in this latest car that the performance would be improved as compared with its predecessor, the ordinary Midget. What is not so much expected is that the performance should have gone up to a genuine 80 m.p.h., the car still retaining tractability and flexibility at low speeds. After testing the machine for sheer performance on Brooklands track, and then observing on the road how it behaves in comparison with other much bigger vehicles, there is every reason for the driver to feel amazed at what has been achieved, and to be led into the impression that the engine must be bigger than it actually is.

Apart from speed, not only on top gear but on the indirect gears, the things that matter most about a sports car are the driving position and controls. The new Midget has a driving position which is exactly right, the back rest of the seat being sloped at a natural angle, while the pneumatic cushions for driver and passenger are separate.

The steering wheel comes within easy reach, is bigger than it was formerly, and, of course, is spring-spoked; the short, stiff gear lever is of the remote control type, with a visible gate; the racing type central hand-brake lever is where it should be; in front of the driver is a big, clear dial, consisting of a combined speedometer and rev. counter, the latter applying to top and third gears, and each of the controls works with a minimum pressure of hand or foot.

The charm of the car to the enthusiast, again, is in the ability, in fact the eagerness, of the engine to turn over at extremely high revs., 5,800 r.p.m. being well within its capabilities. This means that though second and first are comparatively low gear ratios, the car gets going very snappily indeed, for it can be run up to 20 m.p.h. on first, 36 on second, and easily to 60 on third, in which connection it may be mentioned that on the cars delivered second gear will be a higher ratio, which should be a considerable improvement.

A highly commendable feature is that the speedometer read slow throughout

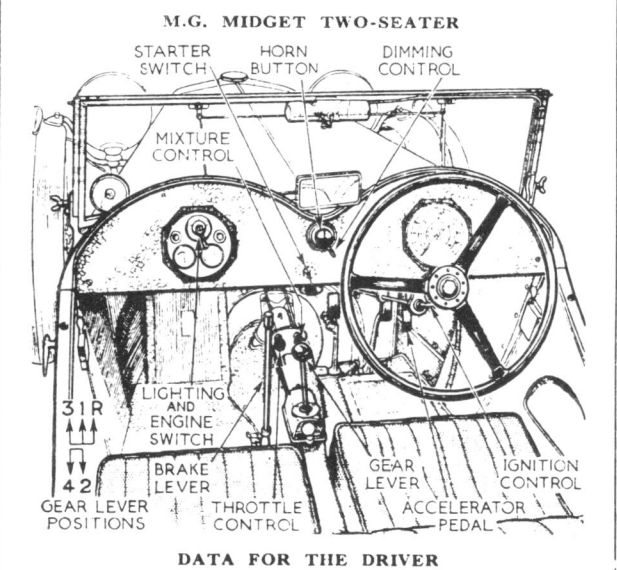

M.G. MIDGET TWO-SEATER

STARTER SWITCH — HORN BUTTON — DIMMING CONTROL

MIXTURE CONTROL

3 1 R
4 2
GEAR LEVER POSITIONS

LIGHTING AND ENGINE SWITCH

BRAKE LEVER

THROTTLE CONTROL

GEAR LEVER

IGNITION CONTROL

ACCELERATOR PEDAL

DATA FOR THE DRIVER

8 h.p., four cylinders, 57 × 83 mm. (847 c.c.).
Tax £8.
Wheelbase 7ft. 2in., track 3ft. 6in.
Overall length 10ft. 4in., width 4ft. 3½in., height 4ft. 4¾in.
Tyres: 27 × 4.00in. on detachable wire wheels.

Engine—rear axle gear ratios.	Acceleration from steady speed.			Timed speed over ¼ mile.
	10 to 30 m.p.h.	20 to 40 m.p.h.	30 to 50 m.p.h.	
19.24 to 1	—	—	—	
11.50 to 1	5¼ sec.	—	—	
7.31 to 1	9¼ sec.	9¼ sec.	10¼ sec.	
5.37 to 1	14½ sec.	13½ sec.	16 sec.	80.35 m.p.h.

Turning circle: 34ft.
Tank capacity 12 gallons, fuel consumption 35 m.p.g. (approx.).
12-volt lighting set cuts in at 12 m.p.h., 7 amps. at 30 m.p.h.
Weight: 11 cwt. 1 qr.
Price, with sports two-seater body, £199 10s.

27 FEET *from* 30 M.P.H.

"THE AUTOCAR" ROAD TESTS

the range, and even during the timed test did not go above 78. The maximum speed and acceleration figures were taken with the windscreen folded down flat on the scuttle.

The new Midget swings along beautifully anywhere from 30 to 60 m.p.h., as conditions permit. Yet immediately the driver wishes to increase the performance still more there is the extraordinarily valuable third gear which is not noisy, the change as a whole being delightful, allowing quick upward changes, though with the higher second gear the change from second to third—an important one—will become more rapid.

There is obviously speed in plenty—to a degree, in fact, which means that for the greater part of the time the car will be driven well within itself. What can be called the secondary appeal of the machine is very strong, too, because there is not that fierceness which, while it may be pleasing to the driver, is not, perhaps, regarded in the same way by a passenger.

The occupants sit well down in the car, the cushions and back rest are deep, the doors are wide and make getting in and out easy, and the real abilities of the car are still further disguised because a particularly effective form of silencer makes the exhaust note at ordinary speeds as quiet as that of many normal touring cars.

On the comfort side, again, the car is good at low as well as at high speeds, with the frictional shock

absorbers not too tightly adjusted. The steering is beautifully light and has a little caster action, the brakes are well up to their work, and the clutch takes up the drive smoothly. On top gear with the ignition retarded the engine will pull down to 8 m.p.h., which is an illustration of its flexibility, but is obviously not a thing which the owner of a car of this nature would wish to do.

From a standing start on first gear the Brooklands test hill, with its average gradient of 1 in 5, was climbed at 17 m.p.h., the speed being maintained steadily all the way up the 1 in 4 section. First gear is a low ratio on which there is an immense reserve of power for this kind of work.

Such points as pockets in the doors, a space for small luggage in the tail, and an easily erected hood and side screens for bad weather have not been neglected; it does not follow that an owner who wants high performance does not also require comfort and convenience in one and the same car. The hood is permanently secured, but is stowed out of sight in the tail beneath a neat cover held by quick-action fasteners; the big rear fuel tank is clearly most valuable, giving a range of something like 400 miles without need for replenishment, and there is a reserve supply of three gallons.

At the back the spare wheel is held securely, and the sensible mountings for the wings and head lamps are noteworthy.

MG Midget J2

Remarkable value for £199 10s, the J2 Midget was announced in August 1932, with its 847 c.c. engine based on the design of the successful Montlhéry Midget derivative of the original M-type. From the start, the little cars represented everything that was "right" in sports car design, embodying rear-mounted slab-tank, quick-action filler cap, centre-lock wheels, spring-spoke steering wheel, fold-flat screen, remote control gear-change—and, if you liked, radiator and headlamp grilles, and a strap over the bonnet . . . such things as Le Mans cars were made of! *The Autocar* staff achieved a mean maximum of 80 mph during the road test—from, it must be confessed, a somewhat non-standard car (though the road test staff were ignorant of the fact). In attempting to emulate this performance, one or two owners discovered the disadvantages of a two-bearing crankshaft! This model was announced in August 1932.

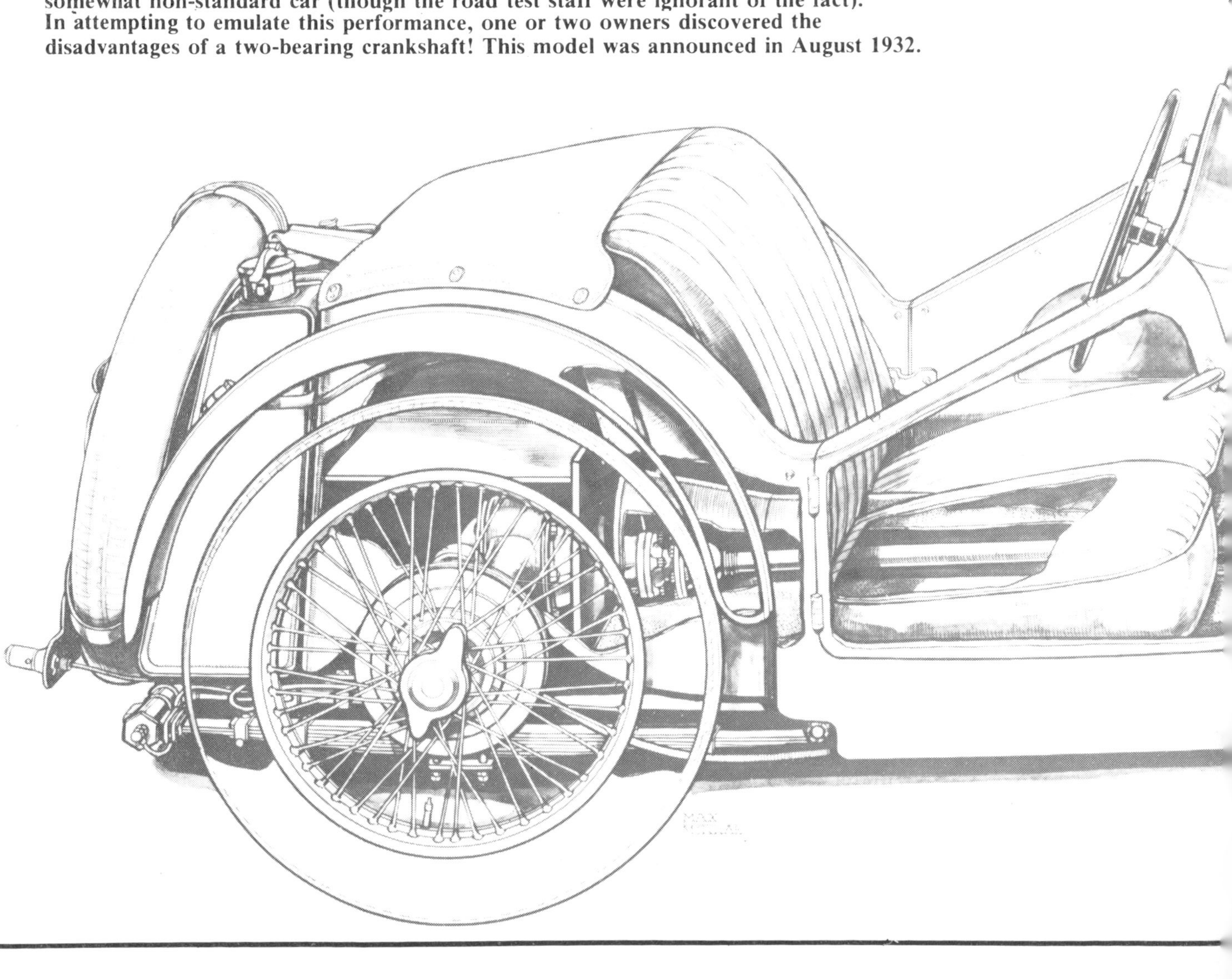

THE SUPERC

S. C. H. Davis at the wheel of G. E. T. Eyston's Magnette at Brooklands.

THE Magnette, with its 1,100 c.c. supercharged engine, is one of the most interesting cars that has been produced for some time, and is really one of the direct results that come from the Tourist Trophy type of race as opposed to the more spectacular but far more expensive product of Grand Prix racing.

Whether a supercharger is actually required for ordinary everyday use, whether, in fact, we should be better or worse if the supercharger had never been adopted for competition work, are questions it is not in the least necessary to discuss or to decide; but this at least can be said, that there is something alive, almost animal-like, wholly desirable, about the small, very fast little car with a supercharged engine, especially when it is being used for racing, and the very "feel" of the car, its tremendous pulling power, and its general fascination alone justify the existence of the type for anyone who realises that a car is something more than just a collection of machinery to carry one from place to place.

Individualism

So long, therefore, as there are enthusiasts in the land, cars of this type will be developed and their development will lift motor car manufacture a little out of the set, and rather tiring, routine which is governed almost entirely by analyses of the cost of production. Be it noted that the Magnette is not, strictly speaking, a racing car, but will give you the joy of a racing car without the latter's expense, for a racing car of the true breed is designed on the drawing board from the very commencement and in every detail for one thing, and one thing only, speed, speed un-

limited by considerations of expenditure, unhampered by the necessity of making the machine reasonably suitable for numerous purchasers. As it is, the speed that is possible with the Magnette varies with the purpose for which it is intended, but what can be done is shown by a lap speed of 115 m.p.h. recorded for one of these machines during a recent race.

The actual car which I drove had been Eyston's in the Isle of Man race, was, in fact, in the condition in which it was prepared for that race, with a low top gear of 4.89 to 1, with a starting motor, but without the battery and most of the other electrical equipment, since the starting motor was arranged to allow the battery to be in the pit and the connection to be made between it and the starting motor in the same fashion that we used to employ with old No. 1 six-cylinder Bentley in the "500."

"Not Easy to Handle" Rumours

Even without this equipment the car is not very light, a material fact when its performance has to be judged, and the performance was interesting, bearing in mind certain rumours that the car was not easy to handle and must necessarily be kept high on the banking. This proved so little true that, at its lap speed of 104.8 m.p.h., the car could be kept almost anywhere on the banking above the sixty-mile-an-hour line, and would actually cross the fork with ten or fifteen feet between it and the near side

of the blue line without pulling out of a natural course.

Actually, the maximum reading on the rev counter, which, because of

wheel slip, is optimistic, meant 114 m.p.h., the probable actual maximum being between 108 and 110 m.p.h., at which speed the engine had the perfect note of a machine going easily at its best, which, at 6,200 r.p.m., is, to say the least, interesting.

Now, it is curious how cars differ, for not ten years have passed since a car of 1,500 c.c. felt, when lapping at over 100 m.p.h., a he-man's job, and

HARGED MAGNETTE

e Car Which George Eyston ce in the Isle of Man

by

S. C. H. DAVIS

it is a bare three since a lap at 110 with 1,100 c.c. was certainly like hard work, yet here was a car which seemed relatively as though it were lapping at 90 m.p.h. Unfortunately, a small difficulty with the revs-speed chart made it impossible to get some of the figures that I had wanted, for taking stop-watch readings from the rev counter of a racing machine is an extremely difficult job, and the faster the car the worse it becomes, with the result that the 10-30 m.p.h. acceleration times were obviously inaccurate.

This had its point of interest also, for the moment the engine really got

with the lever, one can select second while the car is ready to move off on first, and the run from gear to gear is altogether happy and beautiful.

Changing down brings in the controversy as to whether the effect of the self-change box is devastating for the transmission, and from what I tried I should say it might be if the driver took the drastic liberty of using second or first as an exceptionally violent transmission brake by engaging either gear at impossible engine revs. Anyhow, if one uses the throttle with the heel of the right foot while braking with the toe of that foot, and obeys the ordinary rev limit, the change down is not only lightning quick but quite smooth.

Advantages for Racing

I have not the slightest doubt that the gear has great advantages for racing, and the only criticism I would make is an old one, in that I want the gear lever in a gate and not in an ordinary quadrant, especially when the lever has to be used quickly and often. That the brakes stopped the car in 20ft. from 24 m.p.h. speaks for itself. I got the impression, which may be

quite wrong, that for road racing the car is a little heavy in front, and the steering slightly on the springy side, but that is an opinion given without being thoroughly accustomed to the machine, a thing which is necessary for accurate judgment.

Altogether it is a most fascinating little car, and I should think exceptionally interesting on a very twisty circuit. It is easy to drive, easier than most cars, and, because of the very smoothness of the engine, probably quite easy to over-rev.

Constant Performance

Certainly it is the sort of car which one would like in a long race most of all, and there's something to think about when you come to realise what reaching 75 m.p.h. from a standstill in under 15 sec. really means, remembering also that it is easier to repeat that performance on this car than on most, because of the gear change.

The ordinary version of the car, of course, includes lamps, wings, proper upholstery, and such-like touring requisites; obviously, also, that type has a performance which does not require frequent changes from soft to hard plugs, but such a machine should be immense fun in, say, the Land's End, and, anyhow, it is a car the joy of possessing which is great.

hold on first the rev counter needle moved at such a pace that accurate timing on first gear was impossible, but on second, to give you some idea of the car's powers, it took 12⅕ sec. to change from 26 to 66 m.p.h. on third, while the most convincing run of all was from zero to 75 m.p.h. in 14⅗ sec. That showed where the self-changing gear comes in, for, by a little trick

Part sectioned view of the supercharged Magnette as sold to the public.

MONTE CARLO RALLY
and
Mont des Mules Hill Climb

Two firsts
Two seconds

M.G. Magnette makes second fastest time ever recorded for the Mont des Mules Hill Climb, only 10 seconds slower than the 8-litre supercharged car which holds the record.

Also—Fastest time of the day, winning the Automobile Club of Monaco Cup.

Mont des Mules Hill Climb results—

1st	500 - 750 c.c. class	- -	M.G. Midget (s) *Mr. W. C. Platt*
1st	750 - 1,100 c.c. class (record for class)	- -	M.G. Magnette *Mr. G. Wright*
2nd	1,100 - 1,500 c.c. class	- -	M.G. Magna *Mr. M. Lacroze*

Monte Carlo Rally results—

2nd	Braking & Acceleration test	M.G. Magnette *Mr. G. Wright*

(Subject to official confirmation)

JB 1046

SAFETY FAST !

The M.G. Magnette, driven by Mr. G. W. J. H. Wright, which put up the fastest time in the Mont des Mules Hill Climb.

The badge of the M.G. Car Club.

THE M.G. CAR CO. LTD., ABINGDON-ON-THAMES, BERKSHIRE
EXPORT DEPARTMENT - - - - STRATTON HOUSE, 80, PICCADILLY, W.1

SPORTING COLOUR

Previous page: 18/80 Mark II two-seater with dickey—coachwork by Carbodies of Coventry. Only 13 Mark IIs were built with this particular bodywork, of which only four are thought to survive—this car, one in the Doune collection, and two in the United States

Left: One of the most handsome sporting cars of their time—the Speed Model 18/80 which was available on the Mark I and Mark II chassis of 1929 and 1930. This example is owned by Sid Beer

Below: Somewhat non-standard, lightweight version of the MGC, one of those built up by John Chatham from factory parts, using triple Weber carburettors in place of the standard twin S.U.s. Built closer to factory specification than Chatham's other cars, this example was run in the 1970 Targa Florio. **Right:** The standard 6-cylinder Austin engine of the production cars, with twin S.U.s.

LEFT: MONTE CARLO RALLY: Wright's supercharged K3 Magnette started from John o'Groats, completed the Rally successfully, and put up fastest time on the Mont des Mules hill-climb

BELOW: MILLE MIGLIA: One of the three works K3 Magnettes entered for Lord Howe, H. C. Hamilton, Sir Henry Birkin, George Eyston and Count "Johnny" Lurani. The Eyston/Lurani car took first place in the 1,000 c.c. Class, with an average speed of 56·89 m.p.h., followed by the Howe/Hamilton car, 1 min. 30 sec. behind after 1,000 miles

ABOVE: INTERNATIONAL TROPHY RACE, BROOKLANDS: "Bill" Wisdom's K3 Magnette, which took third place in what was referred to as ". . . the most gruelling event ever staged at Brooklands"

RIGHT: LIGHT CAR CLUB RELAY RACE, BROOKLANDS: Left to right, C. E. C. Martin's, G. W. J. Wright's and A. C. Hess' Magnas win the Team Prize

BELOW: MANIN BEG: Cluster of cars headed by Kaye Don's (No. 18), S. A. Crabtree's (No. 19) Magnettes, F. W. Dixon's Riley (No. 7), and Hamilton's (No. 16) and Eyston's (No. 15) Magnettes at Greenshill's Corner, Douglas, Isle of Man. Of the 14 starters, only two cars finished - Dixon's Riley and Mansell's M.G. Midget

M.G. CARS FOR 1934

Slightly Modified J.2 Midget, Continental Coupé Added to Magna Range, Magnette With Greater Engine Capacity, and Pre-selector Gear Box Combined With Plate Clutch

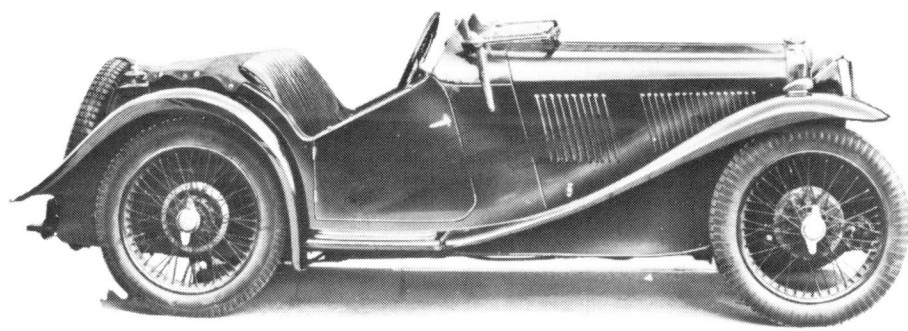

M.G. Midget J2. Two-seater, £199 10s.

VERY little change is being made in the M.G. series of cars for the coming season, for they have been brought to a state of development where extensive modifications are not considered necessary. Prices also are practically unaltered, save for slight variations in the Magnette. The complete range of cars and their prices are as follows:—

M.G. Midget: chassis £160, two-seater £199 10s.

M.G. Magna: chassis £245, open two-seater £285, open four-seater £299, salonette £345, Continental coupé £350.

M.G. Magnette: chassis £340, open two-seater £390, open four-seater £399, pillarless four-door saloon £445.

It will be noticed that there is a departure in the Midget range, inasmuch as the car is now offered as a two-seater only, other bodies being discontinued. The lines are similar to the previous model, but the appearance has been distinctly improved by fitting a modern type of flared wing, and also the addition of running boards makes sure that the car and its occupants are kept clean in bad weather. In order to preserve and improve the snappy and sparkling performance which these exceedingly attractive little cars possess on the road —the four-cylinder engine is capable of turning over at pretty well 6,000 r.p.m. —one or two modifications have been introduced, for example, the connecting rods now have fully floating gudgeon pins, and pistons with controlled expansion skirts included, and the compression ratio also has been slightly raised.

Midget Specification

It is interesting to review the specification of the Midget. It has a four-cylinder overhead-valve and camshaft engine, 57 × 83 mm. (847 c.c.), tax £8. Twin S.U. semi-downdraught carburetters are fitted, and the fuel from the 12-gallon rear tank is fed through an S.U. petrol pump. The engine is cooled on the thermo-syphon system, and in order to avoid waste of power a Burgess straight-through silencer is used. The gear box is a four-speed twin-top type

M.G. PRICES FOR 1934.		
M.G MIDGET.	**£**	**s.**
Chassis	160	0
Two=Seater	199	10
M.G. MAGNA.		
Chassis	245	0
Open Two=Seater ..	285	0
Open Four=Seater ..	299	0
Salonette	345	0
Continental Coupé ..	350	0
M.G. MAGNETTE.		
Chassis	340	0
Open Two=Seater ..	390	0
Open Four=Seater ..	399	0
Pillarless Saloon ..	445	0

provided with a particularly neat remote control which brings the gear lever close up to the driver's left hand. The clutch is a single plate, and the open propeller shaft has Hardy Spicer joints at both ends. Final drive is by spiral bevel, and the road wheels are of the Rudge racing type, fitted with Dunlop tyres. A feature of the car is, of course, the underslung frame, which is responsible for the low centre of gravity, and hence the road-holding qualities. The Midget has a wheelbase of 7ft. 2in. and a track of

3ft. 6in., and the semi-elliptic springs are damped by Hartford shock absorbers.

Marles-Weller steering with a transverse drag link is fitted, and the four wheel brake set is operated through a system of fully enclosed cables provided with proper means of regular lubrication. To handle a Midget on the road is always a pleasure, for the car is fascinating in every way and is not only fast, but has quite a different feel about it from most vehicles. The engine is particularly willing, and also notably smooth for a four-cylinder, and it has a very exhilarating way of going about its work, especially if proper use is made of the gear box.

If a gathering of motor enthusiasts was asked to make a choice out of the M.G. range, the majority would undoubtedly go for the Magna two-seater, for it is a car with just exactly the right balance of bonnet length to body, it sits down to the ground so compactly, and has a distinctly thoroughbred air. That the Magna is capable of doing a great deal more than look well is obvious from the success which it has scored during the recent season—for example, winning the L.C.C. Relay Race, and also the Manufacturers' Team Prize in its group in the International Alpine Trial. Elsewhere in this issue will be found an account of road impressions of one of the current "L" type Magnas.

Magna Revisions

Practically the only alteration to record for 1934 is that larger and more effective head lamps have been fitted. A new type of body, however, is now in production—the Continental coupé. This is a very striking-looking design of two-door four-seater with a large luggage trunk at the back. The interior of the body is most attractively furnished, and there are numerous special points, including elbow rests to the front seats, a sliding roof with windowlets in it, and recessed elbow room. This new body can be finished in black and yellow, in all-black, or various other colours, and is likely to become popular because it is very individual.

Magna Continental coupé.

It will be remembered that the Magna specification includes a six-cylinder engine, 57 × 71 mm. (1,087 c.c.), tax £12, with o.h.v. and camshaft, twin S.U. carburetters, external oil filter, separate dynamo and starter, an Elektron sump holding 1¼ gallons of oil, floating connecting rods, and special pistons with controlled expansion skirts, a gear-type oil pump, and pump water circulation.

Magna Details

Transmission is through the two-plate clutch and four-speed gear box, of the twin-top type, with a remote control gear lever. An open Hardy Spicer propeller-shaft with metal universal joints conveys the drive to a spiral bevel gear, contained in a three-quarter floating design of rear axle. Rudge racing-type wire wheels are fitted and are shod with Dunlop tyres 4.5 × 19in. Jaeger instruments are standardised and include a 5in. diameter speedometer and revolution counter. De luxe equipment is available on all Magna models at an inclusive cost of £11 extra. On the closed cars a No. 5 Philco radio set may also be had at an additional charge of £21, and, incidentally, the salonettes and Continental coupés have, as a part of the standard equipment, an invisible aerial, in case the owner at any time wishes to instal a radio set.

It is in the M.G. Magnette that the most notable changes are to be observed. Following the process of development to which the Magnette has been subjected in the course of racing and other experience, a new type of engine has been evolved for the normal models. The design of this follows very closely on the racing engine, with modifications to make it suitable for the needs of the sporting motorist. The new engine has the same horse-power rating and pays the same tax as the old ones, but its dimensions are 57 × 84 mm. (1,286 c.c.). It has, of course, the usual M.G. type of overhead valves and camshaft, but is fitted

M.G. Magnette K2. Two-seater, £390.

the gear box and the engine a single-plate Don-Flex clutch has been added. This clutch is so arranged that the first movement of the pedal operates the single-plate clutch, and the further movement is then applied to the busbar of the pre-selector gear striking mechanism. Between the pedal and the two systems is an ingenious balancing arm which ensures that the plate clutch shall always work first.

A Smooth Take-up

On the opposite side of the clutch pit to the pedal is a clever tripping cam which again makes certain that when the gear is in neutral position the plate clutch is held out of engagement, but is automatically released ready for use when a gear is being engaged. The object of fitting a plate clutch is to give a perfectly smooth and even take-up when starting from rest or when engaging the lower gears. Also, when the engine is running and the gear is in neutral, the gear box is entirely idle and therefore cannot make a noise. The clutch also makes sure that, should too low a gear be engaged inadvertently whilst travelling at a high speed, the plate clutch is able to slip, and this relieves the rest

of the transmission from what might be excessive stress and strain.

A short run on one of the Magnettes fitted with this device showed that a much more smooth and pleasant take-up is the result when starting from rest and gear changing. The Magnette is made in two lengths of wheelbase, the short being 7ft. 10in., and the long 9ft. The frames of both cars are underslung, and the half-elliptic springs have special slides at their rear ends in place of shackles. To ensure rigidity on the long wheelbase models, a cruciform type of cross bracing is fitted in the centre between the side members, in addition to the usual tubular cross-members. The wheel track of the Magnette models is, by the way, 4ft. For the steering a Marles-Weller gear is used, but the car has a special M.G. patented divided track rod, and this is very effective in practice.

Another minor modification to the Magnette is the provision of a felt-lined tool box in the top of the scuttle, underneath the back of the bonnet.

An Attractive Saloon

Particular interest attaches to the four-door saloon mounted on the Magnette chassis. This body is particularly attractively proportioned, and not only looks well, but allows extreme ease of entry, as it is of the pillarless construction, so that if both doors are open on one side there is nothing in the way of getting in or out. The rear panel of this body can be folded outwards to form a useful luggage carrier, whilst at the same time the spare wheel may be retained in position behind the petrol tank instead of adding to the weight of overhang, as would be the case if the spare wheel were attached to the lid.

Triplex glass is standardised all round on all M.G. models.

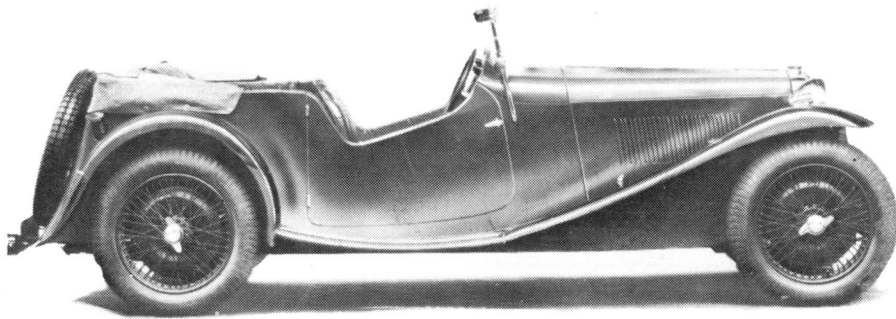

The Magnette K1. Four-seater, £399.

with 14 mm. instead of the more usual pattern 18 mm. sparking plugs.

It is equipped with triple S.U. carburetters and has a special coil and automatic distributor designed to meet the high engine speeds which are obtainable. "H" section floating connecting rods are used, the pistons are of the controlled expansion type, and the same features of Elektron sump, pump water circulation, and external oil filter are employed. The water temperature is controlled by an R.P. Thermostat.

There is a particularly interesting change in the transmission of this car. The four-speed pre-selective self-changing gear box is standardised, but between

Magnette four-door pillarless saloon.

THE M.G. MAGNA FOR 1934.

The Magna
two-seater

The Salonette. One of the close body types on the Magna chassis

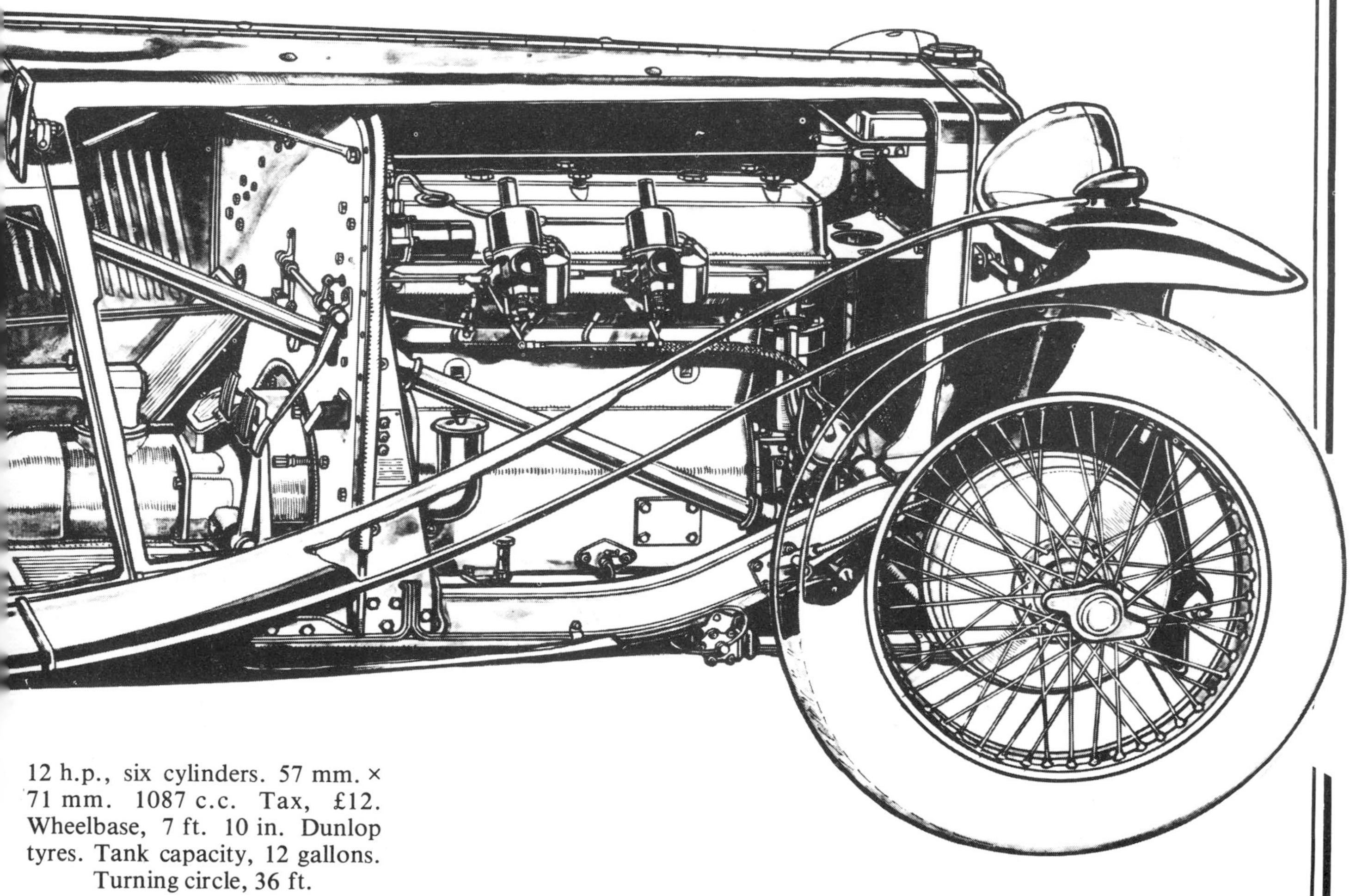

12 h.p., six cylinders. 57 mm. ×
71 mm. 1087 c.c. Tax, £12.
Wheelbase, 7 ft. 10 in. Dunlop
tyres. Tank capacity, 12 gallons.
Turning circle, 36 ft.

Road Impressions of New Models

The M.G. Magna Two-seater

IT is for ever a refreshing experience to change over from the every-day sort of saloon to a piquant and intensely alive little car like the M.G. Magna type "L." The road is no longer a mere highway from place to place, but a path of adventure, as the sea must be adventure to the man who handles a trim sailing craft. There is appeal in the very lines of the Magna, with its long bonnet promising speed, its workmanlike stern view, and long, graceful mudguards. To sense the appeal and try the car is to appreciate in full the very real qualities which are there.

Sitting well down in a deep cockpit, rendered comfortable by pneumatic upholstery, the driver starts the engine, finds a steering wheel tucking itself into his hands, notices the freedom for his arms and elbows, and, looking over the curved scuttle along the shapely snout of the car into the distance of the road, drops his left hand instinctively to the little close-up gear lever. A little light footwork, a snick of the gear lever, a flick of the accelerator, and he is away off the mark with the engine note rising.

Smoothness Outstanding

This modern six-cylinder 1,086 c.c. engine in the Magna is a fine design, and it runs with notable smoothness right throughout its range, from a comfortable toddle on top gear right up to nearly 6,000 r.p.m. when all out. Its flexibility and its freedom from vibration or mechanical noise are remarkable, when taken in conjunction with a big power output in relation to size. It responds instantly to the movements of the accelerator pedal, and, as the acceleration figures show, maintains its liveliness right up through the speed range. The car can be depended upon to reach its maximum on the level without hesitation.

There is a great fascination in driving the Magna. The steering is

DATA FOR THE DRIVER

12 h.p., six cylinders, 57 × 71 mm. (1,086 c.c.)   Tax £12.
Wheelbase 7ft. 10in., track 3ft. 6in.
Overall length 10ft. 10in., width 4ft. 3½in. height 4ft. 2in. Hood up.
Tyres: 4.5×19 on detachable Rudge-Whitworth wire wheels.

Engine-rear axle gear ratios.	Acceleration from steady speed.		
	10 to 30 m.p.h.	20 to 40 m.p.h.	30 to 50 m.p.h.
19.21	—	—	—
11.49	6¼	6¼	—
7.31	10¾	10¾	10¼
5.375	14¼	15¾	17¼

Timed speed over ¼ mile, 75 m.p.h.
With screen down 77.59
Turning circle 32ft. 6in.
Tank capacity 10 gallons; fuel consumption 22-24 m.p.g.
12-volt lighting set.
Weight: 16 cwt.
Price, with two-seater body, £285.
Acceleration from rest through the gears to 50 m.p.h. 18 sec.
Acceleration from rest through the gears to 60 m.p.h. 24¾ sec.
15 yards of 1 in 5 gradient from rest 3¾ sec.

light and quick—at first grasp disconcertingly so—with a strong caster action, but, as soon as it is realised that the wheel is best held with a light grip, the car can be placed neatly, or taken round curves at speed, in an elegant fashion. Although the car is light and lively, the steering has no apparent vices such as incipient wheel tramp, and the radiator and head lamps do not dither about on bad surfaces. Because of the low build and special form of spring anchorages, the car holds the road excellently, and can be driven anywhere with confidence.

One of the features is the four-speed twin-top gear box with remote control. A long extension on the top of the box brings a short gear lever close to the hand, and the gear change is a simple and effective one to handle, whilst the indirect gears are quiet. The ratios are well chosen and the car will reach 40 m.p.h. on second gear, which is pretty useful. The clutch is sweet and light, and is well up to its work. It may be noted that the cockpit of this two-seater does not become uncom-

fortably hot, due no doubt to the metal facings of the dashboard and the rubber sealing around the clutch pit and the steering column, which prevents hot air from blowing through.

Another point which contributes to the general attractiveness of the car is that the large diameter brakes are smooth and progressive, and may be used to pull the car up from high speed without trepidation. Because of the smoothness, they are deceptive in that they pull the car up more quickly than they appear to do, which is always a hall-mark of good brakes. They are armoured-cable operated, but proper provision is made for regular lubrication of the cable sheathing. Except at low speeds, when the shock absorbers can be felt to be doing their work, the comfort of riding is very good, and the stability of the car at any speed of which this model is capable on the track is all that could be desired.

Special Points

There are certain points to attract special attention. The large fuel tank at the rear of the body has a gauge visible on the top, and there is a two-way control which enables some two gallons to be held in reserve. The windscreen is arranged so that it can be folded down flat forwards when needed, and incidentally there is surprisingly little wind when the screen is down, owing to the shape of the dash "humps" and the way that they deflect the wind over the heads of the occupants. It may be mentioned that the maximum speed figure given in the table was an average obtained with the screen down; with it up the maximum was 75 m.p.h.

The speedometer on the car gave a reasonably accurate reading. This instrument is, by the way, a combined speedometer and revolution indicator, for it has separate calibrations showing the engine revolutions equivalent to various road speeds on the different gears. The various controls of the car are well placed and simple to handle; mounted on the tunnel just forward of the gear lever are knobs for the jet adjustment and the slow running setting of the twin S.U. carburetters, the ignition advance is automatic, the lights are controlled from the instrument board, and thus the steering wheel is left quite free of encumbrances.

Taken all round, the open two-seater Magna is a most delectable car with the manners, as well as the air of a thoroughbred.

The Magna L2 two-seater.

GILDING THE LILY

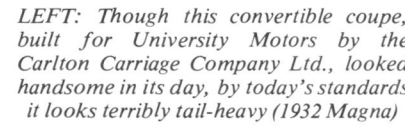
LEFT: Though this convertible coupe, built for University Motors by the Carlton Carriage Company Ltd., looked handsome in its day, by today's standards it looks terribly tail-heavy (1932 Magna)

RIGHT: In the tail of this very pretty body by Stiles, Ltd., of Baker Street, London, there is a single-seater "dickey" providing every comfort - achieved at the expense of hanging the spare wheel very far back, and spoiling the lines (1932 Magna)

LEFT: Though the passenger compartment looks small enough, this was termed a "two-door, four-seater, close-coupled saloon" by its creators, Abbey Coachworks, Ltd., of North Acton, London. With special 8-gallon tank and very full equipment it cost £345 (1932 Magna)

RIGHT: Abbotts of Farnham contributed this drophead coupe body to the wide range of styles available on the Magna chassis in 1932. It cost £325.

LEFT: Windover - a coachbuilder famed for magnificent creations on some of the most costly chassis - bodied this 1932 Magna 2-seater coupe, providing plenty of luggage space by stowing the spare wheel at the side.

NUMBER ONE

Romance of the First Born in the M.G. Magnette Family

by

BARRÉ LYNDON
Author of "Combat," "Speed Fever," etc.

NOW and again the world of motor racing produces a car destined to unusual adventure. It was for such a machine that, at two o'clock in the morning, thousands of enthusiastic Italians waited in an avenue, gazing down a smooth, black road which shone glassily under the stark light of brilliant arc lamps. The spectators were held back by ropes and planking stretched between flag-poles set at the edge of the highway, and the ceaseless, high-pitched drone of their voices maintained an atmosphere of tension and expectation.

Officials hovered beneath a banner strung high above the road, its chequered edging silhouetted against the shadowy trees. Ever and again they looked to where a slender arch straddled the avenue, so placed that it formed an entrance from the deep darkness of the countryside beyond the town.

Without warning a brilliant glare burst from the black distance, rushing towards the arch. The grouped officials broke up.

Magnette No 1 in the Mille Miglia

The standing crowds swayed, and above the noise of their stirring came the blare of a trumpet sounding a long-drawn call, while the blaze of white light rushed nearer. As the trumpet-note died it was echoed by the growing roar of a racing car travelling under full throttle.

Its head lamps caught the arch, silvering the structure's sides. They revealed the animated crowd, lit the scattering officials, and caught the stretched banner as the dark shape of the machine dived through the opening and pitched down the centre of the road. A flag fell in the moment that the car roared beneath the banner, then brakes went on, and men ran from all directions towards the slowing machine.

Proud Bearer of the Union Jack

Beneath its dusty flanks showed the green of England's racing colour. The Union Jack was painted on the bonnet, and on the curve of the scuttle was the Italian flag. Behind the wheel sat Captain G. E. T Eyston, with Count Lurani huddled at his side, both cramped and stiff. In eighteen hours they had covered one thousand and twenty-four miles, and were the first to finish the course for the 1933 Mille Miglia. They had broken all records for 1,100 c.c. machines, and the car they drove was the first of all racing Magnettes.

Such was the *début* of a machine which had been built in record time, and had then journeyed to Italy during twelve stormy days, surrounded by boxes in a vessel laden with china clay. By all precedent a car erected so rapidly, and of new design, should have been subjected to the trials and errors of a dozen events before it ran first past the chequered flag. Yet in its first race it achieved victory in its class, which is unusual.

The crowds swarmed close while Eyston and Lurani were lifted out, and the Italians remained staring at the *vetture Inglese* while other cars came in. They left it only when Tazio Nuvolari raced across the finishing line, but they might have remained could they have known that the future was to link Nuvolari with this dusty green machine

When the crowd had gone the M.G. Magnette was rolled away, returning to the factory to be prepared for the International Trophy at Brooklands. It was driven in this event by Mrs. T. H. Wisdom, who had shown her skill with other machines, including the giant Leyland Thomas. The 1,087 c.c. machine now responded under her hands. It ran faultlessly, stopping only once for fuel and a wheel change, touching 106 m.p.h. down the railway straight, and slipping handily through the turns, aided by its preselector gear box; the car was unique in the fact that it was the first road-racing machine ever to be given this fitment. The slim, black-overalled woman ran the machine into third place, ending a splendid event.

Other Drivers Interested

Mechanics returned the Magnette to the works, and for a month it was used by visiting drivers who wanted to get the feel of this new type of car. It served them on the roads around the factory, and, once or twice, showed its paces on the open track, lapping happily at 110 m.p.h., until George Eyston decided to test its prowess at Shelsley Walsh.

For the first time it met trouble. On the journey down, where the road was narrow, Eyston came fast through a curve to find the way barred by a car backing out of an orchard. The Magnette slowed, but not enough; it dented the tail of the baulking machine and bent its own front axle.

The car went back for repairs, and was soon again demonstrating its capabilities, persuading many to ownership of cars that were duplicates of itself, lacking only its growing tradition. June trailed away, and Eyston entered the machine for the Mannin Beg in the Isle of Man, a race which was something different from anything that the car had yet encountered. *Continued overleaf.*

K & KN MAGNETTES

M.G.'s entirely new 1933 K-Type Magnette, with six cylinders, 1,086 c.c., and triple S.U. carburettors, was announced at the 1932 Olympia Show in October—though the month before *The Autocar's* photographer had spotted an early production model at Beggars' Roost, Devon, and photographed it (shown here). Subsequently in September 1934, in preparation for the Motor Show, a new KN Magnette was announced—with chassis similar in all respects to the K-type, but with the larger, twin-S.U., 1,287 c.c. N-Type engine. The N-Type followed the Midget in body style, with open, sporting two- and four-seater coachwork. The new KN Magnette (shown in the drawing) was aimed at the sporting family owners, with a reasonably roomy, pillarless saloon body, extra elbow room being achieved by fitting sliding windows, with the consequently slimmer doors.

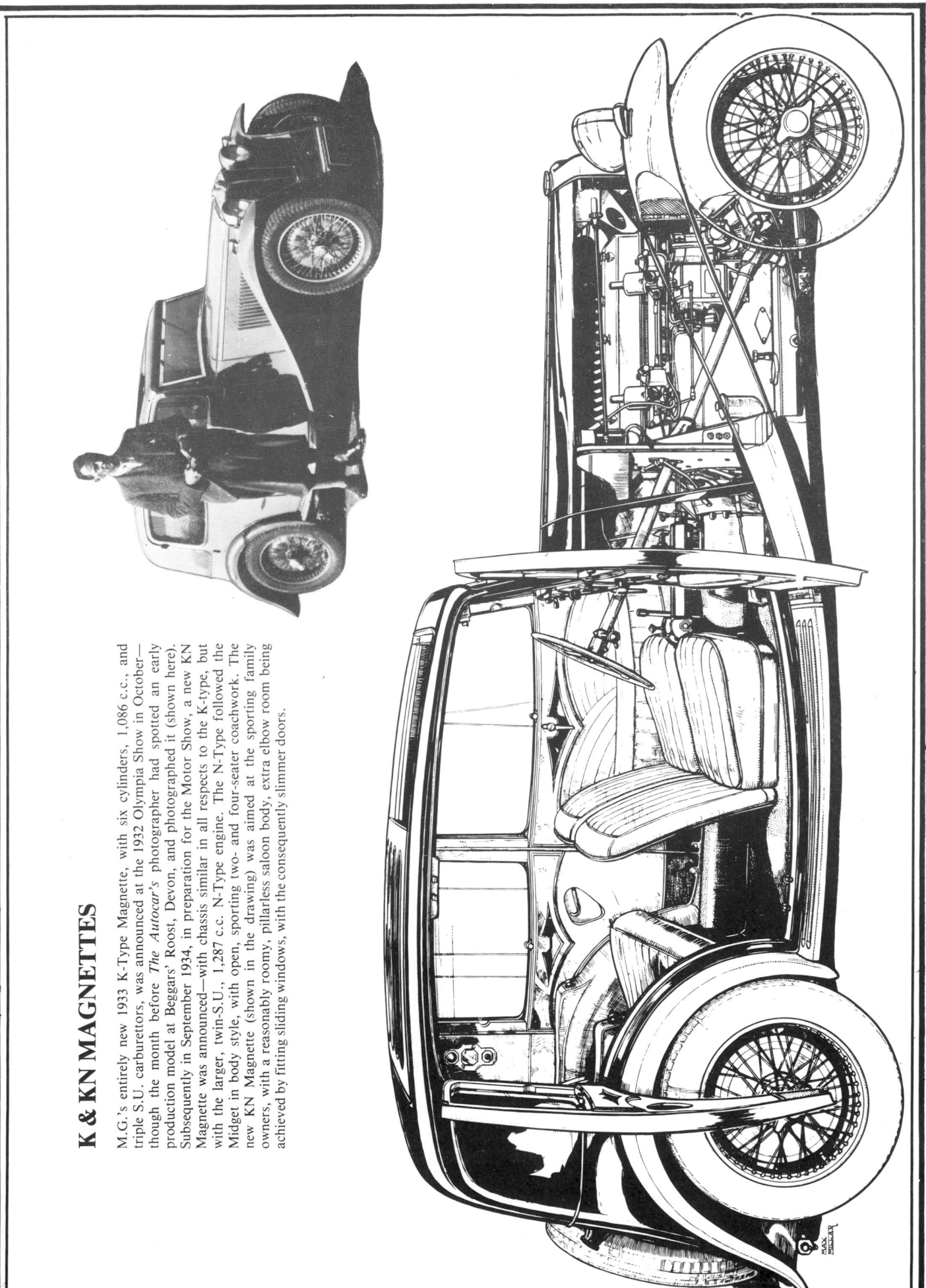

INTO BATTLE

It was an event through house-hemmed streets, with sand-bags to protect spectators and shop windows, with a dozen abrupt corners and endless bends, with tramlines to offer hazards. When the flag fell Eyston let others make the pace, yet lapped only seven-tenths of a mile an hour slower than the leader. Three cars had fallen out before he began to open up; then, on his seventh lap, the engine faltered and went dead. The camshaft drive had fractured.

The car came home again, a little disgraced. It had done good work, but, it seemed, its work was ended. The gruelling of the Mille Miglia had, perhaps, taken too great a toll, and it seemed unwise again to trust its reliability in a race. Mechanics used it for running fast errands, and it was now employed for demonstration only when no newer Magnette was available.

Nuvolari as its Driver

It stood by while other machines were made ready for the Tourist Trophy race. At times it suffered the indignity of journeying to obtain parts that were needed for these cars, of which it was the forerunner. Then, in the midst of the preparations, news came that Nuvolari wanted a wheel for the T.T., and Eyston suggested offering him a Magnette. There was no machine available except the now worn-looking Number One, but there was fine history behind the car and it might respond in the hands of so fine a driver.

Work on the machine—which had descended to a factory hack—was begun at a time when the rest entered for the Belfast race were almost ready. It had less preparation than any, but it looked in fine trim when it came to the line, bearing No. 17, and rightful leader of the four Magnettes which had been entered. Nuvolari had not handled the car before he began practice, and he had never raced with a machine carrying a preselector gear box, but his practice laps were very fast, and he said that he liked the car long before he came to the starting line.

From the fall of the flag Nuvolari began tucking other machines behind his tail, and at the end of half an hour broke his class record with 77.6 m.p.h. After that he put his foot down, and, touching 115 mp.h. along the straight to Comber, lowered his own record on three successive laps, climbing up to third place. He followed Freddy Dixon's Riley, until Dixon lost time through his exhaust pipe coming loose, on which the Magnette again smashed the record on three consecutive laps, snatching the lead which H. C. Hamilton's M.G. Midget had held from the start.

Still the car's speed mounted. Man and machine formed a perfect combination, and Nuvolari broke the lap record yet again when he came round at 81 m.p.h. Two laps later he put up his fastest time, clocking 10 min. 4 sec.— a lap at 81.42 m.p.h. Then, as if to prove that this was no chance performance, the machine duplicated the effort next time round, and, at the end of the following lap, Nuvolari came home victor of the fastest Tourist Trophy race ever run.

The car had broken its class lap record eleven times, and had shown its mettle by finishing the long race at its highest speed.

Italy, Brooklands, Ulster

It had led the rest home in Italy's greatest event, it had taken third place in the International Trophy, and now it had won the finest race the British Isles had ever seen, handled by a man whom many believe to be the world's greatest driver.

THE 1933 TOURIST TROPHY

Driven by no less than the legendary Tazio Nuvolari, with Alec Hounslow of M.G.s as his riding mechanic, a supercharged Magnette won the 1933 Tourist Trophy, 12th in the series, - with H.C. Hamilton's supercharged 750 c.c. Midget in second place, only 40 seconds behind, the issue being in doubt right up to the last minute. But for a delay during one of his pit stops, Hamilton should have won. The race was run on handicap, a supercharged 750 c.c. car being credited with three 13¾-mile laps before the start, and an unblown 1,100 with two.

A MAGIC MAGNETTE, JANUARY 1934: George Eyston's single-seater 1,100 c.c. Magnette under construction - a larger version of the famous Magic Midget, since the car was said to be too small for Eyston's increasing size! The new car had two bodies - one, the single-seater, very similar to the Magic Midget, for track work and records, and the other a road-racing body. This car proved the basis of a remarkable series of record-breakers, driven by Eyston and then by Col. Goldie Gardner.

MILLE MIGLIA, APRIL 1934: The team of supercharged K3 Magnettes entered for the 1,000-mile race, under the leadership of Lord Howe, who had his mechanic Thomas as co-driver; the second works car was driven by Lurani and Penn Hughes; the third, a private entry, was driven by Mr and Mrs E. R. Hall. Lord Howe crashed, the Halls retired, and Lurani and Penn Hughes took second place in the 1,100 c.c. class.

A NEW M.G. MAG

Very Interesting New Design to Take the Plac
Four-seate

FOLLOWING the introduction just recently of the new "P" type M.G. Midget, the progressive spirit of the M.G. Car Company is now responsible for the production of another new model, a six-cylinder Magnette, which is to fill the gap left by an exhaustion of the supply of the Magna two- and four-seaters. This latest new car, which is to be known as the Magnette N type, is every bit as interesting in design as the P-type Midget, and shows several features of new development.

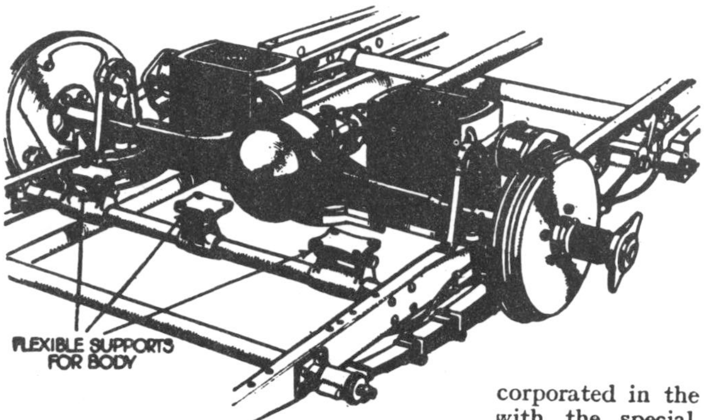

(Below) The rear end of the chassis, showing the special body supports.

FLEXIBLE SUPPORTS FOR BODY

Details of the gear box and propeller-shaft drive. Both butterfly adjustments for the brakes protrude through the floorboards for accessibility.

HAND BRAKE ADJUSTMENT

FOOT BRAKE ADJUSTMENT

Designed and constructed in the light of experience gained by continuous racing and competition work, the six-cylinder engine embodies the latest M.G. practice and has the same inclined overhead valves operated by a single camshaft and light rocker fingers as are incorporated in the new Midget, together with the special feature of ports on opposite sides of the detachable cylinder head, and of a special shape to give a free gas flow. The six cylinders are of 57 × 83 mm. bore and stroke (1,271 c.c.), tax £12.

Extra-rigid construction is a particular feature of the design, for the engine is intended to be able to stand up to heavy duty, and the crankshaft is carried in four bearings. The normal maximum to which this engine may be run is 5,500 r.p.m. on third equivalent to about 63 m.p.h. The engine can be revved as high as 6,000,

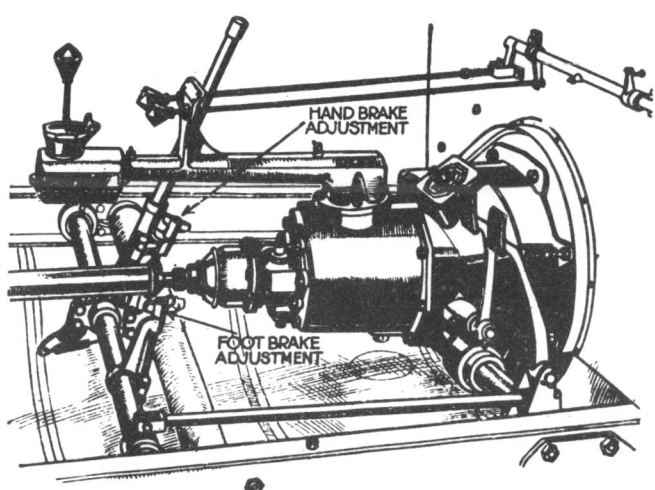

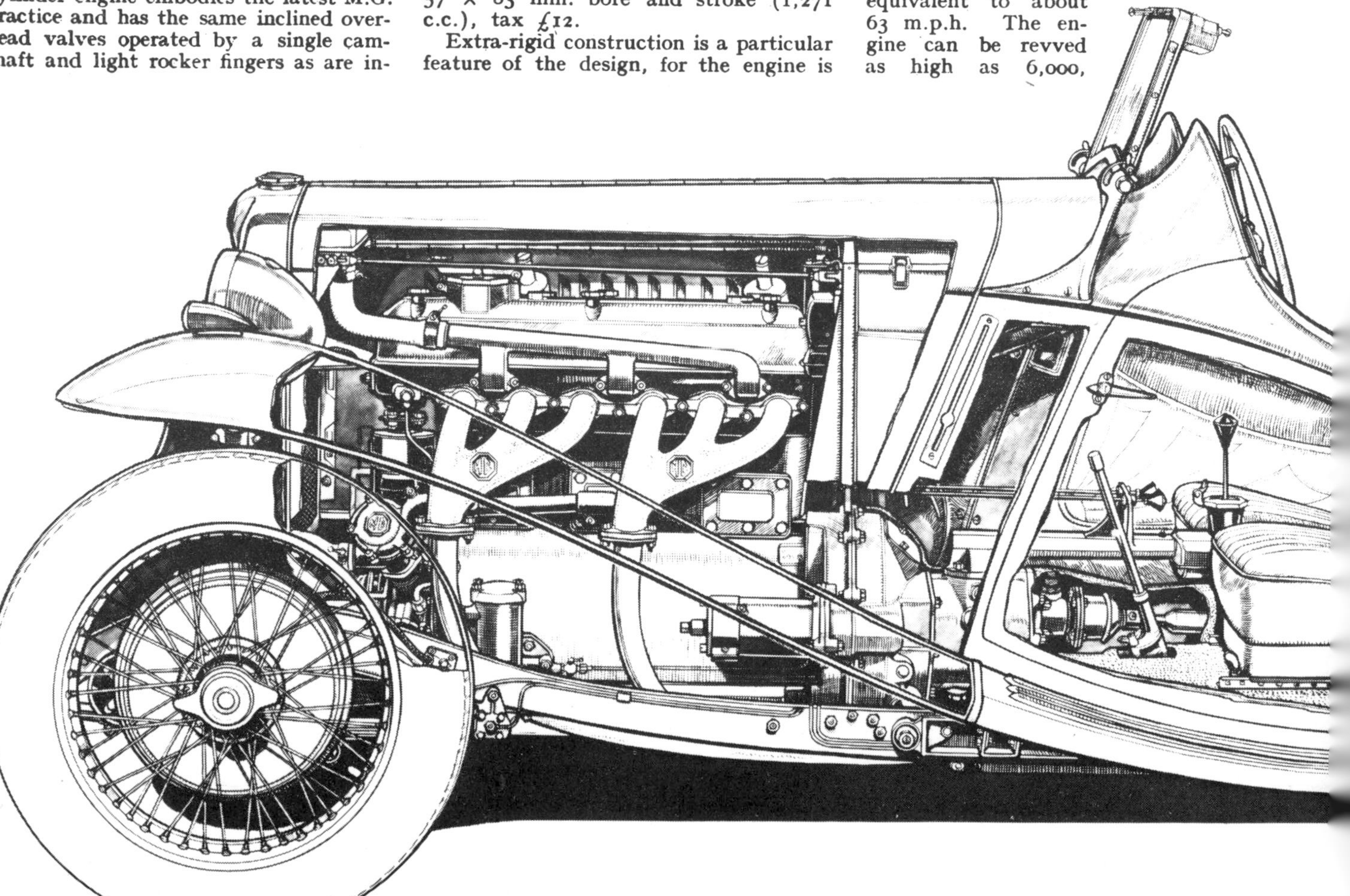

The Magnette four-seater shown in part-section.

but if a regular practice is made of this the life will naturally be lessened.

It is interesting that this latest six-cylinder engine, which conforms to the same general design as the four-cylinder Midget, develops round about 47 per cent. more power than that of the Midget; that is to say, the two extra cylinders are adding nearly one-third more power, and this is distinctly an achievement in small six-cylinder engine design.

The result is secured by attention to many minor points, including valve design and combustion chamber shape, but also by the use of a special form of inlet manifold with twin carburetters. This has an S.U. carburetter, applied not in the middle of each half, but towards the outer end of each, whilst between the two portions is a very special form of balancing port which has been the subject of a considerable amount of research work.

Amongst other minor improvements in the engine design may be mentioned a large oil filler on the top of the valve cover, a breather at the side of the crank case, twin three-branch exhaust manifolds, a large elektron sump containing 1¼ gallons of oil, and ribbed underneath for cooling purposes, an improved type of dynamo in the vertical drive to the overhead camshaft, with a neat enclosed junction box for the wires, and a

The rear seat of the four-seater has been designed especially for room and comfort.

Tecalemit oil filter. Driven from the timing case at the front of the engine by skew gears is a centrifugal pump which attends to the water circulation.

The silencing of the engine is obtained by a Burgess silencer of exceptional length. At the back of the car is a ten-gallon fuel tank which holds two gallons in reserve by means of a special cock and two-level pipes controlled by a handle on the dash in front of the driver. Fuel from this tank is fed by an electric pump through Petroflex tubing to the two carburetters.

In unit with the engine are a four-speed twin top gear box and a new-type single-plate clutch with a laminated centre plate, fabric-faced finger ring, and a new type of grease-retaining thrust race. Mounted on the top of the gear box is the characteristically neat remote gear control with its short lever brought well back within reach of the driver's left hand. This control is of an improved type with a reverse stop on the gate, and a solid bracket formed integrally with the tunnel carries the mixture and slow running controls for the carburetter. The overall gear ratios are: first, 21.94; second, 11.9; third, 6.98; and top, 5.125 to 1. At an engine speed of 1,000 r.p.m. the speed of the car in m.p.h. on each gear is: first, 3.74; second, 6.75; third, 11.5; and top, 15.65.

To carry the engine unit in the frame a special type of mounting is employed which is slightly flexible, but not definitely free. At the front end of the engine a rubber sleeve in a metal housing surrounds the extension of the forward end of the crankshaft centre, whilst passing through the base of the bell housing of the flywheel and clutch, towards the back of the unit, is a stout tubular cross-member which supports the unit through the agency of a rubber bush on each side. The engine unit and the frame, therefore, assist one another as regards general rigidity.

(Right) The flexible rear suspension of the body on three Silentbloc supports.

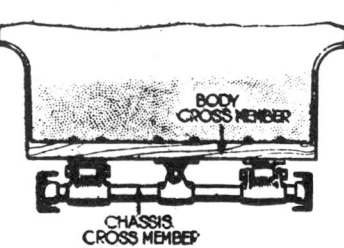

67

Flowing lines are a pronounced feature of the new four-seater.

A New M.G. Magnette

This design is further interesting because of the M.G. method of front end assembly, for the radiator is carried as part of the engine unit assembly, and the radiator, front wings, and the head lamps are braced by tie-bars, so that the front end of the frame itself is relieved of the pendulum or inertia effects which the weight of these accessories would otherwise add. In practice, the front end of these new M.G.s remains perfectly steady even whilst travelling at high speed over bad roads.

Final drive is by means of a balanced open propeller-shaft with Hardy Spicer

The tool case is in the scuttle under the bonnet. Note the position of the traffic signal.

joints, coupled to a spiral bevel drive with a four-star differential in the centre, all contained within a three-quarter floating type banjo rear axle. There are special oil seals to prevent oil from finding its way on to the brake surfaces, and also there is a dipstick in the rear axle centre to show the oil level.

The frame of the N type Magnette is a new one, and is notable for stiff side-members underslung at the rear, and eight tubular cross-members, including one right across the front end of the dumb-irons. One very neat portion of the design is to be found in the brackets which secure the front end of the rear springs to the frame, and which support a very strong tubular member, whilst a continuation of these brackets also carries one end of the special flexibly mounted body frame, which will be referred to later. The tail end of the frame is prolonged some way backwards, in order to give a really stiff support for the back end of the body, especially in the case of the four-seaters.

Wider and longer half-elliptic springs are used throughout and follow the special M.G. practice of having their

sliding ends arranged in roller trunnions in place of shackles, whereby side play due to wear is reduced to a minimum. The forward ends of the front springs have metal bushes, provided with lubricators, whilst the forward ends of the rear springs have Silentbloc bushes. The front springs are checked in their action by large Duplex Hartford shock absorbers, whilst the back springs are regulated by Luvax hydraulic shock absorbers of a special type, in which there

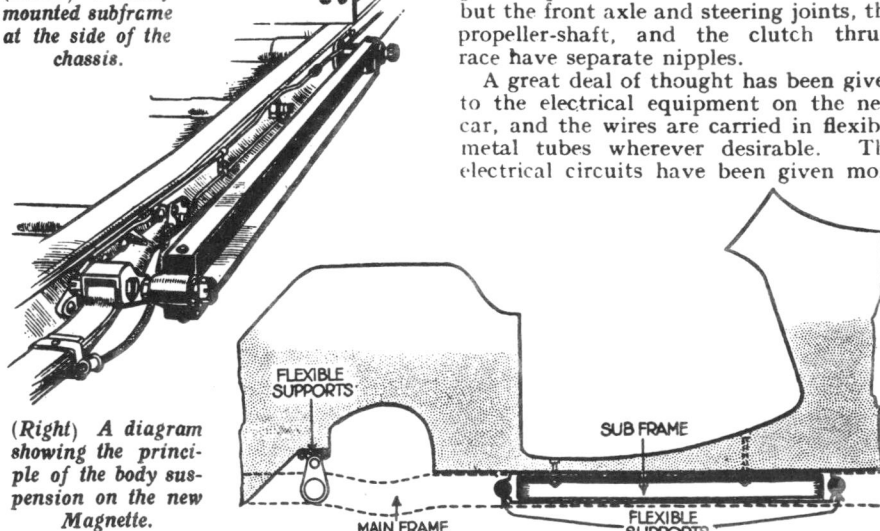

(Below) Flexibly mounted subframe at the side of the chassis.

FLEXIBLE SUPPORTS

MAIN FRAME

SUB FRAME

FLEXIBLE SUPPORTS

(Right) A diagram showing the principle of the body suspension on the new Magnette.

is not only a thermostat control, but also a spring-loaded ball valve control which enables the shock absorber to deal equally well with slow movements as with quick ones. An entirely new Bishop type cam steering gear is employed.

Another interesting feature of the chassis design is that a long undershield protects the underneath part of the car from damage, and at the same time com-

pletely insulates the floorboards and continues the effectiveness of the seal which is made between the dash structure and the engine unit by means of a circular rubber ring round the bell housing. In this way special precautions are taken to keep heat and fumes out of the driving compartment.

Another point is that the batteries are divided into two, and are mounted on each side of the propeller-shaft, close to the rear axle. The system of grouped oil nipples on each side of the forward face of the dashboard attends to the greater part of the chassis lubrication, but the front axle and steering joints, the propeller-shaft, and the clutch thrust race have separate nipples.

A great deal of thought has been given to the electrical equipment on the new car, and the wires are carried in flexible metal tubes wherever desirable. The electrical circuits have been given more

fuses than before, there being a separate fuse for each head lamp, a fuse for the side and tail lamps, a fuse for the horn, and a fuse for the auxiliaries, such as the instrument board lamp, and the plug-in socket. These are in addition to the dynamo field fuse.

Other points in the electrical equipment are a twin electric screenwiper, concealed traffic indicators which are mounted in the scuttle sides, and a stop light. Incidentally, the fog light is a standard fitting, and is carried on a special bar, in front of the radiator, which also carries a horn, and provides a proper anchorage for badges. The windscreen is of Triplex Toughened glass.

The wheelbase of the N type Magnette is 8ft., and the track 3ft. 9in., which figures are slightly increased compared with the Magna, with the intention of giving more body space. Rudge-Whitworth racing-type wheels are fitted, and their 18in. rims carry 4.75in. tyres. The brakes are operated by means of cables enclosed in armoured casings.

The very smart and business-like Magnette two-seater.

TOURIST TROPHY, BELFAST 1934: C. J. P. Dodson driving George Eyston's 1,287 c.c. unblown M.G. Magnette, wins (at 74·65 m.p.h.) the 465-mile race on handicap from E. R. Hall's 3,669 c.c. Bentley after a long and close-fought struggle. The two cars were still so close at the finish that the officials had both Dodson's and Hall's number-boards ready, with the chequered flag. The previous year's Tourist Trophy had been won by a supercharged K3 Magnette, driven by Tazio Nuvolari, with Alec Hounslow as riding mechanic, at 78·65 m.p.h.

Into battle...

Above: 1931: The first 750 c.c. car to achieve 100 mph—the supercharged Midget of George Eyston at Montlhéry which Eyston (in car) and E. A. D. Eldridge (behind car) prepared specially

Below: 1931: MGs dominated the 1931 J.C.C. Brooklands Double-Twelve on handicap, frustrating drivers of the big cars. Tim Birkin, of Bentley fame, talked of a "scurrying kindergarten" of midgets

Below: 1932: Eyston in the specially-bodied, blown 750 Midget at Pendine Sands in February set new records, including a mean of 118.38 mph over the measured mile

Right: 1934: MGs made a great name for themselves in trials in the 'thirties. Here, over typical going, is R. A. Macdermid's PA ascending Hatherland in the Brighton-Beer trial

Above: 1933 supercharged 1,100 c.c. K3 Magnette — found on a scrapyard by Tom David, one of M.G. Specialist Maurice Toulmin's employees, and sold to Michael Elman-Browne, who rebuilt the car, finally selling it to Philip Bayne-Powell, who completed the rebuild to Mille Miglia specification. **Right:** The engine of another example of the K3, owned by Sid Beer and part of a fine collection

SPORTING COLOUR

Below: N-Type Magnette for 1936, first announced in August 1935, the principal external difference from the 1935 cars being that the doors were hinged on their forward edges, the hinges forming part of the styling, and the scuttle line was lowered slightly

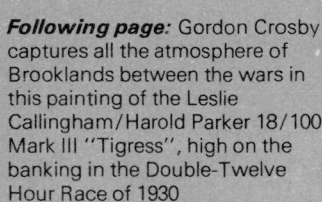

Following page: Gordon Crosby captures all the atmosphere of Brooklands between the wars in this painting of the Leslie Callingham/Harold Parker 18/100 Mark III "Tigress", high on the banking in the Double-Twelve Hour Race of 1930

The Autocar Road Tests

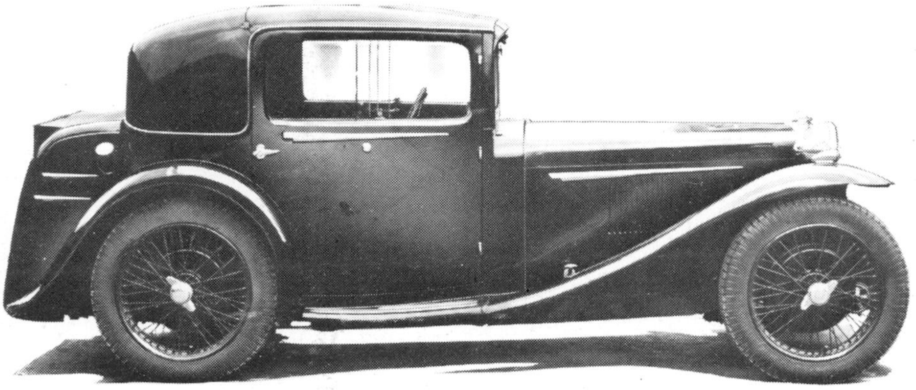

No. 852 (Post-War Series)

M.G. MAGNA CONTINENTAL COUPÉ

Very Comfortable, Beautifully Finished Small Quality Car Which Easily Makes High Averages

SOMEHOW it is natural to think of the M.G. as an open car, but there must be a considerable number of owners who require the various advantages of a closed body, and at the same time appreciate the mechanical qualities of a proved sports engine and chassis design such as the M.G. There are many of the closed models, of various types, in use.

For such people there is the Magna Continental coupé, a smart two-seater salonette which was introduced as a new body type at the last Olympia Show, and which is mounted on the 1,100 c.c. six-cylinder chassis. It is a fascinating little car, which handles beautifully and involves practically no sacrifice of usable performance compared with the normal open models, such is the power developed by the very lively overhead camshaft, twin-carburetter engine.

Especially in acceleration through the gears this car is the match of most small sports-type machines one encounters on the road. It gives all the protection of a saloon without the occupants feeling too much shut in, in which matter the M.G. arrangement of transparent panels in the sliding roof has a considerable influence.

It is a deceptive kind of car in the right sense; for all its power the extremely smooth, quiet engine does not appear to be working at ordinary road speeds. The car floats along happily at 50 to 55 m.p.h. or so without feeling stressed—seems as though it wants to go faster, in fact, besides holding its speed well on gradients, and picking up rapidly after it has been slowed for other traffic.

It is found on a known journey that one has put up an average very nearly as good as that achieved by any type of car one has driven over the same road, yet without effort having to be exerted by the driver or by the car itself. This is an exceedingly valuable attribute and one of the car's principal characteristics.

Whatever may be the conditions of road or traffic, the driver has the most satisfactory feeling that the car will answer exactly. When passing another vehicle at speed, or rounding curves and appreciable corners quite fast, there is still a feeling of certainty and accuracy, yet all the controls are exceptionally light in action. The coupé is as steady to all intents and purposes as an open model, and it rides very well over the wavy type of road which sometimes sets up fore-and-aft pitching in small cars. Friction shock absorbers are used on the M.G.

This Magna exhibits its curious deceptiveness even in the brakes. One discovers that very light pressure on the pedal produces the necessary deceleration for all average requirements, and there is little suggestion of the real decisiveness that the big drums can give until the pedal is pushed hard down for a sudden emergency stop. The figure given in the table, 31 feet from 30 m.p.h., is an average of two tests, and though the braking test had to be made on a wet concrete surface, the car pulled up all square, without grab to either side.

The type of hand brake for long used on M.G.s, in which the lever does not engage with the ratchet unless the knob is depressed, and is freed by a slight backward pull, is exceedingly useful in restarting on a gradient, and the brake holds absolutely firmly.

The other test figures, for speed and acceleration, are increased in value by the fact that conditions at the time were by no means ideal,

M.G. MAGNA CONTINENTAL COUPÉ

DATA FOR THE DRIVER

12 h.p., six cylinders, 57 × 71 mm. (1,087 c.c.). Tax £12.
Tyres: 4.50 × 19in. on knock-off wire wheels.

Engine—rear axle gear ratios.	Acceleration from steady speed. 10 to 30 m.p.h.	20 to 40 m.p.h.	30 to 50 m.p.h.	Timed speed over ¼ mile.
19.21 to 1	—	—	—	
11.49 to 1	6⅕ sec.	—	—	
7.31 to 1	9⅘ sec.	11 sec.	11⅘ sec.	
5.375 to 1	14⅗ sec.	15⅕ sec.	17⅘ sec.	72.58 m.p.h.

Acceleration from rest through the gears to 50 m.p.h., 19 sec.
Speed up Brooklands Test Hill from rest (1 in 5 average gradient), 17.92 m.p.h. (on first gear).
Acceleration up 15 yards of 1 in 5 gradient from rest, 3⅘ sec.
Turning circle: 36ft.
Tank capacity 13 gallons, fuel consumption 26 m.p.g.
12-volt lighting set cuts in at 13 m.p.h., 6 amps. at 30 m.p.h.
Weight: 17 cwt.
Price, with Continental coupé body, £350.

(Latest chassis described in "The Autocar" of September 1st, 1933.)

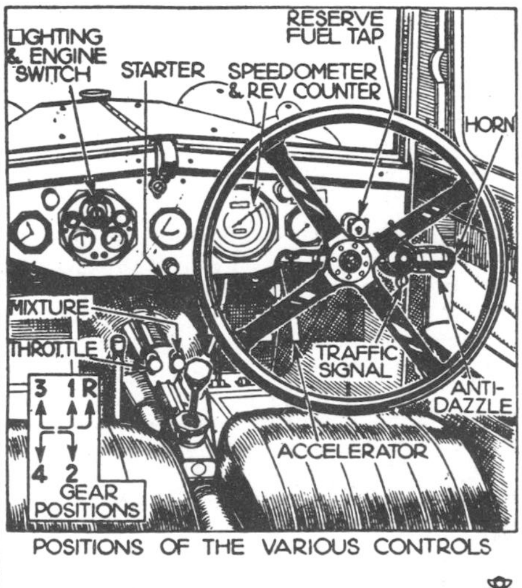
LIGHTING & ENGINE SWITCH
STARTER
RESERVE FUEL TAP
SPEEDOMETER & REV COUNTER
HORN
MIXTURE
THROTTLE
TRAFFIC SIGNAL
ANTI-DAZZLE
ACCELERATOR
3 1 R
4 2
GEAR POSITIONS

POSITIONS OF THE VARIOUS CONTROLS

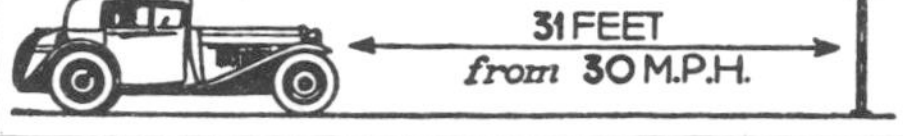
31 FEET
from 30 M.P.H.

since it was raining, and Brooklands track was water-logged in places. Apart from the mean average timed speed given, the best run over the quarter-mile was at 73.17 m.p.h., the speedometer then showing 77.

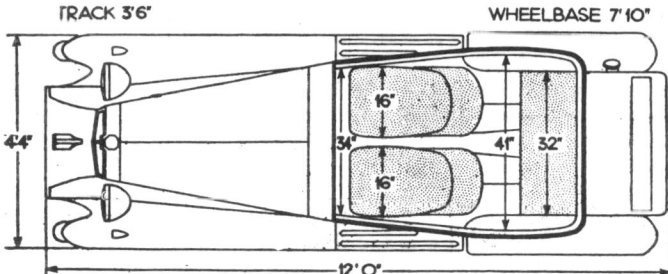

On third gear 40 m.p.h. is reached easily and naturally in accelerating, but an extreme reading of as much as 60 is actually possible on this gear, equivalent to 5,500 r.p.m., according to the calibrations on the speedometer-cum-rev counter dial. On second gear 25 m.p.h. is easy, and 35 is possible, whilst on first about 15 may be regarded as a normal reading, but as much as 22 was held on first up the Brooklands Test Hill. The speedometer proved *slow* at 40 and 50, and only 1.75 m.p.h. fast at 60.

The gear change, with remote-control lever, is a good one; quite rapid upward changing is possible noiselessly. Third is a dead-silent gear, second is more noisy by comparison, and it is only the change down to second at higher speeds which is at all difficult. The spring-spoked steering wheel is brought right back and placed comparatively high, but the driving position as a whole is extremely comfortable, and affords confidence.

There is a host of practical features about the car. Under the bonnet there is at each side a group of three lubricators for the chassis bearings. Particular trouble has been taken to shut off the engine from the body.

Then the body is very tastefully and attractively finished, with leather upholstery and polished wood in the interior, and good detail work. The windows are of the sliding type; the rearward section on each side is fixed. By the use of this type of window several valuable inches of elbow room are saved.

A platform behind the two front seats is valuable for luggage; the container which neatly finishes off the tail houses the spare wheel and conceals the big fuel tank.

It is interesting that the test data were taken after nearly 600 miles had been covered, without adjustment, from the time the car left the works.

A small closed sports car of quality and character.

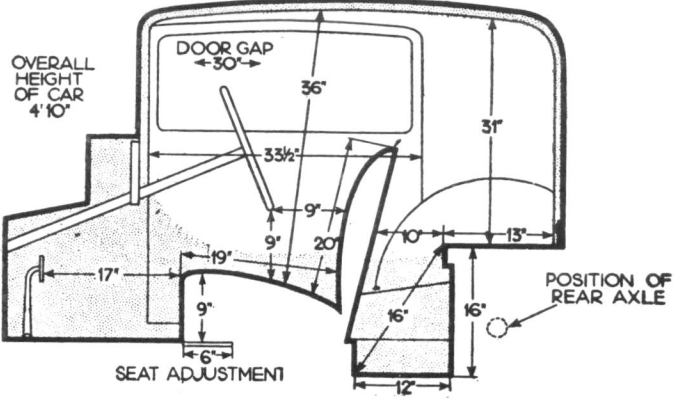

Ex 135 - and the most famous K3 Magnette of all. Radically modified and specially bodied in 1933 for George Eyston, this "Humbug" (so nicknamed because of its lengthwise brown and cream stripes) was designed as a racer-cum-record-breaker with alternative bodies - one very narrow with exposed wheels, the other all-enveloping. It was operated by Eyston in 1934, setting up new Class G records, and winning the British Empire Trophy race. When Lord Nuffield decreed "No more racing by the factory" in 1934, Eyston sold it to Col. Goldie Gardner, who had Reid Railton design a special enveloping body for it, of length 197 in., width 63 in. and height 26 in, the seat being alongside the angled propshaft. Gardner thenceforth, through a steady process of development (including engine changes, blanking-off cylinders to reduce capacity, and further streamlining) entered into a lengthy period of record-breaking through to the war. His first attempt, on the Fankfurt-Dessau road, achieved 187·62 and 186·567 m.p.h. for the flying mile and kilometre - the ultimate maximum achieved by the car being for the mile in 1939, at 204·2 m.p.h.

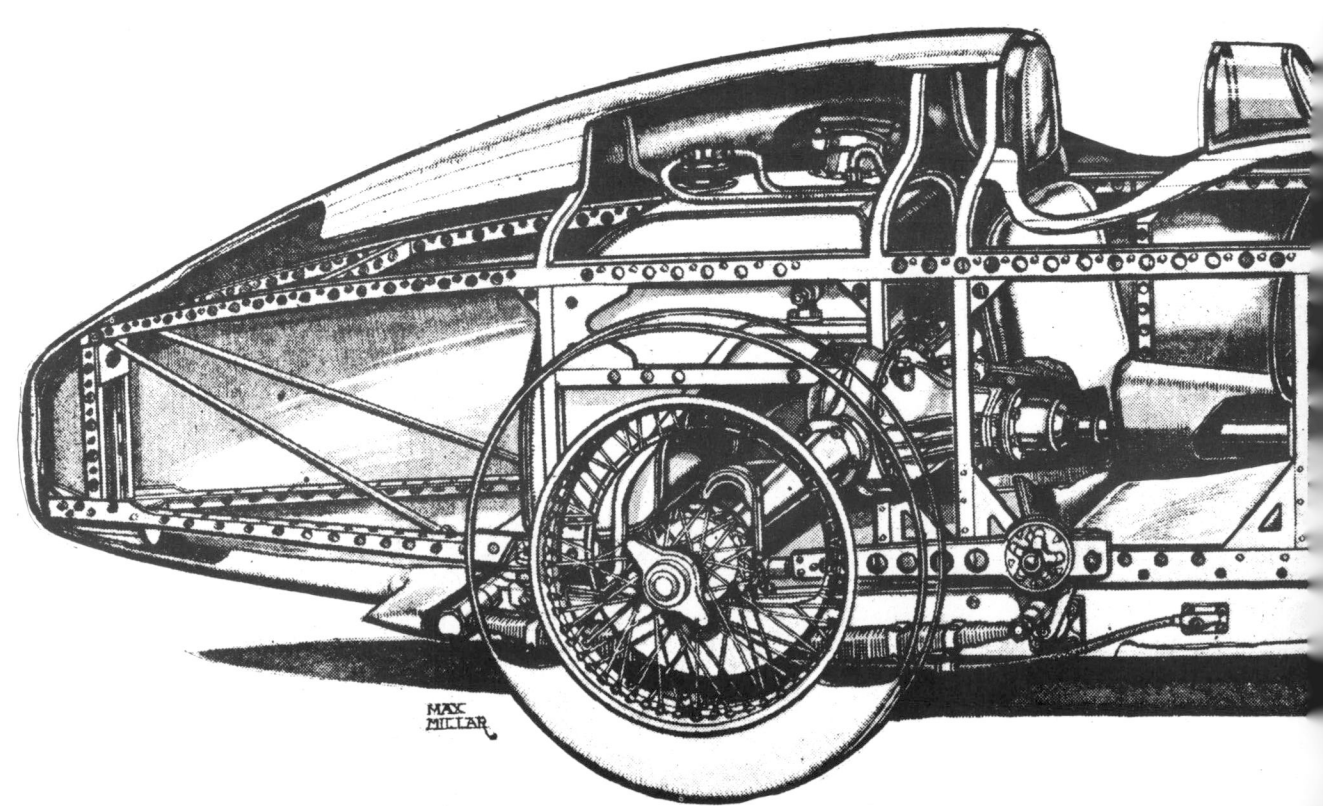

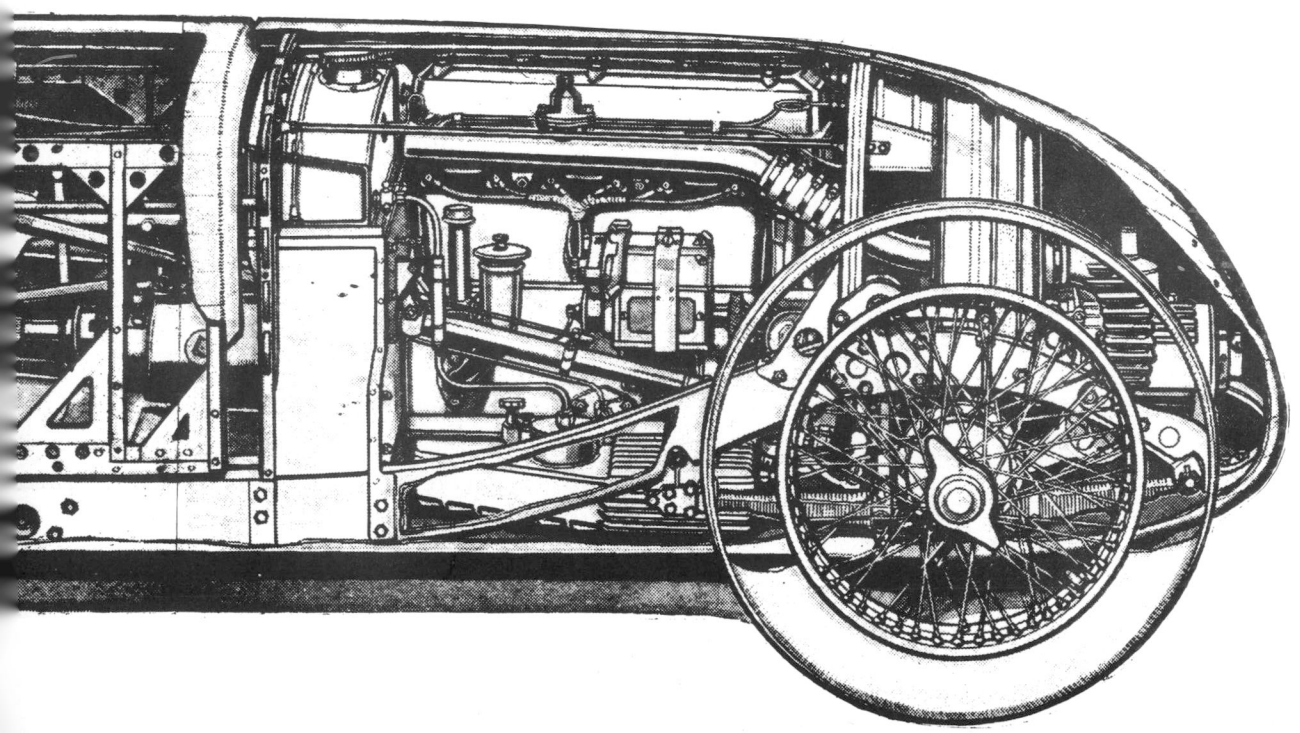

SHELSLEY WALSH, OCTOBER: E. R. Hall's K3 Magnette wins the Midland A.C. British Championship for the fastest sports car, in 46 sec, as well as winning the 1,100 c.c.class for racing and sports cars. It was at this meeting that Hall introduced the special new 3,669 c.c. Bentley with which he had finished second in the Tourist Trophy in September that year - to Dodson's M.G. Magnette.

M.G. MAGNETTE TWO-SEATER

No. 886 $\left(\begin{smallmatrix}Post\text{-}War\\Series\end{smallmatrix}\right)$

WHEN one has had a car in one's care for several days, driving it under the assortment of conditions represented by town traffic, pottering on by-ways, with an occasional steep hill or two, and leavened by sections of good, fast, main-road running, and then, finally, when one has taken the same car to Brooklands and tested it for maximum performance, there is a good basis for fair judgment to be passed. The opportunity is all the better when, as in the case of the M.G., it has been possible in the course of time to follow the successive stages of development through the various models, with plenty of practical experience of their behaviour.

So it is with the latest N Magnette that one comes to it knowing the characteristics of the marque, but naturally expecting to find the most recent model an improvement. Even so, one is not prepared for the very great advance which the N model shows as against earlier types of M.G.s of approximately the same size.

It is not just that the car is fast—its true potentialities in this direction are not easily appreciated until it comes to be taken to the track; it is that it *feels* so very much better. Speed is one thing, and a matter of importance, perhaps sometimes over-rated, to some people; but vastly more important is the manner of a car's behaviour. For, as a rule, it is likely to be driven even by an enthusiastic owner at speeds nearer 50 m.p.h. than its maximum, and the greater part of the joy of owning a real sports car lies in the more normal handling of it.

Acceleration, certainly, is essential to this kind of car, to give which, with a not big engine, revs are the vital essence, and those revs must be maintainable without any suggestion that something is going to break. This engine seems veritably to delight in revs, yet it remains delightfully smooth and quiet, and feels so remarkably happy that the driver quickly gets into the habit of revving "for fun," thereby obtaining a vivid performance.

Latest N Model a Delightful Car to Handle

knowledge of racing, and with the 1,287 c.c. engine that the N Magnette has, it should be capable of giving as high a speed as 80 m.p.h. What comes as a revelation is the ease with which on Brooklands that speed is reached and held, the rev needle hovering between the 5,000 and the 5,500 marks, the whole mechanism feeling as one, and with no sense of adventure attached to such speeds.

It is a sports car, yet it is not harsh in its riding, wherein the use of hydraulic shock absorbers for the back axle no doubt has some considerable effect, the frictional type being retained in front. It is not noisy, either mechanically or in the exhaust; with the same setting of shock-absorbers, the same tyre pressures, and without change of any kind being made anywhere, it is a car perfectly suitable for ordinary running about, for conveying, for instance, an elderly passenger around the country, yet immediately afterwards, and without factory experts being in attendance, the car can be put over the half-mile and record close on 82 m.p.h. (81.45 m.p.h. actually). This was given as the best figure on a practically calm day, with the windscreen lowered but with the normal full equipment in place, the driver only being on board. The best timed speed over a quarter-mile with the windscreen raised normally was 76.27 m.p.h.

On a suitable safe road, with the screen in position in the ordinary way, 75 m.p.h. is a speed which can be got up to with ease and considerable satisfaction. With quite ordinary methods, and changing up fairly early, 50 is registered almost automatically; the way in which the car runs at this speed makes it delightful to keep up, practically irrespective of bend and curve, so rock-steady is the car on the road.

It must not be supposed from what has been said that it is a sixty- rather than an eighty-mile-an-hour car; the distinction lies principally in the road and opportunity available. It is not surprising that with the makers'

M.G. MAGNETTE N TWO-SEATER

DATA FOR THE DRIVER

12.08 h.p., six cylinders, 57 × 84 mm. (1,287 c.c.). Tax £12.
Tyres : 4.75 × 18in. on knock-off wire wheels.

Engine—rear axle gear ratios.	Acceleration from steady speed.			Timed speed over ¼ mile.
	10 to 30 m.p.h.	20 to 40 m.p.h.	30 to 50 m.p.h.	
21.5 to 1	—	—	—	
11.9 to 1	5¾ sec.	—	—	
6.98 to 1	9 sec.	9½ sec.	11 sec.	
5.125 to 1	13 sec.	14¼ sec.	16¼ sec.	80.72 m.p.h.

Acceleration from rest through the gears to 50 m.p.h., 16¾ sec.
Acceleration from rest through the gears to 60 m.p.h., 22¼ sec.
Speed up Brooklands Test Hill from rest (1 in 5 average gradient), 19.37 m.p.h. (on first and second gears).
Acceleration up 15 yards of 1 in 5 gradient from rest, 3¼ sec.
Turning circle : 30ft.
Tank capacity 10 gallons, fuel consumption 24 m.p.g. (approx.).
12-volt lighting set ; 8 amps. at 40 m.p.h.
Weight : 18 cwt. 2 qr.
Price, with two-seater body, £305.

(Latest car described in "The Autocar" of March 30th, 1934.)

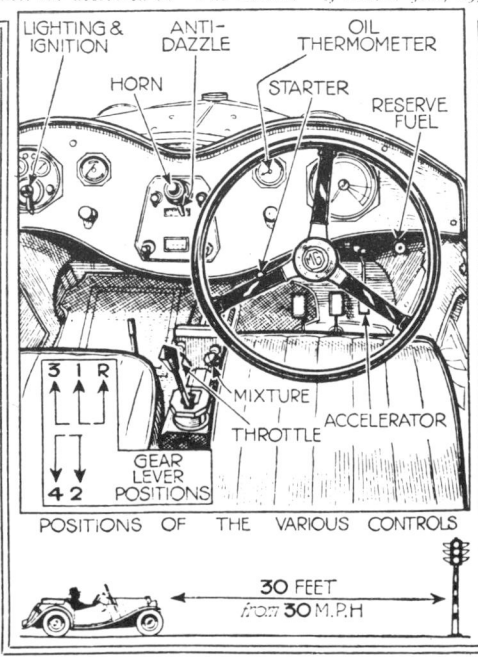

POSITIONS OF THE VARIOUS CONTROLS

LIGHTING & IGNITION — ANTI-DAZZLE — OIL THERMOMETER — HORN — STARTER — RESERVE FUEL — MIXTURE — THROTTLE — ACCELERATOR — GEAR LEVER POSITIONS

30 FEET *from* 30 M.P.H.

M.G. MAGNETTE TWO-SEATER

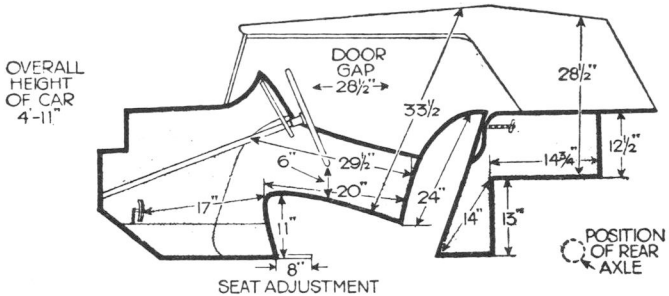

OVERALL HEIGHT OF CAR 4'-11"

DOOR GAP 28½"

28½"

33½"

12½"

14¾"

6"

29½"

20"

24"

14"

13"

17"

11"

8"

SEAT ADJUSTMENT

POSITION OF REAR AXLE

But the difference compared with most ordinary cars is that, when it is wanted, there is instant acceleration available from that speed onwards on top gear ; or, better still, of course, with a quick drop down to third—a movement of sheer joy to the practised driver with the latest gear box, the revs being taken right round to the "five-five" mark if he so chooses—almost exactly 60 m.p.h. on third gear.

To pass, or to climb really fast, in this way is an experience in motoring which is difficult to excel ; the whole running of the car spells efficiency, and, a good point on this N model, there is no ostentation about the exhaust note. Actually, 6,000 is not by any means an unheard-of figure with this engine, but the red marking on the dial leads one to treat 5,500 r.p.m. as a usual limit, which gives 36 m.p.h. on second, and just over 20 on first gear.

The big dial in front of the driver is essentially a rev counter, an intelligent instrument for the owner of a car such as this, but there is an inner ring of readings on which are plotted the equivalent speeds on top gear. The instrument proved very close to accurate in its speed readings,

the maximum m.p.h. figure during the fastest timed run being 83 or so..

Apart from the performance, the most striking thing about the car is its feeling of solidity without, however, seeming "dead." One soon has the feeling of being able to do almost anything with the car on corners. This, and the acceleration, coupled with brakes having big drums of racing pattern, which do their job really well, yet never give the impression of being fierce, make high average speeds a matter of course when required.

An excellent angle has been given to the steering column, the wheel comes in an ideal position for power of control over it, both arms being inside the body of the car. Though very light, the steering is properly accurate. The seats themselves are very comfortable.

Behind the seat there is a genuinely useful-sized compartment for baggage. On the chassis one outstanding provision is a system of grouped lubricators which, communicating by pipe lines to various bearings, reduces lubrication almost to a pleasure.

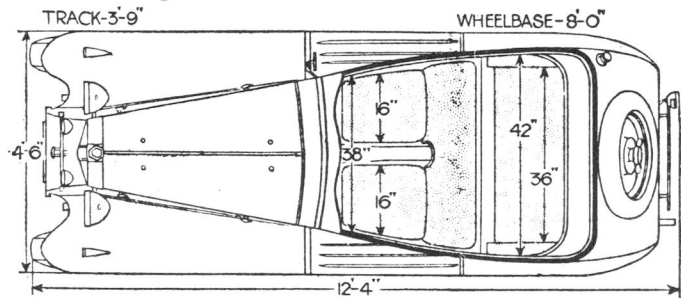

TRACK-3'-9"

WHEELBASE-8'-0"

4'-6"

16"

38"

42"

16"

36"

12'-4"

INTO BATTLE   Man in Beg 1934

As the results show, this event proved a walkover for the supercharged K3 Magnettes! The two illustrations above - both taken at Promenade Corner in Douglas, Isle of Man - show (left) Norman Black (No. 22), the eventual winner, leading Hamilton's car, and (right) George Eyston's very non-standard bodied car.

RESULTS.

Pos.	Car.	Driver.	Time.			Speed.
			h.	m.	s.	m.p.h.
1	M.G. Magnette (S)	N. Black	2	34	37	70.99
2	M.G. Magnette (S)	C. J. P. Dodson	2	36	20	70.20
3	M.G. Magnette (S)	G. E. T. Eyston	2	36	57	69.93
4	M.G. Magnette (S)	C. E. C. Martin	2	41	5	68.11
5	M.G. Magnette (S)	R. H. Eccles	2	44	22	66.78
6	Riley	C. Paul	2	44	25	66.67
7	M.G. Magnette (S)	R. T. Horton	2	44	54	65.55
8	M.G. Midget (S)	W. G. Everitt	2	48	3	63.30

Cecil Kimber, managing director of the M.G. Car Company, with the special supercharged, drophead coupe Magnette he had built for his private use and for experimental purposes

International Trophy, Brooklands, 1934: Marshals had a busy day mending the chicane barriers—scattered here by C. J. Dodson's supercharged K3 Magnette which finished eighth

4 *to* 100 *m.p.h.*

WOULD it surprise your to know that there is in existence a 12 h.p. car which will glide along at 4 m.p.h. in top, and accelerate from that speed, still in top gear, to something in the neighbourhood of 100 m.p.h.? I was in such a car last week, a ladylike-looking four-seater drophead coupé complete with all the amenities, including a Philco wireless set. From the driver's seat one gets an impression that the car is at least a 2-litre job. I have seen it several times, and have had a secret suspicion that it was a new big M.G. Yes, that is what it is, an experimental M.G. Magnette, Mr. Cecil Kimber's own car, which is purely experimental; therefore, it may not even be marketed, for Kimber, as managing director of M.G.s, can build a car for himself just as he wants it.

He had ideas, and set to work to test them out. This car is the result, and has now done 11,000 miles without decarbonising; as he keeps an accurate log, he is able to draw his own conclusions. If those conclusions are the same as my own, he will introduce this model next year for sportsmen who wish to have all the attributes of a sports car combined with a performance at the lower end of the scale suitable for taking the family to church.

In spite of the high wind we did a quarter-mile at over 90 m.p.h. and a lap at an average of over 80 m.p.h. At 6,000 r.p.m. the speed is 99·6 m.p.h. We exceeded that. My first 100 m.p.h.! The wireless control is on the steering column, otherwise I should have turned it off. It was giving us "God Save the King"! Yet that car was as comfortable in town and suburb as my own family saloon: none of that "shockers-too-hard" feeling one experiences with really fast sports cars.

Tourist Trophy 1934: A quartette of Magnettes—Eyston (25), Dodson (27), Handley (26) and Black (28) at Dundonald hairpin. The race was won by Dodson's Magnette, with Hall's 3,669 c.c. Bentley second (on handicap).

M.G. CONTINUITY

No Seasonal Changes, Improvements If and When Desirable

The new KN Magnette saloon, with 1,287 c.c. engine.

AS hard-won racing experience accumulates a fund of knowledge upon which to draw for the purpose of producing cars that are able to maintain with reliability a high performance in the hands of private owners, so does it become possible from time to time for the keen designers to incorporate improvements in existing models or to evolve altogether new ones. These periods of evolution are not governed by the weather, or by the season of the year, but by the state of knowledge, and by the production facilities of the factory, which always will run most economically when working full and regular time.

These are the reasons why the M.G. Company has no new programme announcement to make. New or improved M.G. cars have been introduced at intervals, and each one has marked a very real step forward. When further improvements are discovered, tested, and made commercial they will doubtless be incorporated, but it is definitely the policy not to make seasonal alterations, and thus the existing range of cars remains current. To write of them is an interesting subject.

Full credit must be given to the enterprise and the dogged hard work which

have eventually raised the M.G. racing stable to international fame. How many motorists realise that size for size, M.G. cars can race anything in the world and stand an odds-on chance of winning? Or that in Abingdon, England, they knew more about getting and holding stupendous horse powers out of the smallest of engines than anywhere else? Two hundred brake horse power per litre capacity would have sounded utterly incredible a few years ago, but it is an M.G. hope very near now to realisation. The 750 c.c. engine of the Q-type racer will hold round about 111 b.h.p., suitably tuned, and the car is capable of lapping Brooklands track at 111 m.p.h., and reaching 123 m.p.h. down the straight.

Racing Cars Purchasable

Types of M.G. racing cars can be purchased by anyone in the ordinary way; there are two sizes, the Q-type Midget, four cylinders, 57 by 73 mm. (746 c.c.), and the K3 Magnette, six cylinders, 57 by 71 (1,087 c.c.), the first priced at £550, and the second at £795.

In salient points the design of the two cars is similar. The engines have overhead valves, with straight ports on opposite sides, operated by an overhead cam-

shaft driven by spiral bevel gears through a vertical shaft, dynamo-damped to prevent oscillation. The combustion chambers are of a special shape, and a very special type of gasket is fitted to hand-scraped surfaces between cylinder head and cylinder block-cum-crank case casting. The large size balanced crankshaft is carried in three bearings on the four-cylinder and four bearings on the six.

Engine lubrication is a very important point in cars of this description. A large gear-type oil pump is driven from the crankshaft feeds all the bearings under high pressure through a fine Tecalemit filter. The pump draws through a strainer its supply from an elektron sump ribbed for cooling, and an automatic float feed maintains the oil at a set level from an auxiliary tank in the scuttle. Both engines are supercharged, the blower being driven from the front end of the crankshaft through universal couplings. On the K3 a Roots type is used, with a normal boost of 10 lb. per sq. in. and a maximum of 13 lb., whilst on the Q the compressor is a Zoller with a normal boost of 20 lb. and a maximum of 24 lb. The four-speed gear box is a preselector made under Wilson patents, and is operated from a very neat control in the centre of the cockpit.

The P-type M.G. Midget two-seater,
which goes on without change.

The N Magnette two-seater, which also is unaltered.

of course, the absence of a supercharger. The Q-type machine has been developed from the P.

Materially, the four-cylinder engine of the P is the same, only the stroke is longer, 83 mm. instead of 73 mm., whereby the capacity is put up to 847 c.c. By reason of the rigid construction and the cylinder head and valve design, this engine is

Besides the clutch incorporated in the gear box, the Q has an additional two-plate inoperative clutch in the flywheel, with a pre-determined slip load. The frame of each car is underslung at the rear, and has tubular cross-bracing. An aluminium undershield is fitted flush under the bottom of the chassis to reduce air resistance, and scoops assist the cooling of the gear box and rear axle.

The half-elliptic springs are underslung and flat, and have bronze-lined trunnions at the rear, instead of shackles, to oppose side movement. They are taped and bound, and in the case of the front axles steel cables are carried to the frame to take the torque of heavy braking. On the K3 a very special type of braking is used, consisting of twin cam levers operated through cables and casings in such a way as to double the force of brake application for a given cable load.

The cars are fitted with two-seater bodies of extremely light construction in the form of a beaten aluminium shell, with the fuel tank concealed in a streamlined tail of which the point is hinged. The wings are easily removable, and the body can be lifted without disturbing the mechanism of the car. The body dimensions conform to A.I.A.C.R. regulations.

(Right) Rear end of the Q racing model Midget, showing how access is gained by means of a hinged tail.

(Below) The supercharged 1,100 c.c. K3 Magnette in racing guise. It costs £795.

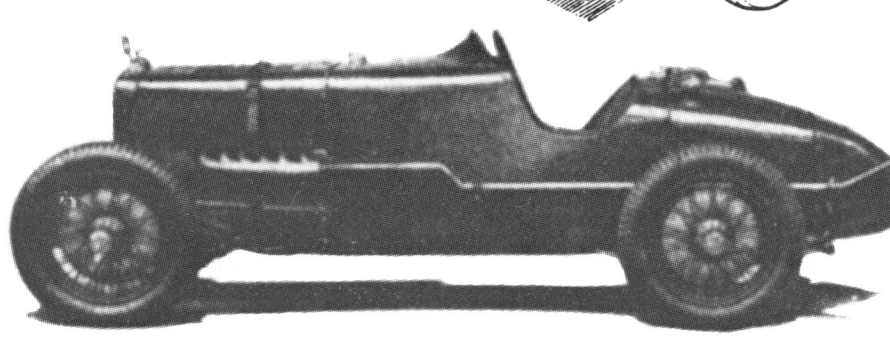

the racing child has really become father to the touring man, meaning that the evolution of both concomitant types is interlocked. For example, the M.G. Midget of to-day, the P type introduced last March, has a very similar chassis to that of the Q type, except only in details, and,

very smooth and has a great capability of revving at high speed. It develops 44 b.h.p. at 5,500 r.p.m. A four-speed "twin-top" gear box, with a specially low first gear is fitted, not a preselective gear.

Remarkable at sight for its trim and alert appearance, the Midget has a number of attractive points apart from the particular qualities of all M.G. cars, namely, that they are designed for fast work and show their mettle best when the speed is high enough to illustrate the

BRAKE
ADJUSTMENT

TWIN FUEL TAPS

(Left) Cockpit of the Q-type Midget. The large-figure instruments, brake adjustment and fuel taps will be noticed.

That is an outline of the general design; there are, of course, numerous other points of special value for racing purposes.

It is perhaps natural for the pen to move first towards describing racing cars, but actually the M.G.s of touring type should have the premier position, because

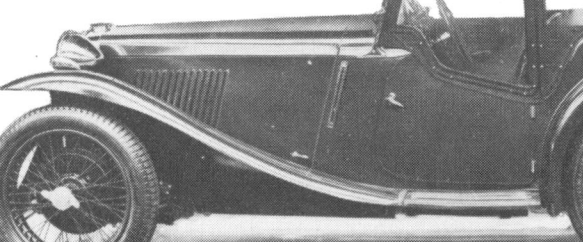

The P-type Midget four-seater.

Interior of the new Magnette saloon.

meaning of a perfect road hold, steadiness in quick curves, a sensitive steering, and brakes that can safely be used at high speed.

The gear control is brought well back into the cockpit, and has a short, stiff lever, the brake lever is of racing type, which is free until locked by the top catch; the instrument board is well arranged, and has a large diameter revolution indicator combined with a speedometer; the screen can be folded flat forward, and the long bonnet, when opened up, gives access also to the interior of the scuttle. The radiator, lamps and wings are mounted in a special way which relieves the front end of the frame of pendulum action, and avoids "front end dither." There is a reserve to the fuel tank with a control in reach of the driver's hand. The driving compartment is sealed off from the

engine by a metal-faced bulkhead, with a rubber annulus around the flywheel housing, and the cable-operated, large diameter brakes have an easy master adjustment. There are three coachwork models of the P type Midget: — two-seater, £222; four-seater, £240; and Airline coupé, £290.

Then come the six-cylinder models. First is the N type Magnette. This again follows normal M.G. practice and is very similar to the Midget, except that it is on a larger scale and has a six-cylinder twin-carburetter engine of 57 by 84 mm. (1,287 c.c.). One additional special feature is the method of mounting the body on flexibly attached side sub-frames and a flexible cross-member at the rear.

The two-seater is priced at £305, the

four-seater at £335, the two-four-seater at £350, and the Airline coupé at £385.

Of other six-cylinder closed models there are the Continental coupé, a two-door four-seater of striking appearance with a large luggage trunk at the back, built on the Magna chassis, which has a 1,087 c.c. engine and a 3ft. 6in. track, priced at £350, and then a new model only just introduced.

This is the KN saloon, which has a K-type Magnette chassis, but the engine is the N type of 1,287 c.c. The KN saloon is likely to attract many purchasers, for it has all the typical M.G. roadworthiness and fast performance, but offers the comfort of a roomy saloon body.

The appearance is not extremist, but very graceful and well proportioned. The seating position is low, but the bonnet and scuttle are also low, so that an excellent forward view is obtained. There are four doors, arranged on the pillarless principle, so that access to the rear seats is extremely easy. In the rear panel is a luggage box, the lid of which can be used as a luggage platform. This car runs quietly and easily, and is very pleasant to handle. The arrangement of sliding windows gives extra elbow room, and altogether the interior is not confined or cramped for either head or leg room. The price is £399.

(A full description of the N-Type Magnette, with cutaway drawing, appears on pages 48 and 49.)

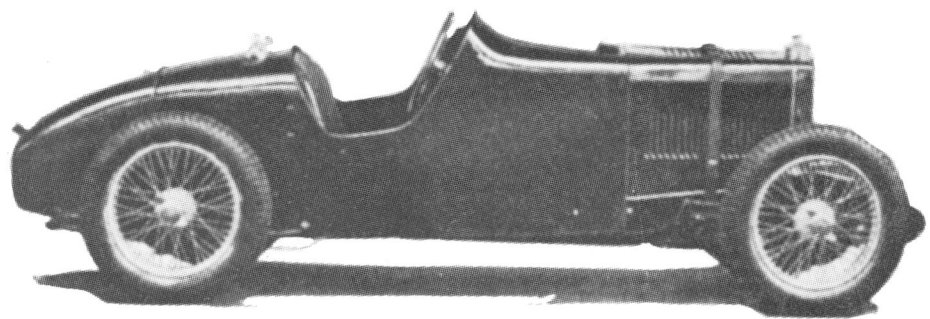

Q-type M.G. Midget competition model, priced at £550.

INTO BATTLE 1935

M.C.C. EXETER TRIAL: S. E. H Bowyer (one of the 276 car competitors; there were solo motorcycles, sidecar outfits and three-wheelers as well!) climbs Ibberton in his M.G. Midget — last hill of the trial. M.G's of various types and sizes accounted for a substantial proportion of the entries for these pre-war, long-distance M.C.C. trials - the Land's End, Exeter, and Edinburgh, as well as the Club's Brooklands one-hour "blind".

The Autocar

Published *The Autocar*
2 November 1934

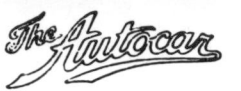

"THE AUTOCAR" ROAD TESTS

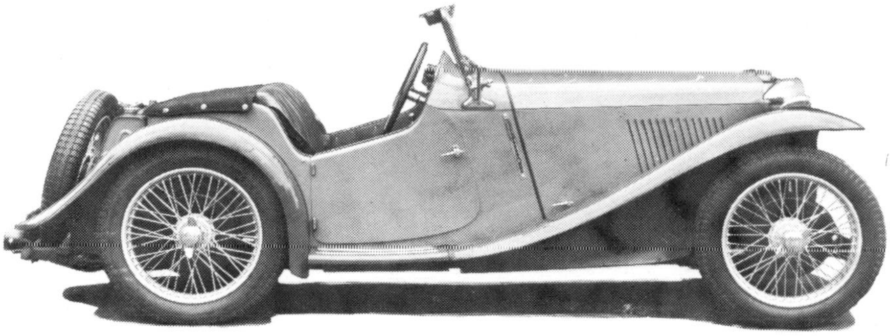

M.G. MIDGET P-TYPE TWO-SEATER

No. 894 (Post-War Series)

Latest Model a Marked Improvement in All Important Respects Over Its Forerunners

THE P-type M.G. Midget is already very well known, but it so happens that only recently has there been an opportunity of carrying out the ordinary Road Test on it. Anyone who has had experience of the various preceding Midget models cannot fail to be struck by the very great improvement which this P-type shows in practically all respects over its forerunners.

One of the greatest things is that the latest engine, with its three-bearing crankshaft and other improvements, is an enormous gain in smoothness, so much so that it seems as happy at high engine speeds as it is lower down the range. This is very valuable indeed, for pre-eminently it is a car which depends upon revs for its performance. If it be driven gently on top gear and with early upward changes, then its performance is much like that of any ordinary small touring car; the gears are definitely there to be used, and thoroughly justify their use.

An excellent gear change, with remote-control lever, is provided, and the engine can be taken up as a regular thing to as much as 5,000 r.p.m., thereby obtaining a performance definitely superior to that of ordinary cars of small and medium size, and very pleasing to the enthusiastic driver because of the remarkable ease with which the engine turns over fast.

There is no doubt that the M.G. people have developed to a fine art the attainment of revs without fuss by engines of small capacity.

The car was driven hard, particularly during the tests on Brooklands, and for several hundred miles on ordinary roads, but at no time did it give any impression that anything was going to break. It seemed, in fact, to defy any such attempts.

On one occasion, on second gear, the revs were taken round to an indicated 6,000 r.p.m. on the instrument, yet still the engine was smooth and apparently contented.

The figure given in the table for maximum speed was taken with the windscreen lowered and with only the driver on board, and represents a mean of several runs in opposite directions. As the best speed under such conditions, but with the wind following, 76.27 m.p.h. was recorded over the quarter-mile. With the windscreen raised a best speed of 69.23 m.p.h. was given over the timed quarter-mile.

It was not a good day for these tests, since a strong cross-wind gave no real help at any time, and was a handicap in one direction. The speedometer did not go above a reading of 78, and a rather remarkable thing about the maximum speed is that, though somewhere about 5,000 r.p.m. is being held, the engine feels perfectly happy. In fact, after several such runs it began almost to feel slow at this speed.

On the gears, using a limit of 5,500 r.p.m. on the combined rev counter and speedometer instrument, readings of 20 on first gear, 36 on second, and 60 on third are given, but there are still revs in hand, and a full 60 m.p.h. on third is possible. The speedometer had an optimistic error not above 2½ m.p.h. at any speed.

Along with this most useful performance the handling of the car is excellent. The P-type feels more comfortable as a touring car, especially at the lower speeds, yet is steadier in the sports car sense at speed. It can be taken round corners with that feeling of rock-steadiness and absolute control which is altogether delightful, and the steering, though very light, is accurate. The brakes, too, are very good indeed. Their full power is not realised until one comes to tread hard on the pedal in making an emergency stop; then it is found that they pull up the car really decisively. The very good figure given was taken using the pedal alone.

With the hand lever as well, which gives an even more powerful leverage, 27ft. from 30 m.p.h. was recorded as the mean of two tests. For ordinary slowing they are really good brakes, too, as the action is smooth and progressive, and the pedal pressure need only be light.

A cruising speed cannot be quoted

M.G. MIDGET P-TYPE TWO-SEATER

DATA FOR THE DRIVER

8 h.p., four cylinders, 57 × 83 mm. (846 c.c.). Tax £8 (1935, £6).
Tyres: 19 × 4.00in. on knock-off wire wheels.

Engine—rear axle gear ratios.	Acceleration from steady speed. 10 to 30 m.p.h.	20 to 40 m.p.h.	30 to 50 m.p.h.	Timed speed over ¼ mile.
22.50 to 1	—	—	—	
12.46 to 1	7⅕ sec.	—	—	
7.31 to 1	12⅘ sec.	12⅗ sec.	13⅕ sec.	
5.375 to 1	19⅗ sec.	19⅖ sec.	26⅕ sec.	74.38 m.p.h.

Acceleration from rest through the gears to 50 m.p.h., 20⅘ sec.
Acceleration from rest through the gears to 60 m.p.h., 32⅕ sec.
Speed up Brooklands Test Hill from rest (1 in 5 average gradient), 18.19 m.p.h. (on first and second gears).
Acceleration up 15 yards of 1 in 5 gradient from rest, 3⅗ sec.
Turning circle: 36ft.
Tank capacity 12 gallons, fuel consumption 35 m.p.g. (approx.)
12-volt lighting set cuts in at 16 m.p.h., 8 amps. at 30 m.p.h.
Weight: 13 cwt. 2 qr.
Price, with two-seater body, £222.

(Latest car described in "The Autocar" of September 14th, 1934.)

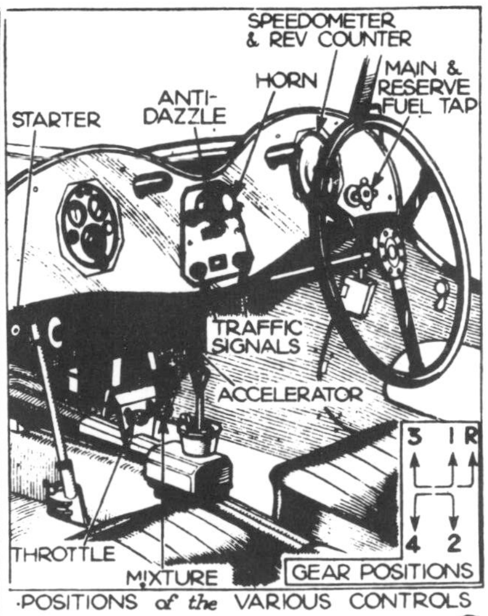
SPEEDOMETER & REV COUNTER
HORN
MAIN & RESERVE FUEL TAP
ANTI-DAZZLE
STARTER
TRAFFIC SIGNALS
ACCELERATOR
3 1 R
4 2
THROTTLE
MIXTURE
GEAR POSITIONS

POSITIONS of the VARIOUS CONTROLS

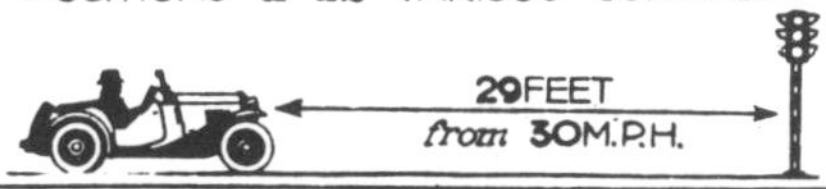
29FEET
from 30M.P.H.

M.G. MIDGET P-TYPE TWO-SEATER

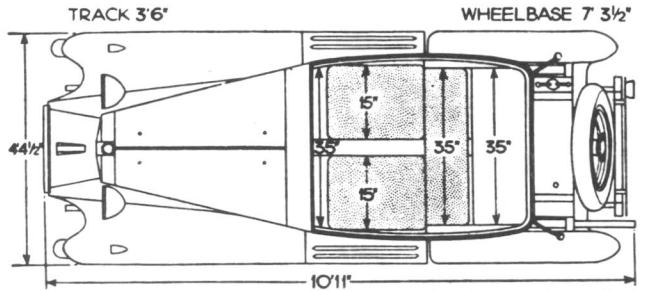

for the Midget in the ordinary way, for it can be taken along at whatever speed within its range the road permits ; 60 m.p.h. is quickly attained on a good open stretch.

The gear change, especially between top and third, is a delight to use, third is barely distinguishable from top in sound ; the upward changes, except between third and top, need a fair pause in neutral. The performance would be still better in acceleration were it possible to get through more rapidly from first to second and from second to third without crashing the gears.

The two-seater body is comfortable and adequately wide ; the windscreen has a double-blade electric wiper, there are recessed traffic signals, and the head-lamp beam is good. An important point which has been noticed in all the normal M.G. models is the instantaneous starting from cold, with very little use indeed of the mixture control.

It is possible to say of this particular car, in a way not always feasible under the conditions of an ordinary test, that the oil consumption was exceptionally light.

The hood is easily raised and lowered, there are good side screens, and a fair-sized luggage space is provided under cover. The seats are very comfortable.

The fuel tank is of a sensible capacity ; a noticeable point under the bonnet is the provision of a fuse to guard each circuit. The new oil filler in the top of the valve gear cover is a great convenience. The exhaust note is quieter than when the P-type was first produced, apart from a period of resonance at about 2,500 r.p.m.

A most desirable little sports car.

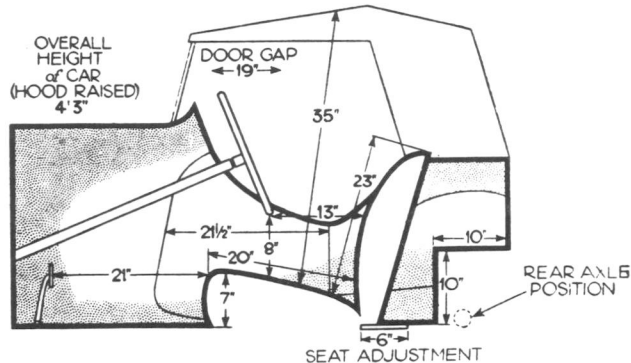

A four seater version of the P-type Midget was also available.

MG P~type Midget

Introduced in February 1934, the P-type replaced the
starker J. Available in two-seater form for £220, 4-seater
for £240, and as the stylish, closed Airline Coupé for
£290, the new model retained the 847 c.c. engine capacity
of the earlier car, though the engine was a new design
with a much-needed third bearing on the crankshaft.
Right: The car in two-seater form, and below, the
construction details of the 4-seater laid bare.

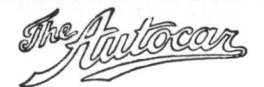

The Autocar Road Tests

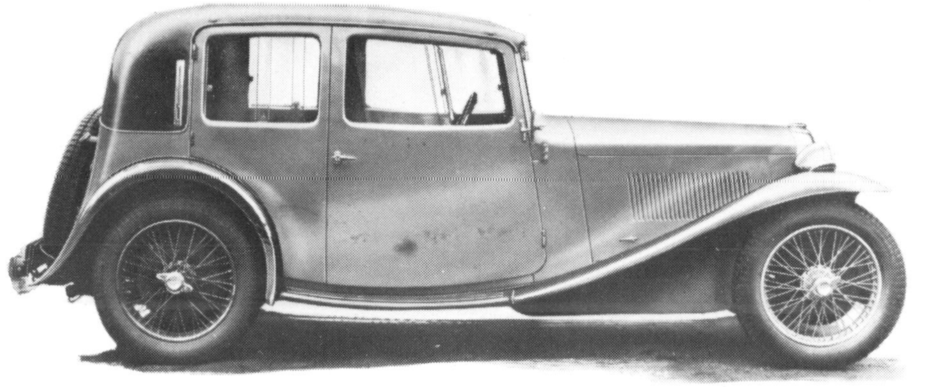

12 h.p. M.G. MAGNETTE KN SALOON

No. 913 (Post-War Series)

Accuracy of Control and a Feeling of Complete Safety Outstanding Features of a Fast 12 h.p. Car

ONE approaches an M.G. saloon in the expectation that it will prove to be decidedly above the average of cars of similar nominal size in regard to road behaviour. In this new KN pillarless saloon the market represented by those who appreciate performance and fine handling qualities in a car is better catered for, one can say, than by any previous closed model on a comparatively small chassis that the M.G. Company have put forward.

One very important underlying reason is that the N Magnette engine, which has been doing so well during the past year, provides ample power for the additional weight of a saloon body. To-day, the makers of these cars have a very varied experience in producing fast cars, that enables them to provide not only a powerful, willing and reliable engine, but to fit this engine in a chassis which as regards stability, braking, and steering, those all-important factors, is in every way excellent.

Experience of the KN saloon, which, incidentally, is on a chassis with a longer wheelbase and a wider track than that applying to the open Magnette models, has extended for purposes of this account over some hundreds of miles, taking in all kinds of conditions of fast motoring, byway pottering, and traffic use, as well as distinct variations in weather.

It happened that a car of this type was driven for some distance on two separate occasions. During the greater part of the time on the first occasion the roads were wet, and there was no opportunity of discovering how the car showed up on a dry road. From the very commencement, however, and this is the important point, a driver new to the car felt that he was able to handle this saloon on surfaces far from ideal almost exactly as though the roads had been dry, either in cornering or under braking, and there was no suggestion at any time that his faith in the road-holding qualities was misplaced.

With the greater confidence of even the experienced driver when eventually it was possible to drive on dry roads, it was found that almost anything could be done with the car on corners, bends being hardly noticed as regards need for conscious steering, whilst on sharper turns taken fast where there was vision ahead the car felt rock-steady.

This question of stability is stressed because in it lies much of the character of the car, and by it is emphasised the natural safety of a machine designed from the start to be driven fast where conditions permit.

12 h.p. M.G. MAGNETTE KN SALOON.

DATA FOR THE DRIVER

12 h.p., six cylinders, 57 × 84 mm. (1,287 c.c.). Tax £9.
Tyres: 4.75 × 19in. on knock-off wire wheels.

Engine—rear axle gear ratios.	Acceleration from steady speed. 10 to 30 m.p.h.	20 to 40 m.p.h.	30 to 50 m.p.h.	Timed speed over ¼ mile.
24.15 to 1	—	—	—	
13.40 to 1	6 sec.	—	—	
7.86 to 1	9⅘ sec.	10⅕ sec.	12⅗ sec.	
5.78 to 1	13⅕ sec.	16 sec.	17⅖ sec.	75.31 m.p.h.

Acceleration from rest through the gears to 50 m.p.h., 18⅖ sec.
Acceleration from rest through the gears to 60 m.p.h., 28⅗ sec.
Speed up Brooklands Test Hill from rest (1 in 5 average gradient), 16.45 m.p.h. (on first and second gears).
Acceleration up 15 yards of 1 in 5 gradient from rest, 3⅕ sec.
Turning circle: 38ft.
Tank capacity 10 gallons; fuel consumption 25 m.p.g.
12-volt lighting set; 8 amps. at 30 m.p.h.
Weight: 21 cwt.
Price, with pillarless four-door saloon body, £399.

(Described in "The Autocar" of September 14th, 1934.)

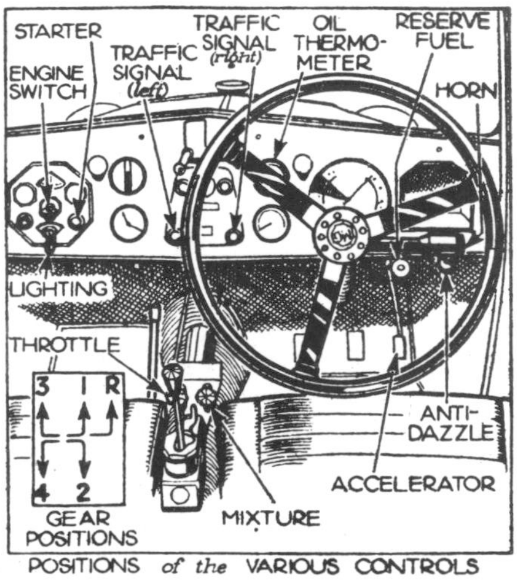

POSITIONS of the VARIOUS CONTROLS

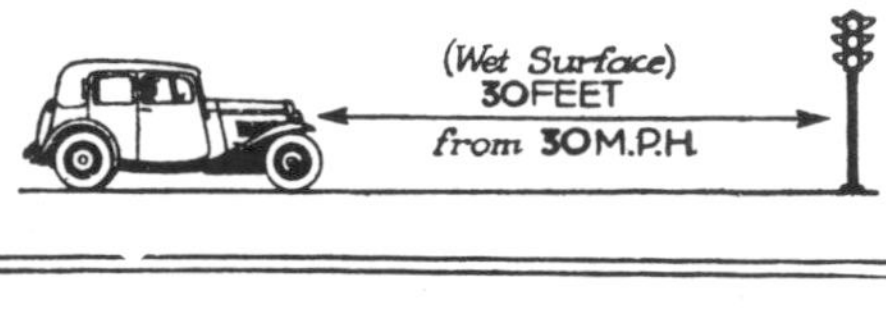

There is that feeling about the steering which enables one to steer to the proverbial inch, at all events, to place the car exactly where one wishes on the road, and as to the brakes, with their large, businesslike-looking drums, they can be put on hard without thought on average roads as to whether the car will remain on a straight course. They are most satisfactorily progressive brakes in that light pressure on the pedal gives ordinary slowing down, and for maximum results heavier pressure is needed.

A rather remarkable feature of the springing is that in spite of the extreme steadiness the riding is not harsh. For all its accuracy, the steering is very light indeed, though not disconcertingly so.

The gear change remains of straightforward pattern; that is, there is no synchromesh or similar device, but third speed has helical-toothed pinions which run in constant mesh. Without being difficult, it is a gear change suited to the car, with its short, stiff remote-control lever, and it handles with exactness.

Third is a quiet gear, second and first are more noisy, but not markedly so. Limits of approximately 16, 35, and 62 m.p.h. are given on first, second, and third gears, up to a full 50 m.p.h. on third without appearing to stress the engine in the least.

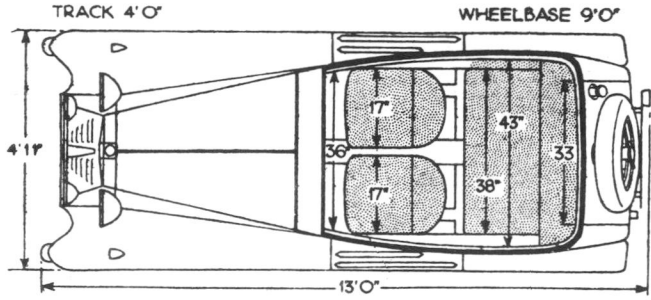

TRACK 4' 0" WHEELBASE 9' 0"

4' 1"

17" 43"

36 33

17" 38"

13' 0"

for the power. The best timed run over a quarter-mile with the wind following was at 78.26 m.p.h.

The standard combined rev counter and top and third gear speed instrument read high by 5 m.p.h. at 60.

The pillarless four-door construction of the body is an asset as regards convenience of getting in and out where a car of comparatively small size is concerned. Pneumatic upholstery is used and is very comfortable, the back rest and cushion being in one, deck-chair style.

Elbow room is conserved for the occupants of the front seats by the use of sliding windows, which obviate winding mechanism in the doors. The driving position is particularly comfortable, with the spring-spoked wheel brought well back and set not too high. The rear view mirror, fitted externally, could be more effective. At the back a platform can be lowered to carry luggage.

A machine for an owner who appreciates a car as a car and not solely as a means of transport.

The manner of one's progression depends almost entirely upon the circumstances. If to go from one place to another is the object, the car responds beautifully, and will hold its 60 m.p.h. or more. On the other hand, it is happy in itself and pleasing to the occupants when running in the thirties and forties, though seeming to express a preference for somewhere about 50 m.p.h. on open roads.

Humming along in its purposeful stride it sweeps up the ordinary kind of hill, helped by the fact that top gear ratio is lower for the saloon model. Often, if slowed by other traffic, it will naturally make a faster climb on third; second, too, is a very valuable gear.

In acceleration the car exhibits a cleanness of carburation, with ready response to the throttle pedal, this on the gears especially, though on top gear, too, the pick-up is satisfactory and it is a machine that can still accelerate usefully from speeds of 40 m.p.h. or so.

For a 12 h.p. saloon which is not particularly light, though material has not been wasted, the speed figures show up outstandingly well. For the test at Brooklands conditions were bad, with a strong head wind against the car in one direction and a wet surface, but the mean speed of several runs, above a genuine 75 m.p.h., speaks well

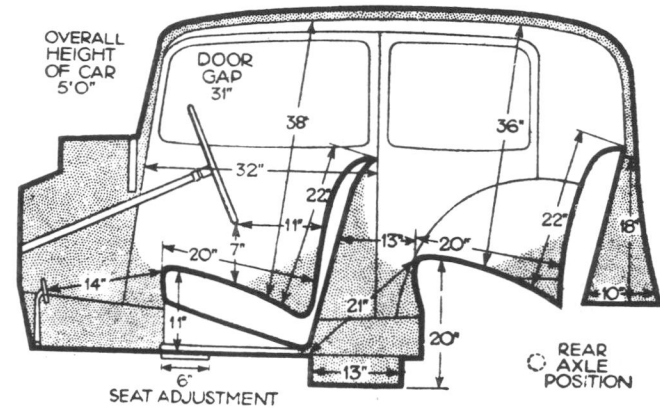

OVERALL HEIGHT OF CAR 5' 0" DOOR GAP 31"

38 36

32"

22"

11" 13" 20" 22" 16"

20" 7"

14" 21" 10"

11" 20"

6" 13" REAR AXLE POSITION

SEAT ADJUSTMENT

THE "CRESTA" MAGNETTE

Special Two-seater Model in Which Both Light Weight and Comfort Have Been Studied

A SPECIAL model of the M.G. Magnette, to be known as the "Cresta" Magnette, has just been placed on the market by the Cresta Motor Company, Ltd., of Worthing. The coachwork, which is shown in the accompanying photographs, has been carried out by E. Bertelli, Ltd., and the two-seater body is designed with a disappearing hood, an occasional seat, ample luggage accommodation, and a windscreen which, when in the raised position, has flanking screens that can be used as miniature windscreens when the main screen is horizontal. A cover is provided for the rear of the car and for the

passenger's seat when necessary, there is a very large tool box under the bonnet, an Ashby or a Bluemel steering wheel is available, the fuel tank holds 11½ gallons, the seats are adjustable for angle as well as for position, and the detail work of the car is carried out very well indeed, weight being kept down by the use of a special grade of aluminium panel. The finish of the upholstery and paintwork adds very greatly to the attractiveness of the car.

The "Cresta" Magnette has a handsome aluminium-panelled body with many excellent features.

M.G.'s Quit Racing

THE decision that the M.G. Company is to cease racing forthwith has come as quite a bit of a shock to a lot of people. The announcement as worded says that the company is to cease building racing cars and concentrate solely on sports cars, but I think it means much more than that, for it affects all racing by the firm's cars, whether they are of the type we call sports cars or not. This is a pretty shrewd blow, but there's no getting away from the fact that racing can be overdone, and I maintain once more that, as far as the real racing machines are concerned, the best policy is to build and maintain one team and to concentrate on that. If the type is interesting and exciting it is bound to have teething troubles before success arrives, and teething troubles are far more serious if there are a great number of these machines in the hands of various people. It's a pity about the Tourist Trophy, though, as the team might have stood a very good chance of pulling it off again, but beyond question the wisest policy for the moment is to concentrate on making money.

TOP *The "Three Musketeers" team of Magnettes—and* Aramis *again—this time winning outright the first Welsh Rally, held in July 1935. The driver, as in the previous illustration, was C. W. Nash*

ABOVE *This illustration—taken on holiday in the I. of M.—of R. A. Yallop's K3 Magnettes seems to sum up all the sporting features and character of these famous cars*

LEFT *NUFFIELD TROPHY, DONINGTON 1935: Reg Parnell's offset single-seater Magnette finds unexpectedly strong opposition in Ian Connell's Vale Special—the Vale finishing the race, while the Magnette retired. The Vale, incidentally, was powered by Triumph Super Seven*

BELOW *Brooklands, Whit Monday 1936: Closely fought Mountain Circuit races were a feature of this meeting, in this case with R. C. Vickers' Type 35 Bugatti being chased by "Bira" and Reg Parnell in Magnettes.*

Thought for many years to be the first-ever MG, this special was driven by Cecil Kimber on the 1925 Lands End Trial

Miss Betty Haig's immaculately preserved 1935 PB Midget

Gilding the Lily?

RX 5974

However goodlooking the production M.G. coachwork, there were always those who thought they could improve on it. Here (left and below) is the Sportsman's coupé version of the 1929 M-Type Midget, complete with unusual sunshine roof

RX 9316

1935: Elegant Airline coupé on the P-type Midget. On the PA chassis this cost £267 10s, and you paid £22 10s more for a PB version

M.G. Announce a Two-litre

A Handsome and Roomy Four-door Close-coupled Saloon on a 10ft. 3in. Wheelbase Chassis

RUMOUR has had much to say of the M.G. Car Company's eve-of-the-Show surprise. It would be this, and it would be that. It would have this feature and that feature. Now, however, the new model is announced, and is seen to be entirely different from the various forecasts.

Briefly, the M.G. Two-litre is a large, roomy sports saloon of the popular four-door close-coupled type, having essentially modern sweeping lines, with a

capacious boot for luggage. It is handsome in appearance, and is equipped in a manner which is usually only found on large and expensive cars, the fittings including Jackall four-wheel hydraulic jacks, twin Lucas Pass lights, and twin Lucas air-operated horns with loud and soft notes. Both the exterior and interior finish are of a high standard, and the size of the car may be judged from the 10ft. 3in. wheelbase and 4ft. 5in. track. This

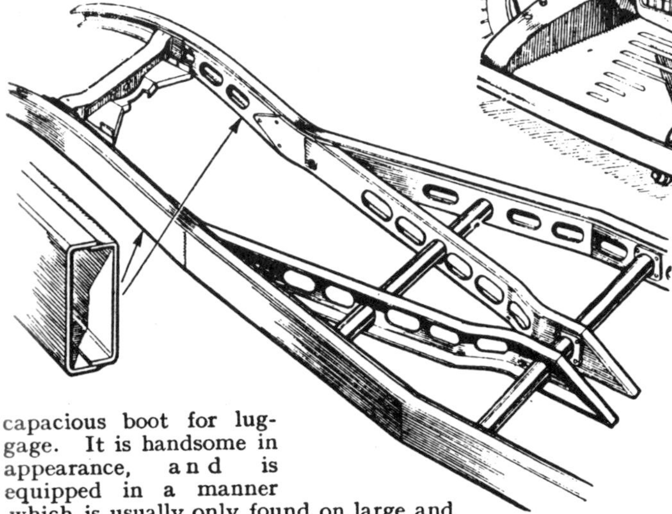

(Above) The twin Pass lights are omitted in this view in order to show the distinctive radiator and the apron.

(Left) The main frame members are of box section, and tubular cross members give additional rigidity.

imposing car—imposing in appearance and specification—costs but £375, and there is no doubt that it represents extraordinary value for money.

In design and construction well-tried features are adhered to. The frame is of the double-dropped type, with main members of box section and three tubular cross-members giving additional rigidity. Furthermore, two channel section stiffening members run from well forward to the second cross tube amidships. Front and rear axles are of conventional design, and the suspension is by long flat half-elliptic springs controlled by Luvax hydraulic shock absorbers. Dunlop Magnum wire wheels carry 5.50in. tyres on 18in. rims, knock-on-type wheels not being fitted as the car is not intended for competitions or racing.

In this frame the power unit is suspended on four rubber mountings. The engine is a six-cylinder of 65.5 × 102 mm. (2,062 c.c.), R.A.C. rating 15.96 h.p., and annual tax £12, with a sturdy crankshaft carried in four large main bearings in a rigid cylinder-block-cum-crank-case casting. Light alloy pistons and steel connecting rods are used, the main and big-end bearings being of white metal.

The detachable head carries overhead valves operated by push rods and

The M.G. two-litre in part section. The s of 65.5 × 102 mm. (2,062 c.c.), cork-faced action for third and top, spiral bevel driv hydraulic four-wheel jacks. Th

rockers from the high-lift camshaft in the crank case. On the off side are twin three-branch exhaust manifolds leading to twin silencers, which are carried by rubber-suspended supports to avoid any exhaust drumming in the body. The

Possessing good lines and proportions the new M.G. is distinctly imposing and is very completely equipped.

manifolds provide hot spots for the induction system, which is fed by two downdraught S.U. carburetters supplied by twin S.U. fuel pumps from the large rear tank.

Lubrication is forced, and all oil passes through a Tecalemit filter. The large aluminium alloy sump is ribbed for cooling, and the oil filler is accessibly placed on the valve cover. Cooling is by pump and fan, the system being controlled by a thermostat, and the radiator is of the well-known and distinctive M.G. design with vertical slats forming a stoneguard.

The electrical equipment includes automatic voltage control of the dynamo, and ignition is by coil, with automatic advance, 14 mm. sparking plugs being used. Twin batteries are

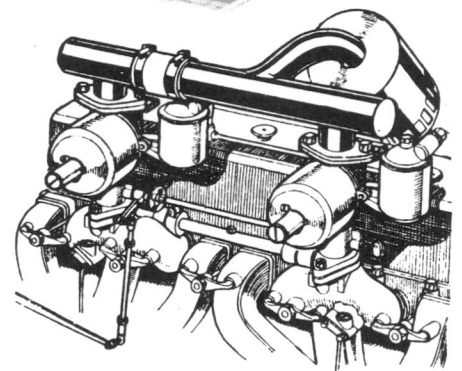

The induction and exhaust system. Twin S.U. carburetters of downdraught type take their air through a large cleaner and silencer.

tion with the spiral bevel-driven three-quarter floating rear axle, are 17.82, 10.15, 6.59 and 4.45 to 1. The propeller-shaft has Hardy Spicer needle roller-type universal joints, which require no attention.

Lockheed hydraulic brakes with 12in. diameter drums are operated by the pedal, while the racing-type brake lever, which lies horizontally along the tunnel between the front seats, operates the rear shoes through cables, and has a very accessible butterfly nut adjustment. Steering is by Bishop cam and lever gear, giving 2¼ turns of the spring-spoked wheel from lock to lock, the turning circle being approximately 40ft.

Chassis lubrication is by grouped nipples on each side of the dash. Large tools are carried in spring clips on the dash, and small tools in a box on the off side beneath the bonnet.

For Four Large Occupants

As regards the body, the occupants sit well within the wheelbase but have ample leg room, while the luggage boot is of unusually large capacity. The front bucket seats are adjustable, and have air bags in the spring cases of the squabs. The rear seat has a wide folding centre arm-rest, and side-rests in which are mounted ash trays. The whole scheme of the seating has been arranged to give ample room and every comfort to four large occupants, with room for their luggage in the boot.

The doors are hinged on the centre pillars, and have winding windows and "no-draught" ventilating windows also. Useful pockets are formed in the leather trimming of the doors, also in the backs of the front seats. Ash trays are also fitted in the front doors. The doors are of good width and give easy access to all seats.

The interior woodwork is of burr walnut, and cupboards are formed at each end of the facia board, in the centre of which the instruments are most attractively grouped. There are from left to right a combined oil pressure gauge and ammeter, a 100 m.p.h. speedometer, a combined rev counter and clock, a combined radiator thermometer and oil-petrol gauge, with switches and controls neatly arranged in a row beneath the instruments. The dials have dull gold

...udes a six-cylinder overhead valve engine ...in oil, four-speed gear box with synchromesh ...lf-elliptic springs, Lockheed brakes, and ...0ft. 3in., and track 4ft. 5in.

carried at each side of the propeller-shaft beneath the rear seat.

From the engine power is transmitted by a cork-faced clutch running in oil to a four-speed gear box with double helical gears and synchromesh action for top and third. The gear ratios, in conjunc-

M.G. Announce a Two-litre

figures and mounts, and at night are illuminated from behind, a refinement being a rheostat to give a graduated light.

The single-pane screen opens to a wide angle, and has twin wiper blades which lie horizontally out of sight, the motor being in front of the driver but below his line of vision. A Weathershields sliding roof is fitted, as are two visors which when not in use lie beneath the cantrails. Two large rear lights give

Side and centre arm-rests are provided. Note the no-draught ventilation panels.

Easy access is given to the seats and the steering wheel is well raked.

The capacious boot gives ample luggage accommodation.

good visibility for reversing, and are fitted with a blind under the driver's control. Trafficators are mounted in the centre pillars, the switch being in the steering wheel boss, also the loud and soft horn switch. A push-switch on the tunnel changes over from head to Pass lights, and vice versa.

There is much that one could say of the style and finish of the coachwork, but the accompanying illustrations show the graceful modern lines and good proportions. The sweeping wings are well valanced and add to the general appearance, as does the extended bonnet with four ventilator panels in each side. The spare wheel is mounted on the lid of the boot beneath a metal cover.

Altogether the new M.G. Two-litre is bound to attract considerable attention by reason of its striking appearance, its very complete equipment, and its most moderate price.

The neat instrument panel with dull gold dials is set in a burr walnut facia board.

INTO BATTLE

LANDS ENDS TRIAL 1936: Vast crowds turned out for these events pre-war; D. H. Fry's Magnette, climbing a dry and dusty Darracott.

Published *The Autocar*, 17 January 1936

The Autocar Road Tests

The Midget taking a mud section, part of the old Pilgrim's Way, near Wrotham, Kent.

No. 991 (*Post-War Series*)
M.G. MIDGET PB TWO-SEATER

A Fascinating Small Sports Car : The Latest Model Shows Marked Improvements in Several Important Points

SOMETIMES the truest expression of opinion upon a car which one has tested in the usual way is to say it is a machine one would like to own oneself. Any such statement is naturally dependent upon the views of the individual expressing it, but, since the M.G. Midget is to be considered as a sports car, appealing to the more enthusiastic type of driver, it is at all events fair comment from someone who tries all manner of cars.

The PB Midget now tested is the model that was introduced just before the last Olympia Show, differing from the earlier P type in having a slightly bigger engine capacity, of 939 c.c. against 847 c.c.—a size retained for what is known now as the PA type. Besides the larger engine there are other points of difference in the PB Midget which contribute towards making it an appreciably improved car.

It would be difficult for anyone free from prejudice and at all capable of being enthused by the performance of a small sports car not to be quickly attracted to this M.G. It does so much for so little. It is almost as fast as can be used reasonably; certainly on either a long or a short journey it covers the ground just about as quickly as any type of car can, and in some circumstances more rapidly than is possible to a bigger, faster but less handy vehicle. Its acceleration is good, and it runs happily at 50, 55 and even 60 m.p.h., for the engine is smooth and will go up to a limit of as much as 5,500 r.p.m. on the indirect gears.

The acceleration shows a distinct gain as a result of the increased engine size—on paper as well as on the road. Not only is the pick-up better from the lower speeds on top and third gears, but in the middle range too, and, if recollections serve, there is a decidedly superior feeling of power in reserve.

Those are points of far more importance than the actual maximum speed. In regard to speed figures, the state of Brooklands at present, undergoing repair as it is, prevented the proper maximum being developed in the available distance. The best that could be managed as a timed speed over a quarter-mile with the windscreen lowered and two up was fractionally below 71 m.p.h.—very definitely that is not the car's limit of speed.

This particular machine was fitted with a speedometer which showed no measurable error at 40, 50, 60 and even 70, and which was slightly *slow* at 30. It is therefore possible to say from the indications the car gave on Brooklands and its subsequent behaviour on the road that the maximum would lie around 75 or 76 m.p.h., given space in which to attain it. That is remarkable for a 9 h.p.-rated car which is flexible, tractable, and thoroughly pleasant for by-way pottering, for instance, and for the slower kind of motoring which often appeals.

Reference has already been made to the high speeds the Midget is capable of keeping up; indeed, about 50 m.p.h seems a natural speed on open roads. Even without ever driving it faster than that there is a charm about the car it is difficult to express, but which no doubt partly arises from the undeniable efficiency of the small overhead camshaft four-cylinder engine.

DATA FOR THE DRIVER

M.G. MIDGET PB TWO-SEATER

PRICE, with two-seater body, £222. Tax, £6 15s.
RATING : 8.9 h.p., four cylinders, o.h.v., 60 × 83 mm., 939 c.c.
WEIGHT, without passengers, 15 cwt. 2 qr. 16 lb.
TYRE SIZE : 4.00 × 19in. on knock-off wire wheels.
LIGHTING SET : 12-volt ; 9 amps at 30 m.p.h.
TANK CAPACITY : 12 gallons ; fuel consumption, 35 m.p.g. (approx.).
TURNING CIRCLE : (L. and R.) 34ft. **GROUND CLEARANCE** : 6 in.

ACCELERATION

Overall gear ratios.	From steady m.p.h. of 10 to 30	20 to 40	30 to 50
5.375 to 1	$15\frac{1}{5}$ sec.	$16\frac{3}{5}$ sec.	$18\frac{2}{5}$ sec.
7.31 to 1	$10\frac{3}{5}$ sec.	11 sec.	$11\frac{1}{5}$ sec.
11.50 to 1	$6\frac{3}{5}$ sec.	—	—
19.24 to 1	—	—	—

From rest to 50 m.p.h. through gears, $16\frac{2}{5}$ sec.

From rest to 60 m.p.h. through gears, $27\frac{3}{5}$ sec.

25 yards of 1 in 5 gradient from rest, $5\frac{2}{5}$ sec.

SPEED

	m.p.h.
Mean maximum timed speed over $\frac{1}{4}$ mile	—
Best timed speed over $\frac{1}{4}$ mile...	—
Speeds attainable on indirect gears—	
1st	22
2nd	37
3rd	55-60
Speed from rest up 1 in 5 Test Hill (on 1st gear)	18.47

Performance figures of acceleration and maximum speed are the means of several runs in opposite directions.

(*Latest model described in "The Autocar" of August 30th, 1935.*)

This unit has been developed to a fine pitch of performance and generally pleasing behaviour. Not only does it give a remarkable power output for its size, but it has been kept quiet mechanically and smooth for an engine of this description.

A good compromise has now been reached in the matter of the exhaust note; just sufficient remains to indicate that this is a sports and not a perfectly normal touring car, and the peak of the note is reached at about 2,500 r.p.m. No sign of pinking was evident from the engine at any time.

The PB Midget does well in running about slowly in speed-limit areas; indeed, its slow-running capabilities on top gear are extremely good in relation to the performance. Also, it shows a good ability to climb comparatively slowly on top gear on those occasions when it is not desired to rush a gradient or to rev on the gears.

An excellent point is the provision of an amber-tinted warning lamp on the instrument board, which lights up at about 20 m.p.h. and then automatically switches out at 30 to attract the driver's attention. Especially at night this is a prominent warning, and removes any perhaps captious criticism there might be that the "30" range of the centrally mounted speedometer is apt to be obstructed from view by the steering wheel. The separate rev counter now fitted is, however, immediately in front of the driver, and thoroughly visible. Whilst on this same subject of driving in built-up areas, it may be mentioned that, even after adjustment, the view given in the external driving mirror is not all it might be.

It is the handling of the car which gives it much of its appeal. The M.G. is low-built, of course, and it feels in "one piece"; the controls are exact, and very soon the driver is at one with the car. The driving position is right, vision is excellent, both wings being seen from the driving seat, and the big-diameter spring-spoked steering wheel comes in just the right place.

Though most satisfactorily light even when manoeuvring, the steering feels firm as well in a way which is remarkably good for fast work. It is by no means unduly low-geared steering, either, for approximately one and a half turns take the front wheels from full lock on one side to full lock on the other side. There is a delightful sense of having absolute control over the car, and, within reason, the road surface, whether wet or dry, makes practically no difference to the driver's handling of it. It rides so firmly, so safely, takes bends to the proverbial inch, and is able to respond completely to the judgment of an experienced driver.

The brakes do all they should do, too, giving an excellent, regularly achieved emergency test pull-up in less

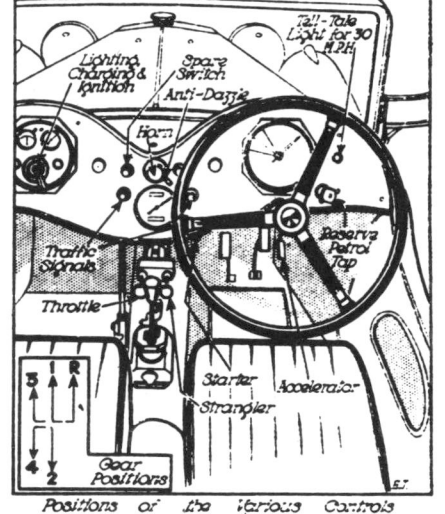
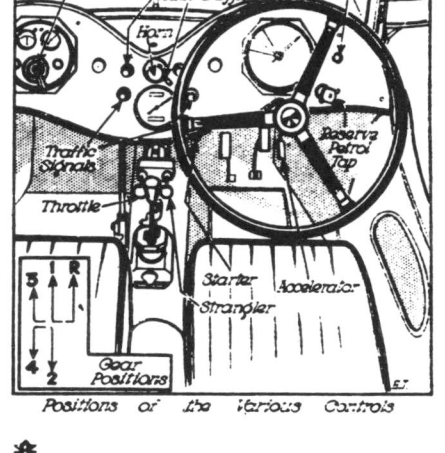
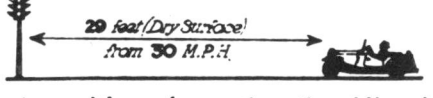

Positions of the Various Controls

29 feet (Dry Surface) from 30 M.P.H.

than 30ft. from 30 m.p.h., yet with little actual feeling of brakes having been applied, and without the least pull to either side. The fly-off racing-type hand lever is excellent for holding the car firmly on the steepest gradient.

One of the improvements concerns the gear change. A lighter clutch driving plate is now used, and, in conjunction with appreciably higher first and second gear ratios, the result is a gear change which can be handled really quickly on the upward movements with no more than mild noise from the teeth, or dead silently with a brief, single-clutch pause. Top and third gear ratios remain as before. This is indeed a gear change that handles beautifully as a whole.

The springing is firm to give the stability that has been mentioned, but not really harsh at any time on surfaces which are at all reasonable. There is at times fairly hard movement, this being principally noticeable in towns, but for a car of this description the riding is comfortable and at its best over the middle range of speed.

The hood, which disappears into the body, is raised or lowered and secured really easily. It is not a very natural position for the driver to have his right arm entirely inside the body. There is fair room for small luggage.

The engine has an extremely good oil filler in the top of the valve gear cover; starting is immediate. Grouped "long-range" lubricators serve chassis bearings which otherwise would be awkward to reach.

A fascinating, satisfying little car.

The trim appearance of the Midget is not lost when the hood is raised.

The Autocar Road Tests

THOUGH there are many changes noticeable in the latest Series T M.G. Midget by anyone who has been well acquainted with its extremely popular forerunners, in character the car remains of the same type. That is, it gives an unusually good performance for its engine size, handles in a distinctly better manner than the ordinary touring vehicle, and possesses those touches in the *tout ensemble* that endear it to the owner with sporting tendencies. In fact, as regards the last-mentioned point, the new car achieves a more "solid" and impressive appearance, the wheelbase being longer and the track slightly wider, with a greater length of bonnet, and the further important practical advantage of a wider and more roomy two-seater body. It will be remembered that the design of the latest car embodies a four-cylinder engine, with push-rod-operated overhead valves, of appreciably larger capacity than the previous model of the Midget possessed.

The M.G. has as background a remarkable hedge, some twenty-five feet high, near Chichester.

On the road the "feel" of the car has undergone a change; the new Midget is softer, quieter, and more flexible at low speeds from the ordinary touring car angle. No car, even a sports machine, is driven fast all the time, and to be able to potter really satisfactorily is a quality worth having. That the sheer maximum possible is extremely creditable with the new engine is shown by the figures in the table, and it is certain, too, that the acceleration has been improved for ordinary purposes, in overtaking and in getting away from low speeds. It was odd to be without the familiar exhaust burble, for there was no real sound from the tail pipe. Ideas in this respect

have considerably altered latterly, but it is understood that slightly more of an "M.G. note" is to be restored; indeed, the same car was tried a second time with this change effected.

It is in itself a tribute to the success and popularity attained by the Midget that in driving this new model one is inclined to be more analytical than usual; in other words, to take more than average interest in the car. Really, of course, it has to be judged as a new car.

Probably the biggest advantage of the larger engine is that it needs to be less highly tuned to give a good all-round performance, is therefore not so sensitive to both fuel and ignition, and gives about as much performance as can be used, with reduced stress upon the mechanism. A good power output is obtained — superior over a normal r.p.m. range even to that of the N-type Magnette—and higher gear ratios are used, which have a notable effect as regards ease of performance, for engine revs are kept lower. In consequence of these points it should be a better machine for the ordinary owner to maintain.

It is still a car which seems to revel in being held at a speed between 50 and 60 m.p.h., and which, given any chance, will run easily up to a good deal more when wanted. The new engine will rev freely on the indirect gears, too, and as a result, coupled with the handy size of

No. 1,058.—10 h.p. M.G. MIDGET SERIES T TWO-SEATER

New Bigger Model, Although Considerably Altered, Remains Essentially of the Same Likeable Style

the car, its cornering capabilities, and hydraulically operated brakes that are fully capable of dealing with the performance, a very good average can be made, even over roads that give little assistance. This car does more than may be suspected until actual measurement of the performance comes to be made.

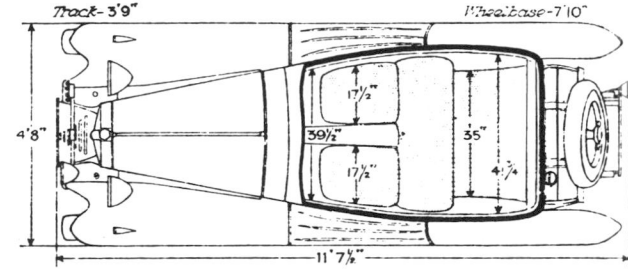

Track–5'9"   *Wheelbase–7'10"*

Seating dimensions are measured with cushions and squabs uncompressed.

General handling is good, for though the springing is a shade softer, and hydraulic shock absorbers are now fitted all round instead of at the back only, the Midget can be put into a fast curve confidently and be swung round an acute turn with a most satisfactory feeling of stability. The steering is firm, more so than formerly, without becoming actually heavy for manoeuvring, and has definite

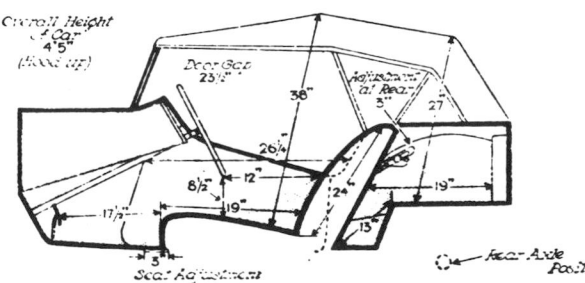

Overall Height of Car 4'5" (Hood up)

Door Gap 23½"

Seat Adjustment   *Rear Axle Position*

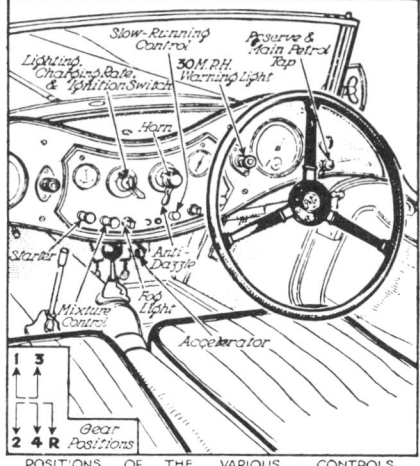

POSITIONS OF THE VARIOUS CONTROLS

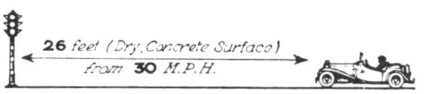

26 feet (Dry, Concrete Surface) from 30 M.P.H.

"The Autocar" Road Tests

caster return action; the latest steering gear ratio is higher, rather less than 1½ turns being needed from lock to lock. The suspension avoids shock to the occupants except in really severe conditions, though on a wavy surface there is sometimes a good deal of motion apparent. The brakes give a most potent power for an emergency pull-up, which can be regularly repeated, and the braking tests were made immediately after 300 miles of road work.

Synchromesh is employed for the gear changes to top, third, and second; there is a new well-placed rigid remote-control lever. Some people may disagree with the use of synchromesh on the Midget, there again indirectly paying tribute to the esteem in which the car has been held by enthusiasts, but there is no getting away from the fact that for general purposes this box handles easily, and at the same time satisfactorily to anyone who takes a pleasure in using the gears of a sports car. Changing up quickly is greatly facilitated, and rapid, quiet, downward changes can be made by speeding up the engine exactly as would be done were there no synchromesh. At lower speeds the synchromesh engages very

vision, being able to see both wings, whilst a decided improvement is that there is more room for the left foot when off the clutch pedal. The clutch action is light and at the same time smooth in taking up the drive. Quite apart from comparing actual measurements, there is the definite impression of more room inside the body, particularly as regards elbow clearance, and the driver can bring his right arm entirely inside the car.

To warn the driver a green-tinted lamp is illuminated as long as the car's speed remains below 30 m.p.h. When this flashes out, he knows that he has gone past the legal limit. This is an excellent idea, but for night work this lamp is a little overpowering. It is understood that the necessary modification has already been incorporated. The instruments are indirectly illuminated with a soft green effect at night. There is also a direct lamp, useful for map reading and so forth. The speedometer proved to be 1.6 m.p.h. fast at 30, 4.8 at 50, and showed a highest reading of 90-91 when the car was being timed in the favourable direction with the windscreen lowered. Tests were made also with the windscreen raised normally, and the car covered a timed quarter-mile thus at 73.77 m.p.h.

The latest hood goes up and down easily and secures quickly to the windscreen frame, whilst the all-weather protection is good, there being two screens at each side which render the interior light with the hood up and at the same time snug. Also, the luggage space behind the seats has been considerably increased. Although there is a straight-across, one-piece back-rest, easily adjustable for angle, separate adjustable seat cushions are fitted. They are very comfortable seats.

There are door pockets, ventilators in the scuttle sides, a twin-blade electric screenwiper, dip and switch head lamps, a fog lamp out in front with a separate switch, and, an extremely good feature, a control on the instrument board to bring a reserve supply of fuel into use, three gallons being trapped.

A "different" Midget, admittedly, but one with some distinctly practical features embodied, and giving plenty of performance in an interesting way.

DATA FOR THE DRIVER.

10 h.p. M.G. MIDGET SERIES T TWO-SEATER.

PRICE, with open two-seater body, £222. Tax, £7 10s.
RATING : 10 h.p., four cylinders, o.h.v., 63.5 · 102 mm., 1,292 c.c.
WEIGHT, without passengers, 17 cwt. 1 qr. 3 lb.
LB. (WEIGHT) PER C.C. : 1.50.
TYRE SIZE : 4.50 × 19in. on knock-off wire wheels.
LIGHTING SET : 12-volt ; 7 amps at 30 m.p.h. ; three-rate charging.
TANK CAPACITY : 15 gallons ; fuel consumption, 27-29 m.p.g. (approx.)
TURNING CIRCLE (L. and R.) : 37ft.   GROUND CLEARANCE : 6in.

ACCELERATION			SPEED	
Overall gear ratios	From steady m.p.h. of			m.p.h.
	10 to 30	20 to 40 30 to 50	Mean maximum timed speed over ¼ mile	77.59
4.88 to 1	13.2 sec.	15.2 sec. 17.2 sec.		
6.46 to 1	9.9 sec.	10.6 sec. 11.5 sec.	Best timed speed over ¼ mile...	79.65
9.85 to 1	6.4 sec.	—		
16.50 to 1	—	—	Speeds attainable on indirect gears : —	
From rest to 30 m.p.h. through gears, 6.1 sec.			1st	17-23
From rest to 50 m.p.h. through gears, 15.4 sec.			2nd	29-39
From rest to 60 m.p.h. through gears, 23.1 sec.			3rd	50-61
25 yards of 1 in 5 gradient from rest, 5.0 sec.			Speed from rest up 1 in 5 Test Hill (on 1st and 2nd gears)	18.91

Performance figures for acceleration and maximum speed are the means of several runs in opposite directions.

(Latest model described in "The Autocar" of June 19th, 1936)

well unassisted, and a sure drop can be made to third or second for extra acceleration or a steep gradient. The gears, more particularly second, are on the noisy side, judged by this particular car. The hand-brake lever is of the familiar fly-off type, operating in the rear drums, and powerful to hold the car on a hill.

The driving position has not been in the least spoilt, again making mental comparison, as seems inevitable with this car; the spring-spoked wheel is set well down in a position that gives the driver power over it, and he has very good

Front or rear, the new Series T Midget is typically an M.G. in lines. The body is wider, and the rear petrol tank is now of even greater capacity than before.

New Cars Described —

Four Types of M.G.s

Prices and Models to Remain Unchanged : A New Larger 2.6-litre Model to Come : New Midget Drop-head Coupé Described

SOME time ago the M.G. Car Company dropped the announcement of a "programme" each year, and, instead, adopted the plan of introducing new series, or editions, of models whenever improvements had been found desirable. Thus the following notes are not a programme announcement, but indications of some new things to come, and a review of current affairs.

Next week's issue of *The Autocar* will contain a description of an entirely new M.G. car of larger size, with body styles similar to the 2-litre, and with a 2.6-litre engine. Meanwhile, a new item to be described is a drop-head coupé on the Series T Midget chassis. Of the current cars the prices and specifications remain unchanged, and the range is as follows :—

RANGE AND PRICES OF M.G. CARS.

Series T.	
Midget two-seater	£222
Midget coupé	Price not fixed
Series V.	
1½-litre chassis	£215
1½-litre four-seater	£280
1½-litre four-door saloon	£325
1½-litre foursome coupé	£351

With Jackall equipment the above prices for the 1½-litre are raised by £5

Series S.	
2-litre chassis	£260
2-litre four-seater	£399
2-litre four-door saloon	£389
2-litre foursome coupé	£415

These prices include Jackall equipment.

The folding-head foursome coupé coachwork is built on the Tickford principles by Salmons and Sons, Ltd., of Newport Pagnell, and the open four-seater tourer body of the 2-litre by Charlesworth of Coventry.

Despite the decrease in general registration figures, 1938 has beaten the M.G. record for previous output.

Deliveries of the new Midget coupé are scheduled to commence in September. This is a most attractive little two-seater and a genuine drop-head coupé without makeshifts or compromises. It can be used as a completely closed car, when the well-padded head with its toggle irons presents a smart appearance, and the solid construction should make it draught-proof, without wind noise, and free from rattles. The car has a windscreen which can be opened right up into the horizontal position (a valuable asset if one is driving through a thick fog) and locked into place by outriggers. Also the windows are of full size and operated by winding handles.

Besides the fully closed position there are two alternatives. In a few seconds the taut peak of the head can be undone, and rolled neatly back to form a coupé de ville. Finally, the cant rails may be undone at the front end, folded back laterally, the toggle irons "broken" and the head folded flat down to open the body completely to the sunshine and fresh air.

To accommodate drivers of different stature, besides the other adjustments, a neat form of telescopic mounting is provided for the spring-spoked steering-wheel.

The direction indicators are concealed in the sides of the scuttle, and are operated by a switch with a red warning light in its centre. Another feature is that the fuel tank, placed at the back, contains no less than 13½ gal.

Various small changes have gradually

A new model is the coupé body on the Series T M.G. Midget.

taken place in other M.G. models since the cars were last described. For example, there is now an extremely wide choice of colour schemes, inside and out, for all models. No fewer than eight cellulose exterior finishes are available, and seven interior leather colours. The exterior colours are blue, red, green, duo green, maroon, black, grey, and metallic grey, whilst the choice of leather colours is biscuit, green, brown, maroon, grey, red and blue.

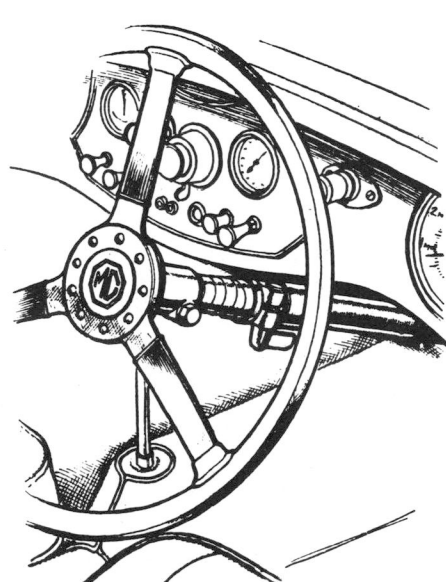

Quick control lever for the adjustable steering wheel.

Any combination of the above colours may be selected for any model except the new Midget coupé, without extra cost, and, furthermore, the body, if desired, can be finished in one of these colours and the wings and fairings in another.

Actually, the metallic grey finish is applied to the body only, the wings being painted to match, but without the metallic lustre. The reason for this is that if "the other fellow" should damage the wings in a cramped parking place it is more easy to repaint them to match. On the Midget coupé the complete range of exterior colours is available, but the leathers are limited to the standard shades of biscuit, maroon, brown and grey.

2-litre Refinements

Of recent times considerable improvements have been effected in the interior finishes of the 2-litre saloon, chiefly in regard to the woodwork. Also the "engine room" has come in for some extra refinement, and, amongst other things, the metal scuttle structure is now painted grey instead of black. Another feature of the 2-litre is that trap-doors in the bonnet sides will be abandoned in favour of louvres.

In conclusion, the specifications of the three chassis may be summarised. The Midget has a twin-carburettor, four-cylinder engine rated at 10 h.p. (tax £7 10s.) of 63.5 × 102 mm. bore and stroke (1,292 c.c.). The overhead valves are operated by push-rods, and the crankshaft is carried in three bearings.

The folding-head foursome coupé on the 2-litre is a real dual-purpose body.

Four Types of M.G.s

a remote gear lever carried on the chassis, and a single-plate clutch. The unit is mounted flexibly on rubber. Transmission is by open propeller-shaft to a spiral-bevel gear. Lockheed hydraulic brakes are fitted. The springs are half-elliptic back and front. Wheelbase is 9ft. and track 4ft. 2in. Centre-lock wire wheels are used and shod with 5.00 × 19in. tyres.

The saloon is of the four-door, four-light style with a luggage boot at the back, in the lid of which the tools are recessed in a tray. This body is notable for large and comfortable seats, neat trimming, large-dial instruments, and a system of no-draught ventilation.

In unit with the engine are a single-plate clutch and four-speed gear box, with synchromesh on third and top, and a remote gear-lever control. The unit is flexibly mounted on rubber. Transmission is by an open tubular propeller-shaft to a spiral-bevel gear in a pressed-steel rear axle casing.

Of box-section, with a forward diagonal bracing and tubular cross-members, the frame is underslung at the rear. Half-elliptic springs are used back and front, and are damped with hydraulic shock absorbers. The wheelbase is 7ft. 10in., track 3ft. 9in., and the tyre size 4.50 × 19in. Lockheed hydraulic brakes are fitted.

The Midget is not sold as a chassis, and, in addition to the new coupé, the standard coachwork is a smart open two-seater with all-weather equipment, having space for luggage in the back behind the seats.

The 1½-litre Model

Next in size, and somewhat different in type, though basically similar in mechanical principle, the 1½-litre M.G. is a sporting style of car rather than a sports car. In short, it is intended to suit those who choose a car for the sake of motoring and not as a humdrum means of transport. So the 1½-litre is typically British and typically specialist, with its long, low bonnet and compact, shapely bodywork. It has been designed for driving fast and in safety, with a weight of experience behind it to ensure that it is up to its specified work. Rated

Most popular of the 2-litre range is the smart four-door, four-light saloon at £389

at 12 h.p. (tax £9), the engine has four cylinders, 69.5 × 102 mm. (1,548 c.c.), with push-rod-operated overhead valves, twin S.U. carburettors, high-pressure lubrication with a "top feed" oil float, full filtration, and an air-cooled sump. It is in unit with a four-speed gear box, having synchromesh on third and top,

The larger M.G. cars, by the way, have a special bulkhead interposed between the engine and the scuttle to prevent undue heat from reaching the interior of the bodywork.

Much that has been said of the 1½-litre applies equally to the 2-litre model, which is a larger car on the same lines, but provided with a more powerful six-cylinder engine. This is rated at 17.97 h.p. (tax £13 10s.) and has six cylinders of 69.5 × 102 mm. (2,322 c.c.). The wheelbase is 10ft. 3in., track 4ft. 5in., and the centre-lock wire wheels carry 5.50 × 18in. Dunlop Fort tyres. The frame is of deep box-section side-members, plentifully cross-braced with stout tubes, whilst the rigidity of the forward end is increased by extra diagonal runners, also of box-section, which form a cradle for the flexibly mounted engine unit. The M.G. 2-litre is a striking and attractive car in its various styles of coachwork.

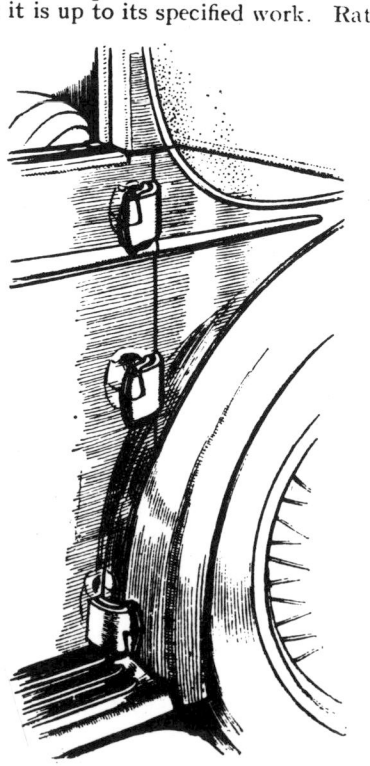

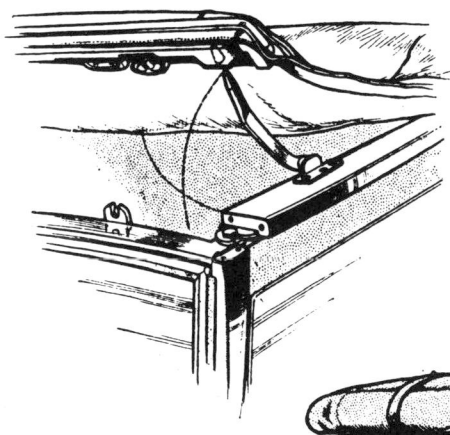

(Above) Fabric tensioning device on the Midget coupé.

(Left) The door of the little coupé is supported by three substantial hinges.

(Right) The rear of the Midget coupé is given up to providing good luggage space for driver and passenger.

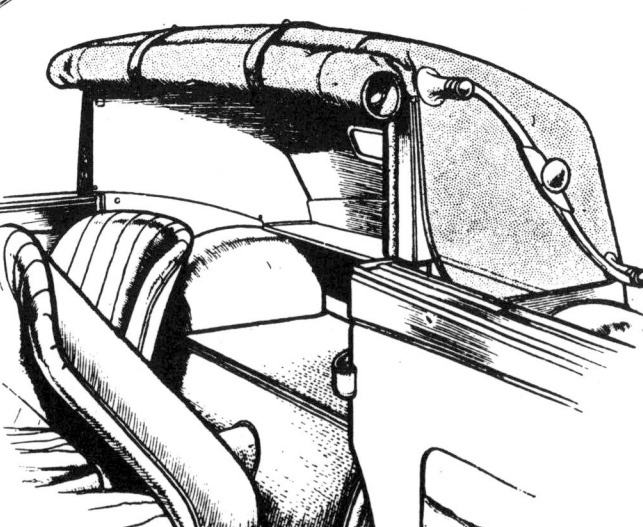

DESSAU DIARY

A Week in the Life of a 200 m.p.h. Motorist

By JOHN DUGDALE

The writer went with Major A. G. T. Gardner to Germany, where the latter broke records with his M.G. last week

IT was astonishing enough last November when Major "Goldie" Gardner averaged 186 m.p.h. with the 1,100 c.c. M.G. So outstanding was his achievement that some thought it must be a fluke or a freak of record-breaking, and when in later statements "Goldie" said he was confident that the car was actually capable of 200 m.p.h., there were those who thought him frankly over-confident.

But now everyone is united in admiration for both man and machine, for—as recorded briefly last week—the tiny 1,100 c.c. M.G., on Wednesday, May 31st, 1939, duly passed the 200 m.p.h. mark just as "Goldie" had said it would. Furthermore, the engine was dismantled, rebored, and reassembled on the day following the record so that it was possible to take three more records last Friday, all at over 200 m.p.h. in the 1½-litre class. The six-cylinder engine which had been bored out from 1,086 c.c. to 1,106 c.c. came technically into the next International Class (F) for cars with engines between 1,100 and 1,500 c.c.

Major Gardner and the M.G. car thus have the signal honour of being the first to exceed 200 m.p.h. in both the 1,100 and in the 1,500 c.c. class.

These records were established on that last word in motor courses, the new double-width *autobahn* at Dessau, and when Major Gardner invited me to accompany him on the trip to Germany I was doubly pleased. Not only did I know that I would thus be right in the thick of things, on what might almost be termed an historic occasion, but, also, I would have an opportunity of seeing the Dessau straight which has been specially designed by the Germans for high speeds. Finally, in view of current strained international feeling I was interested to note the German reaction to an outstanding sports record being established by an Englishman in the heart of the Third Reich. I am glad to say that the reception given to Major Gardner was cordial and sporting in the extreme.

A photograph which shows the generous, over 90ft. width of the Dessau *autobahn*. The mile is timed in the dip seen in the distance.

Major "Goldie" Gardner, who now joins the distinguished ranks of 200 m.p.h. motorists, pictured before an appropriate background.

We crossed the Belgian-German frontiers at Aachen, speeding past the sinister camouflaged fortresses of the Belgian "Maginot" and of the German "Siegfried" line, and stopping the night in Braunschweig, called Brunswick. The next day we went through to Dessau via Hanover, where the road passes the house of the ancestors of our own Royal family. The journey proved fast and comfortable, skimming over the long flat, sunlit straights in an ultra-smooth-running twelve-cylinder Lagonda. Although there was an *autobahn* available almost all the way, we reserved that for the return journey and kept to the old roads.

When we drove into Dessau, the record-holding M.G., packed and sealed in its lorry, had already arrived, together with the four men chiefly responsible for the technical side of the attempt. They were ginger-haired R. C. "Jacko" Jackson and "Sid" Enever, both with long experience of racing with the M.G. Company; Leslie Kesterton, of the experimental department of S.U.'s, a man who has been playing with machines all his life and in the war was responsible for bringing down one of Richtofen's circus; and Chris. Shorrock, the designer of the big Centric Supercharger fitted to the car.

Major Gardner settled down in the hall of the Dessau Hotel, which was picturesquely called The Golden Bottle,

The English party and friends pose with the car after the successful run. From left to right they are : A. Bicknell, L. Kesterton, of S.U. Carburettors, Count Lurani, Major Gardner, R. "Jacko" Jackson and S. Enever, of M.G.'s, a German Dunlop representative, Commendatore Ottolini, John Dugdale, of "The Autocar," C. Shorrock and George Tuck, of M.G.'s.

and forthwith called a conference on the plan of action.

The new *autobahn* was not available until the Wednesday, which left one day for preparation, but it was decided then and there not to unpack the car at all until the morning of the record. That showed the thorough preparation the M.G. had received, and the general air of confidence among the *équipe*.

A trip up to the record section of the *autobahn* was made in the evening, and there was much studying of maps and contours to agree on the lengths of the records to be attacked, and where "Goldie" should decelerate and brake. In high-speed record attempts the pulling-up distance available is the governing factor. It was decided to take the kilometre, mile and five kilometres, all on the same runs, but only to keep the car flat out for the flying mile, which was timed in the middle of the five-kilometre section. This would mean that the speed for the five kilometres would be lower than that of the mile, but that did not matter, as it stood at a very much lower speed, anyway. In the 1,100 c.c. class Major Gardner already held all the records he was attacking at speeds between 143 and 186 m.p.h.

Preparations

On the next day, Tuesday, the mechanics fitted the almost smooth-treaded track tyres and balanced the racing wheels, for Dunlops were insisting on changing all four wheels between each run as a precautionary measure. More visits were paid to the *autobahn* that Tuesday. The distinguishing signs were placed in position to mark the start and finish of the timed sections. A painting machine touched up the triple black line down the centre of the road. Another huge machine swept the concrete dust from the surface. Officials of the O.N.S., the German organisation in control of motor sport, began to arrive, and the atmosphere heightened for that dramatic dash in the early hours of Wednesday morning.

But "Goldie" remained absolutely calm.

I know most racing men, but I have seldom seen one so singularly unmoved as Major Gardner, to all outward appearances, at any rate. I was with him every day for a week, and so could easily mark his changes of mood if there had been any. Even at the uncomfortably early hour of 6 a.m., at which we were constrained to have breakfast on that memorable morning, he was the same as ever, speaking a little and only to the point in his deep,

gruff voice. There were few of those pre-racing signs of tense nerves which reveal themselves in some men, a complete preoccupation on the drive to come so that to talk to them before a race is so much waste of time.

The actual record breaking was conducted with the utmost despatch, though not fast enough for "Goldie."

The crew had the car on the *autobahn* by 6 a.m., and it was standing ready on the road with balanced wheels fitted and track tyres blown up to 60 lb. by the time Gardner and the rest of us arrived at 7 a.m. At that time the atmosphere was almost still and the sun was already bright. But it was another hour before Herr Dienemann, of the O.N.S., was satisfied that the road was properly policed and that the timekeepers were ready. By that time the breeze had increased to a serious extent. "Goldie" sat lounging in the lie-back seat of the record car feeling—but, as usual, not looking—impatient.

At 8 a.m. the car was allowed to be pushed off, and in ten yards that remarkable super-tuned engine broke into life, at first spluttering and coughing after its week-long silence, and then crackling clearly up to 4,000 r.p.m., the limit kept to on the soft plugs. We followed down in the 100 m.p.h. saloon de ville, but the little M.G., even on its limited engine revs, naturally left us well behind. Just before the beginning of the timed section Gardner turned round, paused to tell "Jacko" that all was well and returned to the starting point.

Everything was now ready, and the only comment that "Goldie" had so far volunteered was :—

"I say, 'Jacko,' it's going to take some pulling up! Why, I was only doing 4,000, and she ran the devil of a way."

"Well, Major, you know you're shifting some even at 4,000," was "Jacko's" reply, for 4,000 r.p.m. on the M.G.'s top gear means about 140 m.p.h.—but what is such a speed to a 200 m.p.h. man?

I watched the run from a bridge situated about a kilometre after the end of the timed section. The glare of the sun reflected up from the white concrete necessitated dark glasses even at 8 a.m. Commendatore Ottolini, who had come over with Count Lurani, a German photographer, and an English-speaking Nazi, waited with me. It was a glorious morning, and the countryside looked very fair, a fact which the Nazi (absolutely delighted at the opportunity of discussing his ideology first-hand with an Englishman) rubbed in with relish. His enthusiasm was mercifully silenced by a thrilling distant humming.

The six-cylinder M.G. sets forth on the *autobahn*. In spite of sunny weather a cross-wind made driving tricky.

"Still!" I said. "Der Herr Major Kommt."

Although the car was ten kilometres away you could hear its clean, crisp acceleration rising in a crescendo and then staying level at a high-pitched whine. The small black dot became a little larger, then one distinguished its green colour, noted that it held absolutely steadily to the centre line, and suddenly, with a great blast from the exhaust stumps, which pointed straight at us, the M.G. was under and beyond.

Marvellous!

It was not long before we heard the car coming again from the South, where "Jacko" and other mechanics had taken up a position four kilometres down the 'bahn ready to help turn the M.G. round—steering lock is limited—and to change the wheels.

Round the gradual curve came the small black dot again, and again, with that shattering blast of sound as he passed beneath, he went into the timed section beyond, flat-out. This time, however, the cross and partly adverse wind slowed him slightly and caused the car to swerve. At 200 m.p.h. one does not have much time to correct skids, however, and it is mostly a question of hanging on hard and hoping for the best.

"Goldie" hung on, kept his foot down, and 200 m.p.h. was his!

His comment afterwards, when the Nazis had finished congratulating him and demanding autographs, was:

"You know there's not much difference between 150 m.p.h. and 200 m.p.h. You notice the increase from 100 to 150 m.p.h. all right, but after that it does not grow in the same proportion."

The actual speeds of the runs were as follows, and they show the loss of some 8 m.p.h. on the return run.

1,100 c.c. Class.

1 Kilometre—		m.p.h.
Out, 10.84 sec.		206.36
Return, 11.14		200.78
Mean, 10.99		203.54
1 Mile—		
Out, 17.36 sec.		207.37*
Return, 18.07		199.22
Mean, 17.72		203.16
5 Kilometres—		
Out, 55.44 sec.		201.74
Return, 57.79		193.54
Mean, 56.62		197.54

* Fastest recorded run.

That was on the Wednesday, and that evening the Major drove the sixty miles down the *autobahn* to Berlin, where the B.B.C. reserved a land line and gave him four minutes' talk on the 9.15 news bulletin. Thursday was given over to boring-out the engine slightly so that it just came within the 1½-litre class, to the fitting of the pistons and to a general check over for some more 7,000 r.p.m. running on

the morrow. All this work, by the way, was carried out in the workshop of the local traffic police, just one example of the enthusiastic reception given to the English visit.

Major Gardner, who reckoned the wind had lost him five miles an hour on the mean speed on Wednesday, made a special request for an early start, and on Thursday we breakfasted at the almost impossible hour of 4 a.m. Even now this was not early enough for "Goldie," who would like to have been attacking records in the dawn itself, and, indeed, on Friday, the wind came up earlier than ever and conditions, as far as the wind was concerned, became almost as bad. Once again the engine ran faultlessly and this time, at the end of the mile, instead of easing from his over 7,000 r.p.m. in top to 6,000 r.p.m. or so, he kept his foot hard down in order to study the instruments. As a result of this short look he now averaged over 200 for the five kilometres and his times on the kilometre and mile made him the first man to exceed 200 m.p.h. in the 1½-litre class, thus officially beating Frank Lockhart's Miller record of 164 m.p.h., which has stood since 1927.

1,500 c.c. Class.

1 Kilometre—		m.p.h.
Out, 10.84 sec.		206.35*
Return, 11.05		202.94
Mean, 10.95		204.28
1 Mile—		
Out, 17.46 sec.		206.18
Return, 17.85		201.63
Mean, 17.66		203.95
5 Kilometres—		
Out, 55.10 sec.		202.99
Return, 56.39		198.34
Mean, 55.75		200.62

* Fastest recorded run.

There was some delay between the outward and return runs. In maintaining 200 m.p.h. for five kilometres, "Goldie" had overshot his braking mark. He therefore applied the brakes—rear only—extremely hard and they became very, very hot, as "Jacko" soon found when he came to change the wheels! The return run was made without brakes, but in spite of this the car coasted exactly into the final depot. Nice judgment indeed!

M.G. RECORD CAR EQUIPMENT.

Axles (Wolseley, E.N.V., Laystall and M.G.); ball and roller bearings (Ransome and Marles); bearings material (Glacier metal); body frame (M.G.); body panels (E. G. Brown); brake linings (Duron); carburettors (S.U.); cellulose, alcohol-resisting polychromatic (Nobel Chemical Finishes); chassis frame (M.G.); clutch (Borg and Beck); clutch lining (Duron); electrical equipment (Lucas); camshaft (R. R. Jackson); engine (M.G.); fairing fasteners (Thos. P. Headland); fuel (Shell); fuel pipes (Superflexit).

Gears (E.N.V.); instruments (S. Smith); oil and Adcoids (Duckham); oil seals (Perfect Oil Seals); Aerolite pistons (Light Production); propeller-shaft (Hardy Spicer); radiator and tanks (Morris); shock absorbers (Andre); sparking plugs (Bosch); steering (Cam Gears); steering wheel (Bluemel); supercharger (Centric); suspension springs (R. Berry); tyres (Dunlop); valves—exhaust (British Aero Components), inlet (Hadfields); wheels (Dunlop); windscreen (Triplex Perspex).

For 1,500 c.c. records, Lodge plugs were used, thus making the car all-British in equipment.

The Autocar

The M.G. Programme

Improved Engine for the Midget and Other Modifications to Attractive Range

A handsome foursome coupé the 2.6-litre, priced at £475.

CONCEIVED and built around the ideal of a compact type of car entirely suitable for fast travel, M.G. cars have secured an enviable reputation for success in this country and abroad. The latest and the most amazing M.G. feat was accomplished recently by Major Gardner, who put up the mile record in the 1,100 c.c. class—or about 10 h.p. rating—to the fantastic figure of 203.5 m.p.h. It is with the knowledge and experience of such successful feats as

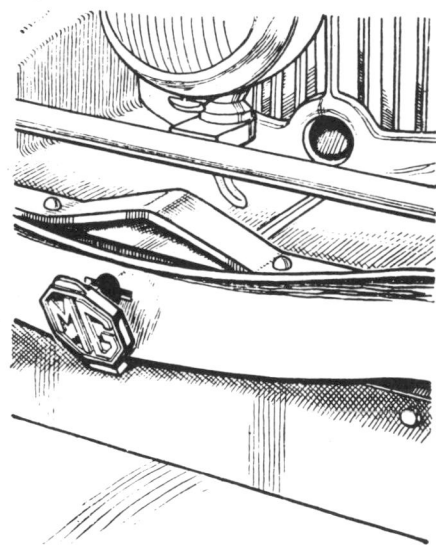

Behind the hinged bumper badge is the hole for the starting handle.

Midget has gone through a regular system of evolution which has kept it in the forefront. The present model, known as the Series T.B., is a development from the Series T, and it is interesting that the Midget, from being at first an 8 h.p. car, has stepped up in engine size until it now has a rating of 10.97 h.p. The engine of the T.B. is different from the T, having four cylinders 66.5 × 90 mm. (1,250 c.c.), whilst the T engine was four cylinders 63.5 × 102 mm. (1,292 c.c.).

From this it will be seen that the improved engine of the Series T.B. has a larger bore, a shorter stroke, and a slightly smaller capacity, and these features have in this modern design secured a considerable increase in power output, accompanied by a greater smoothness of running. This latest engine has a stout balanced and counterweighted crank,

The 1½-litre saloon is smart in appearance and performance. It costs £335.

these that the M.G. normal range of cars is produced. There are four sizes, priced as follows :—

M.G. Midget, series T.B. Open two-seater £225, drop-head coupé £270.

M.G. 1½-litre. Open four-seater £295. Four-door saloon £335. Folding-head foursome £360.

M.G. 2-litre. Four-door saloon £393. Folding-head foursome £425.

M.G. 2.6-litre. Four-door saloon £450. Folding-head foursome £475.

One of the most successful small fast cars ever made in this country, the M.G.

shaft carried in three main bearings, steel H-section connecting rods and aluminium alloy pistons of the controlled-expansion type with three rings, the lowest of the set being an oil-control ring.

Cast monobloc, the cylinders are carefully designed and water-jacketed to prevent distortion under heat, the water circulation being by pump, and having a thermostat temperature control. A fan is also fitted. In the detachable cylinder head the valves are placed overhead. They have triple springs, and are operated by rockers and push-rods from a camshaft driven by duplex chain. Lubrication is force fed and the oil is contained in an aluminium sump ribbed for cooling.

Two S.U. semi-downdraught carburettors supply the mixture through short ports coupled by a balance pipe, and the carburettors draw their air through a large cleaner and filter via a balanced-end type of air intake.

Being essentially a sports car, the Midget has many special features to render it self-supporting on prolonged journeys; for example, the fuel tank at

This is the famous T.B. Midget two-seater, costing £225.

Fast and adequately powered is the 2.6-litre saloon, costing £450.

wheels are centre-lock wire type, and the tyres Dunlop 4.50 by 19. The instruments include a large-dial speedometer, revolution indicator and clock. The wheelbase is 7ft. 10in., and the track 3ft. 9in.

Turning next to the larger cars of the M.G. range: the 1½-litre, although it has built into it the results of great experience with fast cars, is aimed more at luxury high-speed travel than at being a sports type pure and simple. The coachwork is well finished and equipped, and enough room is provided without losing the compactness and the low centre of gravity which are valuable to high performance.

the rear is of extra large size, holding 13½ gal., enough for 400 to 500 miles, according to circumstances. A two-way tap operated from the dash retains three gallons in reserve. The carburettors are fed from the tank by an S.U. fuel pump and flexible piping.

In unit with the engine are the clutch and four-speed gear box. The clutch is also of improved type—a heavy-duty Borg and Beck single dry-plate, in place of the cork insert clutch running in oil which was used on earlier models. Also the gear box has synchromesh on second, third and top. The overall ratios are: first, 17.32; second, 10; third, 6.92; and top 5.22 to 1.

grouped nipples. High-geared cam steering is fitted and a valuable addition is the provision of a telescopically adjustable steering wheel with spring spokes.

The four-wheel brakes are Lockheed

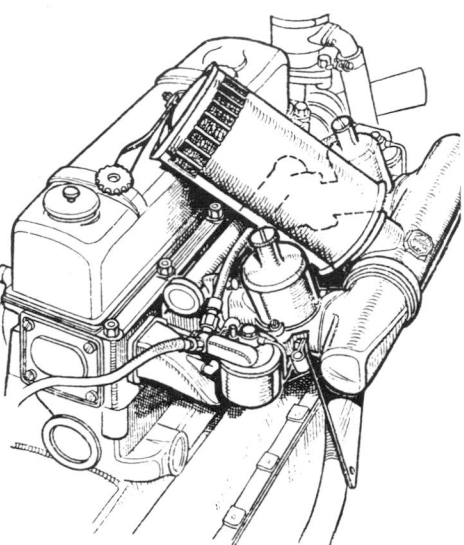

Twin carburettors are fitted to the new M.G. T.B. Midget engine.

Telescopic steering is an M.G. feature.

hydraulic, and the quick-release racing-type hand brake lever applies the rear brakes by independent cable. The

The 1½-litre has also received various improvements. The engine is fitted with a counterbalanced crankshaft, a new type of camshaft, and a dry-plate clutch. The latest Luvax piston-type hydraulic shock absorbers have been adopted, and the Jackall inbuilt jacking system is now standard on all types, as also the new Lund bulb head lamp dipping system in place of the conventional system hitherto used.

Another item is that the interior of the folding-head foursome has been designed to give added accommodation.

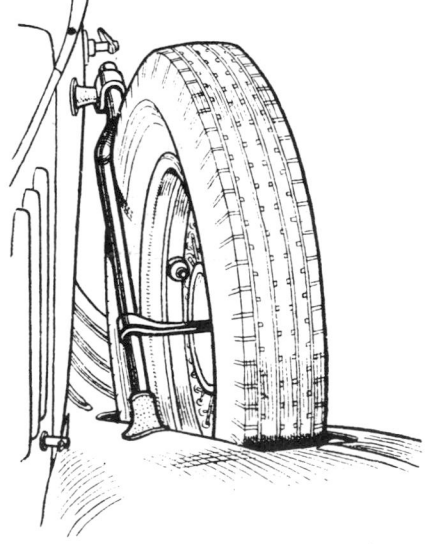

How the spare wheel is mounted on the 2.6-litre foursome coupé.

The gear change has a short lever mounted on an extension to bring it conveniently close to the driver's left hand. Transmission is by a Hardy Spicer balanced propeller-shaft to a spiral drive in a three-quarter floating rear axle.

Box-section side members cross-braced with tubes form the frame, which is underslung at the rear. Half-elliptic springs controlled by hydraulic shock absorbers are employed back and front, and, instead of shackles, sliding trunnions are employed to prevent side play. Chassis lubrication is by a system of

The 1½-litre drop-head foursome coupé, which costs £360.

Here is the M.G. 1½-litre open four-seater tourer, which costs £295.

This is a particularly attractive style of coachwork, as it offers three distinct changes, fully closed, fully open, or partly open as a coupé de ville. The compact low build of the saloon is emphasised by a very clean-cut contour, there being no mouldings on the outside of the body. The rear seating position comes within the wheelbase.

Leading features of the specification of the 1½-litre M.G. are: engine, four cylinders 69.5 × 102 mm. (1,548 c.c.), push-rod-operated overhead valves, single-plate clutch, unit four-speed gear with remote control and synchromesh, rubber unit suspension, twin semi-down-draught S.U. carburettor, 12½ gal. rear fuel tank, high-pressure engine lubrication with constant-level float and 100 per cent. filtration, pump water circulation and thermostat control. The wheelbase is 9ft. and the track 4ft. 2in., and the 5.00 by 19 tyres are mounted on centre-lock wire wheels.

Having the success of several years to its credit, the M.G. 2-litre has reached a stage in development which leaves room only for minor improvements. Recently the externals of the six-cylinder engine have been tidied up, and Luvax piston-type hydraulic shock absorbers have been standardised, also screw-type bearings have been adopted for the spring shackles. A rear bumper has been added to the equipment of all types. On the foursome the spare wheel is now recessed into the near-side front wing.

In the arrangement of the saloon coachwork the underlying principle has been to provide for comfort in the front and back seats throughout the wide range of speed of which this car is capable. To this end the centre of gravity is kept low, the seats are within the axle compass, and the suspension is carefully arranged to give complete stability. The coachwork is panelled in steel on hardwood framing, and is as light as is consistent with proper durability.

Features are: leather upholstery, inlaid walnut fillets, winding windows to all four doors, no-draught ventilating system, adjustable bucket front seats, centre folding arm rest and head cushions in the rear seat, sliding roof, and a luggage boot with a capacity of 11 cubic

The rear seating of the 2.6-litre drop-head foursome coupé.

feet, and a lid which may be used as an extra platform.

Rated at 17.97 h.p., the engine has six cylinders 69.5 × 102 mm. (2,322 c.c.). The wheelbase is 10ft. 3in. and the track 4ft. 5in., the tyres being 5.50 by 18 on centre-lock wire wheels.

Largest of the M.G. range, the 2.6-litre model has met with a marked success since its introduction last year. It is built on similar general lines to the 2-litre, but has coachwork of increased capacity. No changes are being made.

Amongst the special features of this "Safety-Fastest" M.G. model the following may be cited:—Visors, draughtless ventilation by means of triangular panels in each of the four drop windows, folding arm rest and head-rests in the rear seats, and a metal shroud carried by each rear door which keeps the rear wings clean, and prevents clothing from being soiled on wet days.

The luggage boot is of large size, and the lid, which can also be used as a platform, contains a tray into which all the tools are neatly recessed. The spare wheel does not obstruct luggage accommodation as it is mounted in a recess in the front wing.

From the mechanical angle attention is drawn to the high efficiency six-cylinder engine with its twin carburettors, and overhead valves. This engine is able to develop over 100 h.p. The rating is 19.8 h.p. six cylinders 73 × 102 mm. (2,561 c.c.).

Amongst many excellent points it has a constant oil-temperature control operating in conjunction with the water cooling system. Another feature is the use of a "kick shackle" on the off-side front spring, also special cables connecting the front axle to the frame, to take the torque reaction of the brakes. Yet another point is that the electrical wiring is carried out in a manner to avoid interference with a radio set, for on M.G. cars provision is made to render radio installation easy.

The car has a 16½ gal. fuel tank. The wheelbase is 10ft. 3in., front track 4ft. 5¾in., and rear track 4ft. 8¾in.

Instrument board and controls of the 2.6-litre M.G.

ave Cooksey's M-Type Midget, a replica of the team cars
ich won the 1930 Double-Twelve Hours Race at Brooklands

*Two generations of racing MG: Syd Beere's 1933
K3 Magnette (top) and the interior of a 1950s Le Mans
MGA*

Published *The Autocar*, 28 June 1940

Still a

by

H. S. LINFIELD

IT took the mind back over several years, flicking the dust off a certain chromium-plated radiator surmounted by an octagonal cap. The car it belonged to was due to go back to its birthplace the next morning. I remembered doing the same thing, and checking over the oil level, topping-up the radiator, and having a last look round many of its predecessors on similar occasions, and then often starting back to the factory with them early on a summer morning just such as we have had during this sadly troubled June.

Still, I start at the wrong end of the story. The car, of course, was an M.G., one of the last of the current series TB Midgets to come out of the factory before car production had to dry up, for the present, in favour of more urgent calls upon the resources.

Unless you are lucky enough to find one in stock somewhere you cannot now just order an M.G., but there is interest from the road-behaviour angle, and some day these representatives of the British sports car will be in production once again on the old or even a bigger scale.

There is something about the modern M.G. that "gets you," just as perhaps years ago, as in my own case, the earlier models "got" you. An open body always helps, for it is more than a die-hard attitude of mind to consider that open-car motoring has that something in its "fresh-airness" and maximum visibility that no closed body can provide—no, not even a closed M.G. (There is a drop-head coupé Midget model.) One must always qualify this opinion with the proviso—in the right sort of weather.

I will be honest and say I was unusually fortunate with the weather on this recent test run. The petrol position being what it is, there is now none of the opportunity of other days of piling large mileages into a short time, so I took the Midget over for quite a spell, and motored as I could, running it in from practically brand new. It was a fortnight before I had to put up the hood, and as the car was on the road on every day of the fortnight, if sometimes only covering eight or ten miles, it was exceptionally lucky for this country.

But there is more than the appeal of the open car. An unroadworthy M.G. has never been put out—they have always built into these cars an inherent stability, accuracy of steering and power of stopping which make them safe to drive fast. The familiar slogan has more point than most of its kind.

The Series T Midget instituted a new type of Midget, it will be remembered, back in 1936, and the smallest M.G. then became a 10 h.p.-rated machine instead of an 8 h.p. The latest of all, the TB, has a slightly *smaller* engine capacity than the first of the Ts—strictly the type TA The bore was increased from 63.5 to 66.5 mm., and the stroke shortened from 102 to 90 (1,250 c.c. against 1,292 previously), giving a more nearly "square" engine, and, in conjunction with a slightly lower final-drive ratio, correspondingly more zip for low-speed acceleration.

Keeping to 3,000 r.p.m.

Owing to the running-in process I kept the engine speed on this occasion within 3,000 r.p.m. until the speedometer showed between 800 and 900 miles total. This allowed rather less than 45 m.p.h. on top gear and thirtyish on third. Yet it was not irksome driving, largely because the car handled well and allowed the corners to be taken without slackening appreciably below the self-imposed limit. Again, the clearer roads help, for if, as is now possible on even main-road routes, 40 to 45 m.p.h. can be maintained steadily it seems a respectable pace and gets you over the ground.

Once, without exceeding 43 m.p.h., I covered 36 miles in an hour, yet it seemed—and was—leisurely motoring, and because of the rev limit adopted on all gears there was no question of gaining anything by rapid bursts of acceleration or fast climbing.

With the mileage eventually approaching the 1,000 mark I began to give the engine some throttle. It was pleasant to go briefly up to the 60 mark and to use second and third more as they are intended to be used. The engine never felt really stiff from the first, but there was that slightly hot smell of new paint after a run, and its freedom after

Midget

M, 12, P, PB, T, and Now TB—M.G.'s Have Run Through the Alphabet! : The Latest Model on the Road in Wartime

1,000 miles or so was distinctly noticeable in contrast with the earlier stages.

During the last two days before the final scene with which this account opens I discovered something of what the Midget could do, though never in these times does one feel justified in holding full throttle for any appreciable distance when 45 or 50 will do just as well. There was, however, a rather joyous mile or two of by-pass, a perfect surface, clear of traffic, and with a beautifully radiused right-hand bend that you can take hard over to the right-hand kerb since it is a twin-track road. For that short time and one other brief section the M.G. came to life for the first time in its career, which I hope will be a satisfactory one, and never allow it to be said that this was a car that was " beaten " when it was young! My conscience is clear.

There is no sideways " give " when cornering fast, and the steering, though light, is nicely accurate and firm, but the springing is a great improvement for comfort over the old types. You notice the difference between various kinds of surfaces, and feel fairly appreciable movement over the less good, but never real shock.

Praise for the Hydraulic Brakes

I liked the Lockheed hydraulic brakes a lot. All through the run the linings must have been bedding down from the new condition, but the brakes did not become soft and always had a reserve. In the last fifty miles a quick stop was necessary at traffic lights on a de-restricted road that I had not been watching closely enough, and the M.G. pulled up right on the line, dead straight. The hand brake is still the fly-off pattern, that you pull on to release without touching the knob, always the best kind when restarting on a gradient. The synchromesh gives really nice " slicing " changes up and down, and covers the useful second gear. The steering wheel is telescopically adjustable over a useful range.

The car came to me first of all with all the side screens in position but the hood down, and though I think I have never previously driven an open car for more than an hour or two in this rig I found it a good one—and one's wife appreciates it! It stops nearly all draught. These particular screens are metal-framed, with a big clear area, and if securely clamped on to their clips do not rattle.

There *is* a flap in the right-hand one for signalling, but its use I found a little irksome. As a matter of fact, I got into the habit of watching the useful external mirror more even than usually and gave up signalling except on the most obviously important occasions! I do not necessarily advocate the plan and never felt really easy about it, but it brings home to you how much of the signal-flapping and hand-waving is strictly superfluous. The hood is an easy enough one-man affair and is neat when down, besides allowing plenty of head-room when up. There is handy luggage space beneath the " tonneau " cover, of leather material rubberised on the inside, which conceals it.

The " Thirtilite " that M.G.s have had for a long while proved a blessing. Consisting of a small green lamp in front of the driver, it was set to light up at 20 m.p.h. and go out at 30. Thus, when driving slowly at night, striving for a level 20, you know that if there is no green tell-tale you are O.K., and that in 30 m.p.h. stretches if there *is* a green light you are below 30 m.p.h. Altogether an excellent thing, now doubly useful, though for driving on really dark nights I should experiment with a view to somewhat reducing the brightness of the green illumination.

In the practical M.G. style a rev counter is fitted, and the red line on its dial is placed at 4,800 r.p.m. In the later stages of the run I found that this gave 72 or 73 by speedometer, but that it could be exceeded without apparent distress. Limit recommended revs mean a comfortable 50 on third, but 60 can be seen by winding things up.

When you come to driving it fast you realise what a reserve the car possesses, and it can obviously hold 55 or thereabouts all day on a suitable road without fussing itself. Shades of the past and hopes for the future!

Highly Satisfactory M.P.G. Figures

A 13½-gallon tank is a grand feature of the Midget—if you can legitimately get it filled these days. For driving in the wartime manner, but by no means crawling about, a full tank means a mileage approaching 500. I made a number of successive tests by quart tank over different routes and the average of six checks worked out at 37.6 m.p.g. The conditions included 20 and 30 m.p.h. driving in town areas, steady 30 m.p.h. runs for a specific purpose, and 50 to 60 m.p.h. work with fair use of the gears, *but* always taking advantage of coasting possibilities without letting the speed come down so much as seriously to slow the general rate of progress.

I should regard the all-round average as being 36 m.p.g. in normal conditions. At 30 m.p.h. steadily held the figure was 39.6 m.p.g. I devoted one quart of petrol to a test in the full-throttle style of driving that has been forgotten for the moment—pedal hard down wherever possible, second and third gear used at roundabouts on a by-pass and for accelerating away from them, and generally reverting to pre-war style when in a hurry. Even then the Midget gave 30.4 m.p.g., which is remarkable. All this was done as part of necessary journeys, not as special test runs.

It would be difficult to find a car of similar liveliness and all-round performance—interesting performance—that would be as economical, and this was with a barely run-in engine that had not had any special settings. . I came to agree with the makers' policy on the Midget of fitting a reserve petrol tap, but not a gauge. There is the big tank to start with, and the reserve system traps the exceptional quantity of three gallons. The control tap is on the instrument board, right in front of the driver. You can go a long way—several days of running around—without having to think about petrol, and then when the S.U. pump begins to " tick " you turn over to reserve and have 90-110 miles in hand.

Especially on a car that has as good a consumption as the Midget's I would personally sooner have the reserve supply and no gauge, than a gauge and no reserve. I found one other thing about this arrangement, that it avoided the plaguey gauge-watching habit one has got into since a gallon of petrol came to mean so much—a practice which does no good in any case, and is irritating, yet almost impossible to avoid nowadays.

This engine proved to be another example of the fairly high compression sports type that takes no violent exception to the present-day petrol A certain amount of pinking occurred when accelerating, but never excessively. I think that the alleged evils of Pool were overrated at first, though probably it is desirable to decarbonise more frequently than in the past.

Published *The Autocar,* 17 October 1947

No. 1339
TC M.G.
MIDGET
TWO-SEATER

The Autocar ROAD TESTS

DATA FOR THE DRIVER

TC M.G. MIDGET.

PRICE, with open two-seater body, £412 10s, plus £115 6s 8d purchase tax. Total, £527 16s 8d.

RATING : 10.97 h.p., 4 cylinders, overhead valves, 66.5 × 90 mm, 1,250 c.c. **TAX** (1947), £13.

BRAKE HORSE-POWER: 54.4 at 5,200 r.p.m. **COMPRESSION RATIO:** 7.25 to 1.

WEIGHT, without passengers : 16 cwt 19 lb. **LB. PER C.C. :** 1.45.

TYRE SIZE : 4.50 × 19.0in on knock-off wire wheels.

LIGHTING SET : 12-volt. Automatic voltage control.

TANK CAPACITY : 13½ gallons : approx. fuel consumption range, 28-34 m.p.g.

TURNING CIRCLE : 37ft (L. and R.). **MINIMUM GROUND CLEARANCE :** 6in.

MAIN DIMENSIONS : Wheelbase, 7ft 10in. Track, 3ft 9in (front and rear). Overall length, 11ft 7½in ; width, 4ft 8in ; height, 4ft 5in.

SCREEN WIPER — CHOKE — STARTER — HORN & ANTI-DAZZLE — LIGHTS & IGNITION — SLOW RUNNING — 30 M.PH. WARNING LIGHT — FOG LAMP — GEAR POSITIONS — HAND BRAKE — THROTTLE — FUEL WARNING LIGHT

ACCELERATION			
Overall gear ratios	*From steady m.p.h. of*		
	10 *to* 30	20 *to* 40	30 *to* 50
5.125 to 1	12.1 sec.	13.5 sec.	14.9 sec.
6.93 to 1	8.9 sec.	9.5 sec.	10.3 sec.
10.00 to 1	6.2 sec.	6.6 sec.	—
17.32 to 1	—	—	—

From rest through gears to : —

30 m.p.h.	.. .. ..	5.7 sec.
50 m.p.h.	.. .. ..	14.7 sec.
60 m.p.h.	.. .. ..	22.7 sec.

Steering wheel movement from lock to lock : 1⅜ turns.

Speedometer correction by Electrical Speedometer : 10 (car speedometer) 7 ; 20 — 22 ; 30 — 29 ; 40 — 41 ; 50 — 50 ; 60 — 59.5 ; 70 — 70.

Speeds attainable on indirect gears (by Electrical Speedometer) :

M.p.h.		
	normal	and max.
1st	.. .. ..	15 — 25
2nd	.. .. ..	32 — 40
3rd	.. .. ..	52 — 61

WEATHER : Dry, warm ; wind light.

Acceleration figures are the means of several runs in opposite directions.

Current model described in " The Autocar " of October 12, 1945.

IN a motoring world in which there is so much talk as there is today of rationalization, and in which cars tend more and more to resemble one another in appearance as well as in performance for a given size, the M.G. Midget two-seater stands unique. Yet an interesting point, as shown by recent public utterances on export subjects as well as by other sources of information, is that this car does not appeal only to the trials-minded and youthful fraternity of motorists in this country. On the contrary, it is gaining more and more of a following in other countries, including the U.S.A., and has reached a position where it can be regarded as one of our more exportable cars in terms of proportion of total output of the model.

Today it is certainly a class alone among cars made anywhere in the world as a sporting type retaining the conventional outward appearance of the " real " car dear to the hearts of enthusiasts in years gone by—that is, by displaying its radiator, or at all events a normal grille, and lamps, and in not having gone " all streamlined." It is a model, too, which more than most cars has evolved through the years, with its beginnings in that much smaller Midget of seventeen years or so ago that instantly registered a success. No car has done so much to maintain open-air

motoring and to support the demand that exists all over the world for sports car performance and characteristics in a car of not exorbitant first cost and at moderate running costs.

It offers a great deal in sheer performance, yet is not just a sports car with an appeal limited to special occasions; instead it is in every way a perfectly practicable car for all occasions where two seats are sufficient and the fresh-air style of progress is preferred. Actually, the all-weather equipment is good, the hood being easily erected and the side screens likewise, and they turn this car into a very reasonable imitation of a permanently closed car for bad weather use.

The Midget is in no way more difficult to drive than the ordinary family saloon, but given the type of driver who usually falls for such a machine—not necessarily a youngster—and who likes to use the gear box, the performance becomes quite vivid. That is not to suggest that the gear box has to be used in the manner of a pump handle whether the driver chooses or not; the 11 h.p.-rated engine that the TC Midget possesses has quite a range of flexibility on top gear, and the car is tractable in traffic. On the other hand, with an engine that will rev very freely without

Autocar ROAD TESTS

complaint much more can be made of the performance, of course, by using indirects that offer maxima as high as 60 m.p.h. on third and 40 on second.

Owing to the handy size of this car, its ability to pass safely where a bigger car would be held back, and the way in which it regains its cruising rate after it has been checked by other traffic, the Midget is almost as fast a car, over British roads, as can be found today. One feels, too, from its ability to take hard treatment and to hold speeds between 60 and 70 m.p.h., apparently for as long as roads in this country permit such motoring, that stretches of motor road offering far more opportunity of sustained speed than ever is found in this island would not "melt" a Midget engine.

The handiness of the car, the way in which it helps the driver in its manner of cornering, its "quick" steering, are big factors in giving it unusual average speed capabilities without an extremely high maximum speed being attained. The present car has been handled over a considerable distance in conditions which provided crowded roads, and also over routes on which traffic had been thinned by seasonal and petrol considerations. In both circumstances the average speeds were exceptional, a 40-miles-in-the-hour showing seeming always to be within its reach on a journey of any length, while, when roads are clear, figures such as 44 and 46 m.p.h. averages have been obtained. When the car was being timed by *The Autocar's* electrical speedometer to be travelling at 75 m.p.h., the car's speedometer showed only 73 an unusual state of affairs. In other more helpful road conditions subsequently the car's speedometer was seen at the 75 mark.

Sense of Accurate Control

Always one has the feeling of being able to make a fast run easily in the Midget, for it responds so readily to all the controls and is so quick—eager, it seems—to get moving. The biggest factor in this and other directions, apart from the actual performance available, is the complete sense of command which the driver feels he has over the car at all times, including the major features of brakes, steering and road holding on corners. The Lockheed brakes deserve special mention, for they deal most effectively with high-speed braking, and also are powerfully smooth in low speed applications.

Merits and demerits of normal versus independent suspension can be argued, in the main to the latter's marked

With a hinged-down-the-centre bonnet and normal wings it is easy to reach the engine, and accessibility of the individual components that require periodical attention is well above the average of presentday standards.

advantage, but there is no doubt of one fact in this connection. The normally sprung car, rather hard sprung, as in this instance, does let the driver gauge within close limits the speeds at which he can corner safely fast. After a little experience of it one finds oneself holding quite high speeds round bends in the Midget, and the car steering to a close course only a foot or two out from the near-side verge. Such a half-elliptic suspension has, of course, the counter-balancing feature that it is on the harsh side over poor surfaces, but on the Midget this tendency is by no means excessive.

It is a trim and appealing little car in its general arrangement and very practically laid out, besides offering a considerably higher accessibility factor than is usual today. One quickly comes to feel an affection for its efficiency and willingness, and in all respects, including performance, it is "man-size," with no suggestion of the tiny car about it.

Driving Position and Controls

Doubly important in a car of this type is the driving position. The Midget is provided with an adjustment for the seat back rest, which is in one piece, although there are two separate cushions, whilst also the spring-spoked steering wheel is telescopically adjustable and can be placed ideally for full power of control. A feature much appreciated or disliked, according to the point of view, is the fly-off type of hand brake lever—in *The Autocar's* view a form of control to be highly commended for its certainty and positiveness of operation. A more comfortable position for the left foot off the clutch pedal would be welcomed.

The gear change has synchromesh on second, third and top, and with a short vertical lever, which is well placed, this works very well for really quick upward and downward changes when the utmost is being made of the performance potential. The instruments include a rev counter, and the engine can be taken round to 5,500 r.p.m. with celerity, and it will readily go beyond that figure.

One does not think of this car in the usual way in terms of top gear climbing ability. Actually, however, the capabilities in this direction are good, for the power-to-weight ratio is favourable, but it is a delight to drop to third and fly over the gradients that bring the speed down at all appreciably on top. As to steeper gradients, second gear lets the car tear up a hill of 1 in 6½ calibre.

The head lamps are good for fast night driving. Starting from cold is immediate, and not much use of the mixture control for the twin S.U. carburettors is needed before the engine will pull properly. An excellent point, of value here, but still more so in territories where filling facilities are widely spaced, is the big petrol tank, giving a range of action of approximately 400 miles.

FRONT TRACK 3' 9"   WHEELBASE 7' 10"   REAR TRACK 3' 9"

4' 8"   17"   17"   41"   6"   44"   32"   1½"   19½"   11' 7½"

OVERALL HEIGHT OF CAR 4' 5"   2½"   35½"   DOOR GAP 27"   1¼"   10"   23"   17"   12½"   3"   24"   19½"   6"   19½"   17"   7½"   5"   REAR AXLE POSITION   4"   SEAT ADJUSTMENT

Measurements are taken with the driving seat at the central position of fore and aft adjustment. These body diagrams are to scale.

TALKING OF SPORTS CARS (No. 293)

A Brace of M.G

Late and Early Exam

BRITISH racing prestige was at a very low ebb in the early 1930s. The glory of the Bentleys had departed and British drivers were mostly racing foreign cars, for in spite of the critical letters this action provoked in the Correspondence columns they had no alternative if they wished to compete in Continental events with any chance of success.

Then in the winter of 1932 the M.G. company, heartened by its successes with its 747 c.c. Midget, produced a blown 1,100 c.c. car, the K3 Magnette. The new model made its first appearance in the Mille Miglia, entered by Earl Howe, and won not only its class but the team prize as well. This was but the first of a long list of successes, for the K3 has been winning ever since. Most of those still competing have been extensively modified and as a result have grown steadily faster as their age increased.

The two cars described this week belong to Frank Kennington, of Weybridge, whose burly form is often to be seen at Prescott and elsewhere hurrying to the top of the hill to the accompaniment of many revs and a shrill scream from the blower.

This year Kennington won the Baines Trophy awarded for best aggregate time by a visitor at Prescott's three open meetings. VIZOR.

● ● ● ● ● ● ● ● ● ● ● ● ● ● ● ●

"ALTHOUGH the two K3 Magnettes under review were both complete and distinct entities when they came into my possession," Kennington points out, "their life story, so far as I am in a position to tell it, is somewhat complicated by the fact that they have been the subject of wholesale merging of identities. The earlier car, JB 1269, was the first K3 ever built and served as practice machine for the M.G. works team in the 1933 Mille Miglia. The later one, HJJ 870, was one-from-last in the K3 series and dates from 1934; it was first registered as late as 1940, which ex-

plains its 'modern' registration number.

"For quite some time after its Italian sojourn, JB 1269 remained the property of the makers, leading a life of obscurity until its acquisition by Yallop, who in the mid-'thirties drove it in the Mannin races and elsewhere. There was a third owner whose name doesn't strike any familiar chords—he laid it up for the war period—and then the car passed to Jack Bartlett, from whom I bought it in the summer of '46.

"Without replacing anything except piston rings we ran the car in four 1946 sprint events, scoring class wins twice at Prescott, once at Bouley Bay and running second in the 1,100 c.c. supercharged sports class at Brighton. (To do both these M.G.s justice it should be borne in mind that 'eleven-hundreds' run in the 1½-litre category at Prescott).

"In the winter of 1946-47 JB 1269 was stripped down to the last screw and rivet, a process revealing the fact that the crankshaft had at some time broken and been welded together again; as we had repeatedly run the engine up to 6,500 in the course of sprints and a re-

spectable road mileage (the car being in daily use for general hacking) one may conclude that the welder knew his job. The Mille Miglia edition of the K3, of course, with its comprehensive road equipment and full-width body, was in no degree less habitable than milder M.G. models such as the L-type Magna two-seater, which it somewhat resembled, although to outward appearance of slab type, actually had a large and invisible forward extension, giving a total capacity of 26 gallons.

"Neither trouble nor expense was spared on the winter rebuild, an operation which can be very briefly summarized as follows: Laystall crank, Martlett pistons and a probably unique set of heavier-than-R-type connecting-rods installed (the base of the bores had to be relieved by interminable filing to give these rods clearance); water feed to engine drastically revised (standard system employed a single duct to the middle of the block, whereas ours used a four-branch pipe to the off side of the head,

Right: Alongside E. G. Pool's elderly Bugatti HJJ 870 begins the preliminary lap before the start of the Manx Cup race, during which it oiled three plugs.
Below: The older car, JB 1269, setting up a new Prescott record for blown 1½-litre sports cars at the July meeting with a time of 51.33 sec. The Arnott blower was in use on this occasion.

leaving virtually static water around the bores); standard blower, a Powerplus No. 10, scrapped in favour of a big Arnott Type 2800, driven at engine speed—as against a small reduction with the Powerplus—and giving a top boost of 23lb; inlet manifolding entirely redesigned in conjunction with Robin Jackson and coming into line with Goldie Gardner practice, i.e., blower delivers to No. 1 manifold pipe; that one in turn feeds through one port to pipe No. 2, which in its turn connects through two ports to pipe No. 3, whence the charge enters the head itself (this system effectively corrected an earlier tendency for plugs Nos. 5 and 6 to swamp, because of mal-distribution); head lapped direct to block; E.N.V. self-change gear box fully overhauled by makers, and crown wheel and pinion replaced.

"In its new form the K3 would run happily up to 7,500 r.p.m. and, in addition to being a uniquely exhilarating road car, promised reasonably well, we felt, for the 1947 racing season. Incidentally, owing to the difficulty of obtaining

K3 Magnettes

a Potent Blown Eleven Hundred

The Marshall-blown HJJ 870 has the more streamlined body and the revised braking system.

The big Arnott blower fitted to JB 1269. Note the oil feed to the nose of the blower from an auxiliary oil tank on the left and the large S.U. carburretor.

benzole in quantity, our fuel, for road -work as well as such competitions as give *carte blanche*, has been 60 per cent methanol, 30 per cent benzole and 10 per cent Pool.

"So far as sprints were concerned the K3's 1947 score was satisfying; class wins at two Prescott meetings and second place in another; two seconds off the class record for the hill; fastest 1,100 c.c. sports car at Brighton and Merston. The three actual races entered, however, brought negative results, though through no fault of the car's. At Gransden, acting on a false hunch after fifteen trouble-free practice laps, I increased the rate of oil flow to the blower, and promptly drowned two plugs in the race. At Rheims, on the extraordinary pretext that the M.G. 'looked too old-fashioned' and therefore 'wouldn't be a credit to Britain if it won,' the organizers refused to allow it to start, although it had made third best practice time. (After the race, incidentally, in support of the Speed-through-Chagrin movement, we motored the 179 miles from Rheims to Dieppe, two up, wing-less and with open pipe, in three hours dead—departure and arrival times both independently verified.)

"Our last race of the season was the Manx Cup; but first, to keep the chronology straight, HJJ 870 must come into the picture. This car, of whose past history I know little, apart from the fact that it belonged latterly to a Mr. Phillips, was acquired in May, 1947. With its narrower, doorless body and faired tail its appearance is, of course, quite different from the Mille Miglia model, although both are painted the only possible colour, British racing green.

"With the Manx race in view we in-

stalled the souped-up JB 1269 engine in the 1934 car, thus availing ourselves of the new-found maximum speed and acceleration, while also harnessing the HJJ 870's lighter weight, smaller frontal area and better brakes; the later K3s, it will be remembered, had scissors-type brake actuation, giving roughly a 100 per cent increase in retarding effect for a given pedal pressure.

"For the Isle of Man the axle ratio was raised from 4.89 to 4.33 to 1, but was subsequently changed back for the September Prescott meeting. On the 4.33 ratio 6,100 r.p.m. were realized, equal to about 120 m.p.h. with the size of tyre then fitted. Because of the impossibility of transmitting the available power—roughly 130 b.h.p.—through the standard 4.75 by 19in covers, we are using 6.50 by 16in at the rear.

"But to revert to the Douglas meeting. During practice, two days before the race, the blower seized at 7,500 r.p.m. In response to an S O S Charles (Carter Paterson) Brackenbury flew out from home base at Weybridge with a Marshall as replacement. This supercharger had never been run but by working through the Wednesday night we were just able to 'be and appear' at the pits on the Thursday in time for the parade lap. The Marshall, as you would expect, had spent its life submerged in oil, a fact of which, in all the frenzy of the preceding thirty hours, we had forgotten to take account, with the result that three plugs oiled up on the ceremonial circuit at 25 m.p.h. It being impossible to pull back the lost time in so short a race as this (about 46 miles) I decided to cut my losses and retire.

"A single-seater racing car, utilizing the JB 1269 engine but in other respects almost entirely original, is now in the early stages of construction. At the time of writing, however, a few days before Black Sunday, November 30, the one complete K3 in day-to-day service is the outcome of the marriage between this same JB 1269 engine and the 1934 chassis and body. When the single-seater becomes a *fait accompli* we intend compounding a road car from the Mille Miglia chassis and engine—Marshall-blown with some 15lb maximum boost—and the 1934 body.

"To date the two K3 Magnettes have aggregated something like 12,000 road miles, and neither engine—discounting the supercharger seizure mentioned earlier—has suffered a breakage of any sort. Starting, except occasionally in freezing weather, is instantaneous, tractability is adequate and many a well-cared-for family saloon produces more mechanical engine noise; admittedly, of course, this mechanical reticence can only be appreciated on the over-run, for under any other conditions the exhaust note, negligibly subdued by a Brooklands silencer and fishtail, tends to divert attention from fainter phon sources.

Fast Motoring

"The contemporary K3, pulling the 4.89 to 1 axle ratio, more than once registered 6,300 r.p.m., equal to about 114 m.p.h., in the course of a pre-Abolition run from Weybridge to Dorchester-on-Thames. R. M. Oliver, the Prescott Bugatti man, who once kept station with the M.G. on this trip, spoke afterwards of the 'furry black lines' left by our rear tyres up to a speed of 75 m.p.h. on dry tarmac.

"Fuel consumption under road conditions averages a surprising 15 m.p.g. As regards general creature comforts, there is a hood, but, as only a Maskelyne could get into or out of the car with the roof erected, it stays furled. The full-width screen is also kept permanently flat. A passenger-side tonneau cover being a fixture on all solo excursions, it is found easier to take the quickly detachable steering wheel on and off for ingress and egress, rather than unpress the dots. The instruments, reading from L to R, are an ammeter, oil thermometer, water thermometer, boost gauge, engine oil pressure gauge; second row, blower oil pressure gauge, fuel tank ditto. All the foregoing are small and matching; at the extreme right presides a soup-plate rev counter.

GILDING THE LILY

Above: In search of a "production-type" supercharged sports car, in 1939 W. E. C. Watkinson bought this ex-Charles Martin supercharged K3 Magnette, K3025—which, driven by Charles Martin and Roy Eccles, had taken fourth place at Le Mans in 1934—and had it rebodied by Jensens, of West Bromwich. The car lay forgotten for many years at Abingdon until, in 1960, the factory restored it completely to its original racing specification for its present owner Kjell Qvale

Below: Smart lines on a Swiss drop-head coupe on an M.G. 2·6-litre chassis

---

Autocar   AUGUST 1, 1947

Gardner Takes 500 c.c. Records

Successful Attempt on Belgian Motor Road

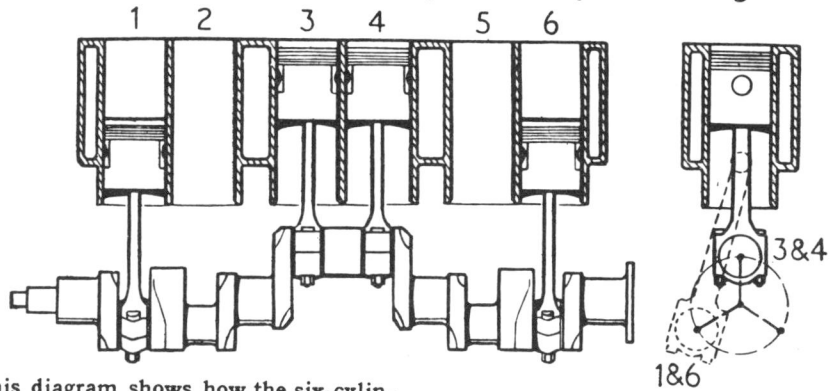

This diagram shows how the six-cylinder 750 c.c. engine of Gardner's car has been converted into a four-cylinder 500 c.c. engine, in order to take records in the 500 c.c. class. Pistons have been removed from cylinders two and five.

In this form it raised the 1,100 c.c. record, first to 186 m.p.h. and later to its present figure of 203.54 m.p.h. on the Dessau autobahn. On that occasion the engine was at once bored out slightly, whereupon the car took the 1,500 c.c. record, which it still holds at 204.28 m.p.h.

ᴇARLY on the morning of Thursday, July 24, a little green car bearing the crossed flags of England and Belgium on its nose snarled along the Jabbeke-Aeltre motor road near Ostend to take four new records in Class I, the international 500 c.c. class, for its owner-driver, Lt. Col. A. T. Goldie Gardner. They were the flying kilometre at 118.016 m.p.h., the flying mile at 117.493 m.p.h. the five kilometres at 114.117 m.p.h., and the five miles at 110.544 m.p.h. His fastest recorded single run was 126.166 m.p.h.

Since it was built for George Eyston by the M.G. company in the early months of 1934 to attack 1,100 c.c. records the car has had a long and illustrious history, including the winning of a long-distance Brooklands race, the British Empire Trophy. When it passed into Gardner's hands in 1938 it was extensively modified and fitted with its present beautifully streamlined body.

Mechanics and Belgian officials crowd round Lt. Col. Goldie Gardner to congratulate him after his successful attack on Class I records.

Published *The Autocar*, 15 May 1953

No. 1497: M.G. MIDGET SERIES TD TWO-SEATER

Though the body is wider, nowadays giving ample elbow room for two passengers, the familiar lines of the Midget are preserved. Bumpers with substantial over-riders cater for the relatively large overseas market that the car enjoys.

The *Autocar* ROAD TESTS

FEW cars, if indeed any, can claim to have fostered enthusiasm for sports cars to the extent that the M.G. Midget has done. In April, 1929, the first of these cars, a Series M Midget, left the M.G. works and started a line of small sports cars which, under various type letters, but always with the suffix Midget, has continued unbroken to the present day. Many different models have made up this succession; some, notably the Montlhéry J4, Q and R types, were out and out racing cars, but their less stark and highly tuned counterparts, too, have been competing in races, rallies and trials ever since.

It is likely that a car with a lineage of this sort should possess qualities in handling and performance that are out of the ordinary; the relatively large market for the current model, the Series TD Midget, in America is evidence of this fact, and the car can claim to have played a fair part in the present rapid growth of enthusiasm for sports cars amongst the American public. That this model has continued virtually unchanged since it was introduced early in 1950, and has lost none of its popularity, is further evidence, if such were needed. It is interesting to try to analyse the points which, collectively, make the TD such fun to drive.

The feel of the car on the road inspires confidence and there is the impression that even an indifferent driver could make a good showing behind the wheel; however long the journey, the actual driving of the car is beguiling all the way. In traffic its small size and good visibility make it very manoeuvrable and the flexibility of the 1¼-litre engine is such that one can trickle along at 10 m.p.h. on top gear, using the lively acceleration on third and second gears to pass through comparatively narrow openings in the traffic. For the daily shopping it could not be more convenient; its small size and good steering lock make parking an easy matter.

The high-geared rack-and-pinion steering is light, accurate and sensitive, and small movements of the wheel produce a quick response. On the open road it is necessary only to hold the wheel very lightly, and long, fast bends are taken more by leaning the body into the corner than by steering round it. A slight tendency to oversteer at the recommended tyre pressures, particularly with a full tank, was cured by increasing the rear pressures to 20 lb. One of the few major departures from the design of the earlier cars lies in the front suspension, which is independent, using coil springs and wishbones; leaf springs are used at the rear, though not of the short, stiff variety on the Midget's forebears. In operation, the suspension is sufficiently stiff to reduce roll on corners to a minimum and it gives a comfortable ride over rough surfaces, though there is a certain amount of vertical motion over roads with undulating bumps.

Speeds up to 65 m.p.h. are reached easily and a cruising speed of 60-65 m.p.h. can be maintained whenever conditions allow. Above these figures, however, the increase is slower and to reach 75 m.p.h. on the slightly flattering speedometer requires a fair length of road. With the windscreen flat and only the driver in the car a true speed of 78 m.p.h. was reached on two occasions on level ground. Without unduly stressing the engine or the driver it is possible to put upwards of 45 miles into the hour in normal road conditions. Main road hills are taken easily on top gear and it is very seldom indeed that it is necessary to drop below third gear for gradient alone. For normal use the top gear ratio of 5.125 to 1 is about right, but for extensive main road driving, particularly on the long straight roads of Europe, one feels that a slightly higher gear would be useful.

The gear box, with synchromesh on second, third and top,

Accessibility at its old-time best. Regular maintenance of the auxiliaries and components of the 1¼-litre engine is encouraged by neat layout. Dipstick, oil filler, oil-bath air cleaner, distributor, sparking plugs, fuel pump, battery and tool boxes are all accessible.

and its short, remote control, central lever, are a joy to use—to such an extent that one tends to use third gear more than one needs. For normal purposes the synchromesh is adequate but, in the conditions of recording the performance tests where full use of the performance was made, it was quite easy to override it. In this connection, too, it was found that, in taking the acceleration figures, when full-throttle gear changes were made there was a tendency for the clutch to spin. In a car of this type which is bound to be used in competitions by many owners, stronger clutch springs would be an advantage; this would be particularly necessary in a car which had been subjected to the stage-by-stage tuning which can be carried out under the guidance of the M.G. company and which was fully detailed, with its results, in *The Autocar* of July 18 and 25, 1952.

The Lockheed hydraulic brakes, with two-leading shoes at the front and leading and trailing shoes at the rear, are amply adequate to the car's performance. Heavy pedal pressures are not required and, as a test, the brakes will stop the car in a straight line from 50 m.p.h. with the driver's hands off the wheel. There was no sign of fade in the arduous conditions of the test, and after extensive use both while taking the performance figures and during many miles of normal motoring, they did not deteriorate nor did the pedal travel increase to any great extent.

Noise Levels

Mechanically, the engine is agreeably quiet and the exhaust note is subdued and pleasant; even on the intermediate gears between high buildings there is no back echo. Inevitably there is a certain amount of wind noise in an open car at high speeds, but this is not worrying and conversation can be maintained without the need to shout; gear noise is confined to a pleasant whine on the intermediates. The engine starts easily from cold and the mixture control is required only for the initial start. It is sensitive to fuel and, on a low-grade diet, it pinks readily. At speeds not exceeding 50 m.p.h., maintained over a long run, the fuel consumption worked out at a little under 30 m.p.g.

The driving position is good and the seats are adjustable —together, not separately, because of the one-piece back rest—to an extent to suit drivers of widely different heights; the steering column, too, is adjustable for individual reach. Space is rather cramped round the pedals and there is barely enough room for the left foot when it is not on the clutch pedal. Both front wings are visible from the driving seat,

Still undisguised, the radiator has changed little since the days of the first series M Midgets ; the flat, octagonal filler cap is functional, not just ornamental.

though the left wing view is in line with the driving mirror. The 5in speedometer and revolution counter dials are directly in front of the driver, though it is felt that they could both be moved over to the right, as the higher readings on the speedometer are hidden by the rim of the steering wheel. On a panel in the centre of the facia are grouped the remaining instruments : a combined radiator thermometer and oil pressure gauge, ammeter, horn button, lighting and starter switches, mixture control, rheostatically controlled facia lighting switch, ignition warning light and a green light which warns the driver when the level of fuel in the tank drops below 2½ gallons; a fuel gauge is not fitted. There is an additional switch for a spot lamp if one should be fitted, though such a lamp is not standard. There is a deep cupboard in front of the passenger, though its lid is not lockable; upholstery and interior trim are in leather and the seats are comfortable, well padded, and give ample support to the extent that, after a long drive, no signs of stiffness are felt. The windscreen wiper motor is placed at the top of the fold-flat windscreen, in front of the passenger, and the twin blades clear a wide area of the screen. At high speeds, with the blades in the parked position, and occasionally when they are in operation, the blade on the driving side disappeared above the screen; a stop to prevent this would be valuable.

The weather equipment, once in position, is excellent and free from draughts and rattles, and the side screens are rigid and fit well; soon after raising the hood the interior becomes almost as warm and comfortable as that of a convertible. At high speeds the canvas of the hood vibrates and produces a fair amount of noise, but the side screens remain well

All the attributes of an enthusiast's car : a good driving position with the pleasant, long bonnet stretching away in front of the driver, accessible spare wheel, external slab tank with quick-action filler cap, and adequate luggage space. In closed form the car is proof against the worst weather, and is warm and comfortable.

fitting and they do not flap. The hood and side screens take a fair time to un-stow and erect; against this, however, must be balanced the pleasant thought that, in fine weather, one has the joy of driving along in the sunshine and, given warning of the weather's more obscure moods, one has first-class protection available against them. Adequate luggage space for two large suitcases is provided behind the seats and it is fully protected by the hood.

The double-dip head lights give a good beam which is adequate for any speeds within the car's range; a conveniently placed dip switch lies to the left of the clutch pedal. In general, the finish of the car is first-class and in keeping with the better traditions of British craftsmanship and quality-built British cars. A minor criticism in this connection is that the washers under the chromium-plated screws on the apron in front of the radiator are inadequately plated, if indeed at all, and rust very quickly.

From the point of view of the owner who carries out his own maintenance, the accessibility of the engine and its auxiliaries could not be better. The gear box has a dipstick which is reached through an inspection cover in the floor above the gear box; the rear axle, too, is easily checked for level and replenished by removing the floor of the luggage compartment.

The Midget is a survival of what, in the opinion of many people, is the right sort of small sports car. It caters for those who look upon motoring not as a means to an end, but as an end in itself. Many thousands of these little cars are succeeding admirably in providing their owners with something that will, at one moment, journey forth and do the shopping and, at the next, take part in serious competitive events or tackle a 400-mile journey with zest; and this at a price which, in modern times, amounts to a very modest outlay.

M.G. MIDGET SERIES TD TWO-SEATER

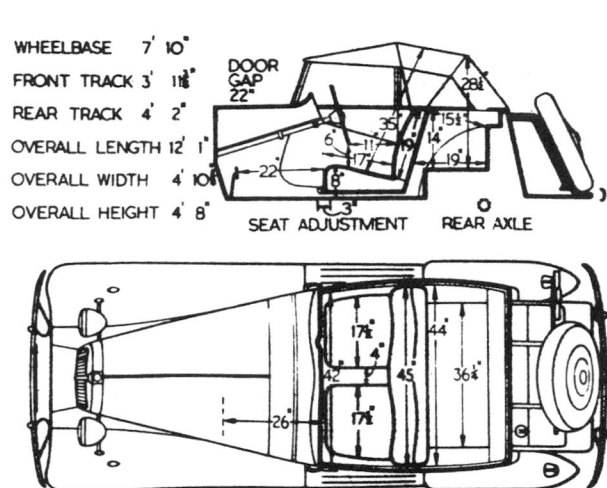

WHEELBASE 7' 10"
FRONT TRACK 3' 11½"
REAR TRACK 4' 2"
OVERALL LENGTH 12' 1"
OVERALL WIDTH 4' 10½"
OVERALL HEIGHT 4' 8"

DOOR GAP 22"

SEAT ADJUSTMENT   REAR AXLE

Measurements in these ⅛in to 1ft scale body diagrams are taken with the driving seat in the central position of fore and aft adjustment and with the seat cushions uncompressed.

PERFORMANCE

ACCELERATION : from constant speeds. Speed, Gear Ratios and time in sec.

M.P.H.	5.125 to 1	7.098 to 1	10.609 to 1	17.938 to 1
10—30	11.7	8.6	6.1	—
20—40	12.4	8.9	—	—
30—50	12.6	9.8	—	—
40—60	15.1	—	—	—
50—70	22.6	—	—	—

From rest through gears to :

M.P.H.				sec
30	..	..	..	6.3
50	..	..	..	15.6
60	..	..	..	23.9
70	..	..	..	39.6

Standing quarter mile, 23.4 sec.

SPEED ON GEARS :

Gear		M.P.H. (normal and max.)	K.P.H. (normal and max.)
Top	(mean)	73.5	118.3
	(best)	75	120.7
3rd	..	48—59	77—95
2nd	..	30—38	48—61
1st	..	16—20	26—32

TRACTIVE RESISTANCE : 26 lb per ton at 10 M.P.H.

TRACTIVE EFFORT :

			Pull (lb per ton)	Equivalent Gradient
Top	..	..	179	1 in 12.5
Third	..	..	257	1 in 8.5
Second	..	..	390	1 in 5.6

BRAKES :

Efficiency	Pedal Pressure (lb)
96 per cent	130
78 per cent	95
35 per cent	53

FUEL CONSUMPTION :

25 m.p.g. overall for 320 miles (11.3 litres per 100 km).
Approximate normal range 23—29 m.p.g. (12.3—9.7 litres per 100 km).
Fuel, First grade.

WEATHER : Dry surface, light wind.
Air temperature 55 degrees F.
Acceleration figures are the means of several runs in opposite directions.
Tractive effort and resistance obtained by Tapley meter.
Model described in *The Autocar* of January 20, 1950.

SPEEDOMETER CORRECTION : M.P.H.

Car speedometer	..	..	..	10	20	30	40	50	60	70	80
True speed	..	..	..	10.5	19.8	29	38	48	57.5	67	77.5

DATA

PRICE (basic), with open two-seater body, £530.
British purchase tax, £221 19s 2d.
Total (in Great Britain), £751 19s 2d.

ENGINE : Capacity : 1,250 c.c. (76.28 cu in).
Number of cylinders : 4.
Bore and stroke : 66.5 × 90 mm (2.62 × 3.54in).
Valve gear : Overhead ; push rods.
Compression ratio : 7.25 to 1.
B.H.P. : 54.4 at 5,200 r.p.m. (B.H.P. per ton laden 50.8).
Torque : 63.5 lb at 2,600 r.p.m.
M.P.H. per 1,000 r.p.m. on top gear, 14.5.

WEIGHT (with 5 gals. fuel) : 17¾ cwt (1,995 lb).
Weight distribution (per cent) 50.2 F ; 49.8 R.
Laden as tested : 21¼ cwt (2,395 lb).
Lb per c.c. (laden) : 1.9.

BRAKES : Type : F, Two-leading shoe. R, Leading and trailing.
Method of operation : F, Hydraulic. R, Hydraulic.
Drum dimensions : F, 9in diameter, 1.5in wide. R, 9in diameter, 1.5in wide.
Lining area : F, 52.5 sq in. R, 52.5 sq in (98.1 sq in per ton laden).

TYRES : 5.50—15in.
Pressures (lb per sq in) : F, 18. R, 18 (normal).

TANK CAPACITY : 12¼ Imperial gallons.
Oil sump, 10½ pints.
Cooling system, 12 pints.

TURNING CIRCLE : 31ft 3in (L and R).
Steering wheel turns (lock to lock) : 2¾.

DIMENSIONS : Wheelbase, 7ft 10in.
Track : 3ft 11¾in (F) ; 4ft 2in (R).
Length (overall) : 12ft 1in.
Height : 4ft 8in.
Width : 4ft 10½in.
Ground clearance : 6in.
Frontal area : 16.6 sq ft (approx), with hood erected. 13.0 sq ft (approx), with hood and windscreen down.

ELECTRICAL SYSTEM : 12-volt ; 51-ampère-hour battery.
Head lights : Double dip, 42—36 watt.

SUSPENSION : Front, Independent ; coil springs and wishbones.
Rear, Half-elliptic springs.

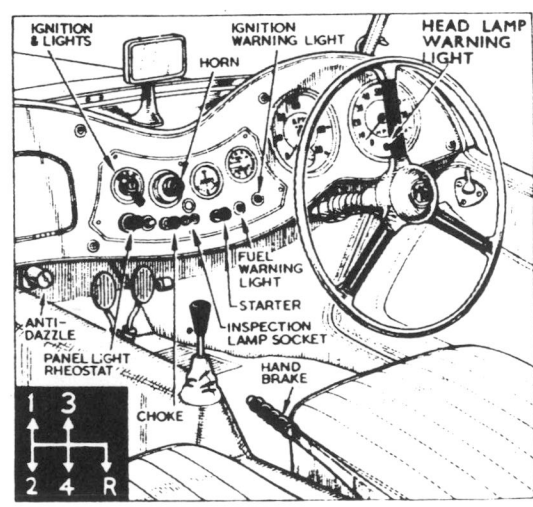

Published *The Autocar*, 23 September 1955

The Autocar ROAD TESTS

THE NEW M.G.

ON THE ROAD

TO confound the critics who say that racing teaches no useful lessons comes the brand-new M.G. sports two-seater. Designated the model A—thus starting afresh after the long line of M, J, Q and R racing cars, and TA, TD and TF Midgets that rolled out of the Abingdon works—the new car is a very close development of the M.G.s that did so well in the 24-hours race at Le Mans this year.

There are naturally some differences between the racing car and the production model, but the road holding, braking and steering are unaffected and in these respects the M.G. A recalls very intimately the Le Mans car, road impressions of which were published in *The Autocar* of July 29, 1955.

The immediate impression on sitting in the driving seat was that the car had been tailored to fit, of which more later. Starting the 1½-litre B.M.C. engine presented no problems. A radiator blind, as fitted to the test car, is available as optional extra equipment and is easily operated by a control below the right-hand corner of the facia. This blind facilitates the warming-up in which any right-thinking enthusiast will indulge, although even without its use operating temperature was reached very quickly.

On opening the cable-operated throttle there came the familiar M.G. exhaust note. At no time did this become objectionable to others, and there was no annoying boom to be heard with the hood up. The car will drift along through residential areas on a whiff of throttle and with no unwelcome attention attracted.

There is immediate response to sudden pressure on the accelerator and the getaway from rest is very good, 70 m.p.h. being reached in just over 21 seconds. On wet roads, which were experienced during the taking of the acceleration figures, wheelspin was very apparent, and black lines can be left on a dry surface if the start is abrupt. At the end of the standing quarter mile the M.G. was travelling at very nearly 70 m.p.h., and this was very creditable with the load carried. Performance figures were taken with hood and sidescreens erected, except for some

runs to determine maximum speed, when a small racing-type screen was fitted.

With this small screen and a tonneau cover over the passenger seat, the best speed reached was 96 m.p.h., as against 99 m.p.h. with the hood and sidescreens in position. At such high speeds the M.G. A is very stable and the driver is able to concentrate on the rev counter needle as it climbs to the orange 5,500 r.p.m. mark on the dial, and the road shooting past him and away under the nose of the car. On Continental roads it was possible to cruise for mile after mile with the speedometer needle between 90 and 100 m.p.h. The oil pressure and temperature gauge needles remained steady in spite of a considerable amount of high-speed driving.

The M.G. A is, in fact, one of those cars whose cruising speed is determined by road conditions, and this became very evident after driving fast over the French and Belgian roads. But there is no feeling at the end of a hard day that the driver has been doing most of the work. Long, winding hillside roads are a joy to traverse; the car rockets to the top in third gear, and this gear is also extremely useful for overtaking other traffic and for town use. Yet it is possible to accelerate smoothly from 12 m.p.h. using the 4.3 to 1 top gear, and the car can be very pleasant when used in a gentle fashion. The engine is no temperamental unit, liable to behave only when it thinks it will.

Fuel consumption benefits from the body shape; driving at 50 m.p.h., with short periods at 70, resulted in a figure of 30.8 m.p.g., which was achieved on a give-and-take main road in Great Britain where to maintain the predetermined average speed the available acceleration had to be used.

The road holding and steering are of a high order. Even with the tyre pressures set for fast driving, there was no feeling of discomfort or pattering when on *pavé* and other poor surfaces. Fast cornering was a joy, the driver being able to position the car exactly where he wanted, and exit from a corner is also very satisfactory. On roads just wet ter a sudden rainfall, the tail of the car would swing out ightly, but correction brought an immediate response and here was no lack of control. Suspension and damping is uch that the whole car feels in one piece and the front end oes not hop about.

The rack and pinion steering, with one of the æsthetically etter types of present-day steering wheel, has a good, easy ction with very little lost motion. There are two and three-uarter turns from lock to lock and the car proves to be uided by a slight motion of the hands rather than turning he wheel through a number of degrees.

Control is helped at all speeds by the excellent driving osition previously mentioned. The seat is low down, elow the level of the frame, and the driver's legs stretch omfortably to the pedals. The steering wheel (non-djustable column) is at a good angle and there is plenty f room for the driver's elbows. The sight line of a tall river is well below the top of the windscreen, and there space for large feet in the neighbourhood of the pedals. he short remote control gear lever comes immediately to and and the movements are precise and extremely satis-actory, the results being equally so! Occasional difficulty as encountered in engaging first gear from rest. The everse stop spring on the car tested was also rather stiff, ut experience of a similar gear box has shown that this tiffness wears off. The clutch is hydraulically operated nd has a nice feel. It is capable of enabling very quick ear changes to be made without slip.

Racing experience shows in the M.G. A braking, which all that could be required for very fast road work. wo-leading shoes in the front brakes, with leading and ailing shoes working in the rear, give the driver all the etarding power he is likely to need in normal circumstances. Jo fade was experienced during the test, and only when he brake performance figures were being obtained did any nevenness set in. The fitting of centre-lock wire wheels, n optional extra, would assist in cooling the drums as well s improving the already attractive appearance of the car. he hand-brake lever lies horizontally by the side of the ropeller-shaft tunnel and has a fly-off action. It is easily eached and does not get in the way of the driver's leg.

Fast night driving is quite safe with the beam of the head ghts, but the foot-operated dip-switch is placed rather igh and is difficult to reach. It would be considerably etter if it could be adjacent to the clutch pedal. There is rheostat for the instrument lighting, and at one position f the switch the speedometer alone is illuminated. The nly reflection in the windscreen comes from the tonneau over studs immediately in front of the steering wheel. With he hood up and head lamp beams reaching away in front, he M.G. A is as comforting to drive at night as it is ex-ilarating by day.

Both seats have adequate adjustment and the back rest at a comfortable angle. Some drivers would prefer more upport for the thighs. The passenger has a grab handle nd this also forms the windscreen frame support. As is o be expected, it is easier for two persons to erect the hood rom its stowed position behind the seats, but the driver lone can manage it. The sidescreens, which have a pring-loaded flap, are simple to put into position and emove; they are each locked by one turnbuckle. Some

A new slant on the familiar M.G. front, successfully adapted

wet came in between the windscreen and front edge of the sidescreens when travelling fast, and in extremely heavy rain water dripped on to the driver's right leg from a point under the scuttle. There is a very reasonable amount of head room with the hood erect, and there was no instance of the driver's head hitting the hoop sticks when going over a bump. At speeds between 70 and 80 m.p.h. the hood

Seats tip forward if required. Instruments confront the driver but the horn is in the centre of the facia

For a sports car, luggage space is reasonable. Hood up, the new model loses nothing in smartness; the rear window is flexible

material vibrated on the frame but this noise was not experienced at lower speeds.

There is no cubby-hole in the facia; the space occupied by the radio fitted on the test car is blanked by a plate with an M.G. motif when there is no radio. A large pocket in each door is sufficient for maps, torch and the usual odds and ends crews require for a few days away from home. The pockets remain dry in rain when sidescreens are not fitted. The door handle cord is slung across the inside top of the pocket and can be reached by inserting a hand underneath the flap of the sidescreen. There are fitted envelopes behind the seats for the side curtains and these envelopes neatly conceal the hood when it is folded away.

The release handle for the luggage locker lid can be reached behind the passenger seat; there is room in the locker for a suitcase and small articles. Strapped on the rear bulkhead is the tool roll, containing the lifting jack and wheelbrace. The jack, surprisingly enough, is of the old-fashioned screw type. A starting handle is supplied and is clipped to the back of the locker. Nine points require attention with a grease gun every 1,000 miles and the twin six-volt batteries are housed beneath the luggage locker. They can be reached by removing the spare wheel.

A heating and demisting unit, available as an optional extra, was fitted to the test car. It worked well, and draws in fresh air via a long duct through the engine compartment. On the left side of the radiator, fresh air is ducted to the intakes of the twin S.U. carburettors. Hot air and fumes from the engine compartment are cleared by a vent on each side of the bonnet. As is usual with these B.M.C. engines, the oil filler is accessible, though it is difficult to see why the oil level dipstick could not be two inches longer, raising it clear of the sparking plug leads. Dynamo belt adjustment is not particularly easy with the standard tool kit.

M.G. TWO-SEATER (SERIES A)

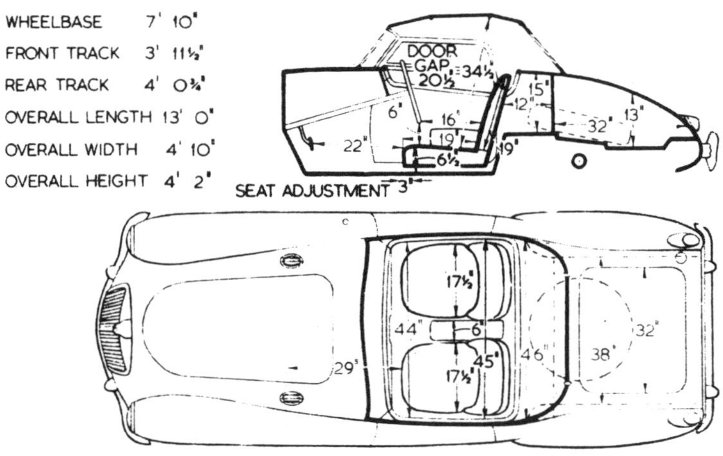
WHEELBASE 7' 10"
FRONT TRACK 3' 11½"
REAR TRACK 4' 0¾"
OVERALL LENGTH 13' 0"
OVERALL WIDTH 4' 10"
OVERALL HEIGHT 4' 2"
DOOR GAP
SEAT ADJUSTMENT 3"

Measurements in these ¼in to 1ft scale body diagrams are taken with the driving seat in the central position of fore and aft adjustment and with the seat cushions uncompressed

PERFORMANCE

ACCELERATION: from constant speeds.
Speed Range, Gear Ratios and Time in sec.

M.P.H.	4.3 to 1	5.908 to 1	9.520 to 1	15.652 to 1
10—30..	—	8.2	5.0	—
20—40..	12.2	8.0	4.8	—
30—50..	12.3	8.4	—	—
40—60..	13.1	9.1	—	—
50—70..	15.0	10.7	—	—
60—80..	18.1	—	—	—

From rest through gears to:

M.P.H.	sec.
30	4.9
50	11.0
60	15.6
70	21.4
80	32.1
90	50.1

Standing quarter mile, 20.2 sec.

SPEEDS ON GEARS:

Gear		M.P.H. (normal and max.)	K.P.H. (normal and max.)
Top ..	(mean)	98.0	157.7
	(best)	99.0	159.3
3rd		58—70	93—113
2nd		38—44	61—71
1st		20—26	32—42

TRACTIVE RESISTANCE: 20 lb per ton at 10 M.P.H.

TRACTIVE EFFORT:

	Pull (lb per ton)	Equivalent Gradient
Top	203	1 in 11.0
Third	303	1 in 7.3
Second..	455	1 in 4.9

BRAKES:

Efficiency	Pedal Pressure (lb)
85 per cent	100
77 per cent	50
58 per cent	25

FUEL CONSUMPTION:
27 m.p.g. overall for 672 miles (10.46 litres per 100 km).
Approximate normal range 25–38 m.p.g. (11.3–7.4 litres per 100 km).
Fuel, First grade.

WEATHER: Overcast, wet surface.
Air temperature 68 deg F.
Acceleration figures are the means of several runs in opposite directions.
Tractive effort and resistance obtained by Tapley meter.
Model described in *The Autocar* of September 23, 1955.

SPEEDOMETER CORRECTION: M.P.H.

Car speedometer	10	20	30	40	50	60	70	80	90	100
True speed:	11	20	29	38	48	58	68	77	86	96

DATA

PRICE (basic), with two-seater body, £595.
British purchase tax, **£249 0s 10d.**
Total (in Great Britain), **£844 0s 10d.**

ENGINE: Capacity: 1,489 c.c. (90.88 cu in).
Number of cylinders: 4.
Bore and stroke: 73.025 × 89 mm. (2.875 × 3.5in).
Valve gear: o.h.v., push rods.
Compression ratio: 8.3 to 1.
B.H.P.: 68 at 5,500 r.p.m. (B.H.P. per ton laden 70.6).
Torque: 77.4 lb ft at 3,500 r.p.m.
M.P.H. per 1,000 r.p.m. on top gear, 17.0.

WEIGHT: (with 5 gals fuel), 17¾ cwt (1,904 lb).
Weight distribution (per cent): F, 51.5; R, 48.5.
Laden as tested: 21 cwt (2,254 lb).
Lb per c.c. (laden): 1.51.

BRAKES: Type: F, two-leading shoe; R, leading and trailing.
Method of operation: F, hydraulic; R, hydraulic.
Drum dimensions: F, 10in diameter; 1¾in wide. R, 10in diameter; 1¾in wide.
Lining area: F, 67.2 sq in. R, 67.2 sq in (112.6 sq in per ton laden).

TYRES: 5.60—15in.
Pressures (lb per sq in): F, 17; R, 20 (normal). F, 18; R, 23 (for fast driving).

TANK CAPACITY: 10 Imperial gallons.
Oil sump, 6½ pints.
Cooling system, 10 pints (plus 0.65 pints if heater is fitted).

TURNING CIRCLE: 28ft 0in (L and R).
Steering wheel turns (lock to lock): 2¾.

DIMENSIONS: Wheelbase: 7ft 10in.
Track: F, 3ft 11½in; R, 4ft 0¾in.
Length (overall): 13ft.
Height: 4ft 2in.
Width: 4ft 10in.
Ground clearance: 6in.
Frontal area: 13.77 sq ft (approximately) (with hood up).

ELECTRICAL SYSTEM: 12-volt; 51 ampère-hour battery.
Head lights: Double dip; 42–36 watt bulbs.

SUSPENSION: Front, independent, coil springs. Rear, half-elliptic leaf springs.

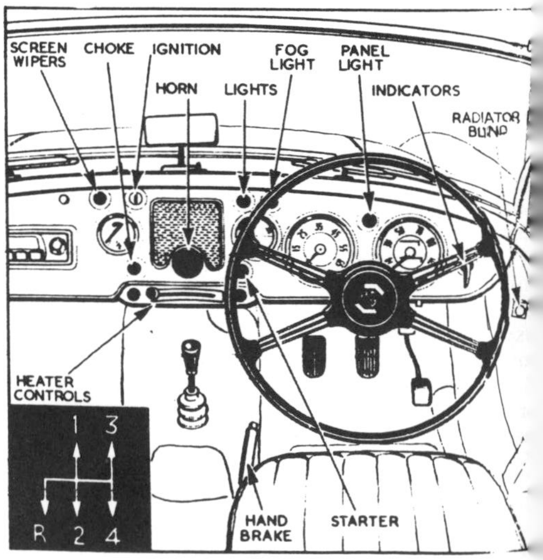
SCREEN WIPERS
CHOKE
IGNITION
FOG LIGHT
PANEL LIGHT
HORN
LIGHTS
INDICATORS
RADIATOR BLIND
HEATER CONTROLS
1 3
R 2 4
HAND BRAKE
STARTER

Published
The Autocar,
18 July 1958

The radiator grille bears the well-known M.G. octagonal motif. On each side of the bonnet are vents to allow hot air to escape from the engine compartment. Direction indicators are combined with the side lights

Autocar ROAD TESTS

M.G. Twin Cam MGA

OPEN TWO-SEATER

BY producing a high-performance model to partner the successful MGA two-seater, the M.G. Car Company, Ltd., has filled a gap which has been evident to overseas and competition-minded motorists; the new 1,588 c.c. twin overhead camshaft engine will enable the car to compete on equal terms in the 1,300-1,600 c.c. class with Continental-built cars. As described in preceding pages, this engine is a development of the special power unit used in the record-breaking M.G. EX 181.

The new model also has Dunlop 10¾in disc brakes, centre-lock steel wheels and Road Speed tyres, which are not fitted to the standard MGA. The road test car was an open model equipped with hood and side screens and all optionally extra equipment. A coupé version of the car is available.

Powered by the twin carburettor version of the 1½-litre B series engine, the standard MGA coupé is capable of slightly more than 100 m.p.h.; the new 1,600 c.c. unit gives the open car, with hood and side curtains in position, a maximum of 114 m.p.h. It is faster than the 1½-litre car by 7sec to 60 m.p.h., and by 15sec to 90 m.p.h.

The engine starts easily and quickly reaches working temperature. It revs freely, and the limit marking on the tachometer is 7,000 r.p.m.; it was taken up to this limit repeatedly during the test.

Engine vibration was noticed at 2,500 and 5,500 r.p.m.; at maximum speed in top gear the tachometer reading was 6,500 r.p.m., and this was held for approximately 5 miles on a level stretch of *autoroute*.

Power builds up noticeably after the engine tops 3,500 r.p.m.; by the time 4,000 r.p.m. is reached it really takes hold and the little car begins to show its potential performance. In first gear it gets very quickly to 30 m.p.h., and a fast change to second gear is needed to avoid exceeding the rev. limit. The comfortable minimum speed in top is 18-20 m.p.h., and in traffic, second and third gears are most used. In open road cruising, 80-90 m.p.h. can be held indefinitely, with plenty in hand for use when required. The car was quite happy at 100 m.p.h. for long stretches on Continental roads, although to maintain high engine speeds has a marked effect on the fuel consumption, of course,

and above 90 m.p.h. the driver has the feeling that the engine is working much harder.

There is a constant, rather obtrusive background of mechanical noise; most of this can be traced to the valve gear, particularly the tappets, which have a recommended clearance of 0.018in, but there is also a "ring" associated with the first stage of the timing gears. Nor can it be said that the engine is smooth or silky. Exhaust-wise, the car is not objectionable, and it can be driven through city traffic without attracting undue attention. This car had a loose silencer baffle. Carburettor intake noise is not noticeable, although only small flame-trap type air cleaners are fitted.

From the performance and maintenance angles, the MGA has an enthusiast's engine. Many of the ancillary units are not easy to reach, as the underbonnet space is filled by the engine itself. The distributor is located below a camshaft housing (it became covered in oil during the test), and the coil is tucked away under the heater trunking. The oil level dipstick would be easier to replace if its containing tube were a little longer. An oil cooler, which is an optional extra, was mounted in front of the radiator, but no oil temperature gauge was supplied.

All maximum speed and acceleration tests were carried

When the side curtains alone are used, the crew can enjoy fresh air motoring with some measure of protection from draughts. The Twin Cam insignia appears beneath the motif on the tail panel

The hood and side curtains are a snug fit and follow closely the contours of the body. There is no exterior door handle. Three large windows at the back of the hood are made of flexible Vybak. Bumper overriders are standard

out with 100 octane petrol. With this, and Belgian premium petrol (89 research octane rating), the engine tended to "run on" after being switched off. It also used a considerable amount of oil; five pints were added to the sump during one journey of 800 miles, and an overall oil consumption figure of 1,020 m.p.g. was recorded—approximately one quart of oil each time the petrol tank (capacity 10 gallons) was refilled.

Once accustomed to the controls, an experienced driver can get off the mark with very little wheel spin, but it was felt that more suitable gear box ratios would give an even more sparkling getaway, without losing the benefit of easy fast cruising—there is a very noticeable interval between first and second, and between second and third. An owner using the car for circuit racing would, no doubt, prefer a gear box with closer ratios. A 4.55 to 1 axle ratio can be fitted in place of the standard 4.3 to 1 ratio at an extra cost of £10 2s 6d.

Apart from occasional difficulty in selecting first gear when the car is stationary, the gear box is generally pleasant to use. The short, remote control lever has precise movements between the ratios, and very fast changes can be made. One notices a slight difficulty—not uncommon in B-series gear boxes—in getting through the gate transversely, particularly when the gear box is hot. This sometimes makes difficult the change from third into second, and there is a risk that the lever may overshoot into the reverse quadrant. The top of the lever is close to the steering wheel when the latter is set near the facia; it is also well placed in relation to the driving seat. There was no vibration from the transmission, and the axle was silent.

Free from slip during full-bore gear changes, the clutch transmitted the engine power without judder under all conditions. Some adjustment was found necessary to take up pedal movement, but once attended to the need did not recur. Positioning of the pedals is good, although to clear the clutch pedal, the left foot has to be placed beneath it rather than to the left. The accelerator, which is connected to the throttle by a cable, works smoothly, and delicate, progressive control can be achieved.

Among the most delightful features of the MGA are its road-holding and cornering. The manufacturers' well-known motto—Safety Fast—is particularly pertinent to this new model. Changes in road surface have little effect on the manner in which the car sits firmly on the road, and its behaviour on a streaming wet road is equally good, although the tail will swing slightly if the throttle is opened suddenly when cornering. Power can be used judiciously to help the car round a corner, in fact progress on a winding road is all the better if this technique is applied.

There is strong self-centring of the steering, and there is no lost motion to impair its accuracy; from lock to lock requires only 2¾ turns of the wheel, and although the turning circle is greater by 4ft 6in than that of the 1½-litre-engined car, the Twin Cam model can be manœuvred easily in narrow streets.

A slight heaviness in the steering was noticed with the tyres inflated to the normal recommended 18 lb front and 20 lb rear; when pressures were raised by 4 lb sq in, this heaviness disappeared and the ride was not uncomfortable.

With full load, or with the driver only in the car, there is a satisfactory firmness about the suspension, which reaches an excellent compromise in a car which may be called upon to take the owner to work during the week, and yet be driven in races at the weekend. Stability is first class and there is no heeling-over on corners, although brisk progress is marked by excessive tyre squeal; the latest pattern Road Speed tyres were not fitted to the test car.

The driving position is well suited to most drivers, but a person of small stature would be happier with a higher seat cushion. The steering wheel can be set close to the facia by a lock-nut and bolt fitting; in this position of adjustment the driver has fingertip control of the horn button and indicator switch. The thin-rimmed wheel is set at an ideal angle for control, being almost vertical; it does not obscure the instruments.

Fitted to the test car were the competition-type seats, which have a padded roll round the edge of the back rest, and long cushion; they proved most comfortable and provided firm support at a good angle. Driver and passenger are well held when cornering fast, and long distances can be covered without fatigue. The proximity of the engine and gear box can bring about an uncomfortably high temperature around the legs and feet; it is probable that owners in hot climates will call for separate fresh air ventilators. On the other hand the warmth would be appreciated in winter conditions.

All the advantages which this car affords for fast motoring would be wasted if the braking system was not up to the same standards. It is becoming increasingly the practice for 100 m.p.h. cars, whether they are large saloons or agile two-seaters, to be fitted with disc brakes. The Dunlop 10¾in diameter discs fitted to the Twin Cam MGA are adequate to all they are called upon to do in wet or dry. The pedal has a good feel to it, being neither spongy nor too hard, though loads are rather high in normal traffic stops; this is normal with discs, which have no self-servo effect, and is noticeable

A cover encloses the spare wheel, on top of which is strapped the tool kit. The petrol filler has a quick release cap

M.G. Twin Cam MGA . . . .

The polished aluminium covers of the camshaft housings dominate the under-bonnet view

when there is no external servo assistance, as in the case of the MGA. Maximum braking brought the car to a standstill all square, and the brakes could be applied hard when the car was being driven fast on wet roads. There was no noticeable increase in pedal travel after 800 miles of fast driving. The front discs did show signs of scoring, which has not been noticed on other cars.

The parking brake is controlled by a fly-off-pattern lever, in which the button is pressed to lock the brake on. The lever is placed between the transmission cover and the driving seat, and the hand falls readily on it.

At night reasonable use can be made of the car's performance, although more powerful head lamps would be appreciated for speeds close to 100 m.p.h.; the dipped beam did not inconvenience oncoming traffic. The Twin Cam MGA is one of the cars which really do require a hand dipper switch. When driving on the open road at night, one needs two left feet to operate the clutch and the foot dipper, for the driver always seems to need to change gear and alter the light setting at the same moment. The positioning of the pedal and switch are such that the changeover cannot be made on the instant.

Facia instruments are well lit, and the switch is fitted with a rheostat. There is a small map light, with a separate switch on the left side of the facia. Self-parking wipers are fitted, and although they are powerful and silent, they are up against an unusual handicap—in heavy rain, water is blown off the bonnet on to the screen and the wipers have difficulty in clearing it. An owner could perhaps prevent this by fitting a shallow Perspex deflector across the bonnet to deflect the air stream up and over the screen.

With the hood and side curtains erected, the car proved weatherproof except at speeds over 90 m.p.h., when wind pressure tended to lift the hood above the middle of the windscreen; rain found its way in there, and also through the scuttle on to the passenger's legs. Although there were gaps between the windscreen frame and the side screens,

rain did not penetrate here. The hood is comparatively simple to erect and can be folded away neatly behind the seat backrests. A plastic bag, secured to the bodywork behind the seats, provided stowage for the side curtains.

With the hood and side curtains erected, a tall driver has no difficulty in getting into or out of the car, and there is ample headroom. In this condition, the occupants find the interior rather warm, and it was not possible to obtain a flow of cool air through the vent above the gear box cover. A heater—part of the extra equipment—proved amply efficient in the moderate temperatures encountered during the test.

Accommodation for maps and small articles is provided by a deep pocket in each door, but as the doors cannot be locked, it is not advisable to stow valuables in these pockets if the car is left unattended. Only the Twin Cam models and the 1½-litre coupé are supplied with a leather-covered facia. A large proportion of the luggage compartment is occupied by the spare wheel and tool kit, and it is not easy to find room for a large suitcase, but a number of small bags and boxes can be stowed away. If coats and soft travelling bags are fitted in carefully, more can be carried than at first appears likely.

The tool kit includes a starting handle and, surprisingly, an old-fashioned, screw-type lifting jack. Two 6-volt batteries are located just forward of the rear axle; to service them the spare wheel and a panel in the floor behind the seats must be removed. The high-pressure electric fuel pump is close to the battery on the right side of the frame. Nine lubrication points require grease gun attention every 1,000 miles.

In the road test of the 1½-litre MGA coupé it was stated in summary that the car was capable of holding its own against more powerful vehicles; this applies even more markedly to the 1,600 c.c. Twin Cam model. The extra performance is matched by the road-holding, steering and brakes, and this car maintains the M.G. tradition of good looks coupled with a very fine performance.

Left: Competition seats, an optional extra, are contoured to give extra support in cornering, and under the thighs. Right: This is a functional facia, with neat, easily read dials. The main switches come quickly to hand. The steering wheel is shown in its nearest adjustment to the facia. The plated support on the left of the windscreen forms a useful grab handle for the passenger

ENGINE

No. of cylinders	...	4 in line
Bore and stroke	...	75.4 x 88.9 mm (2.97 x 3.5in)
Displacement	...	1,588 c.c. (96.91 cu in)
Valve position	...	Twin O.H.C. Hemispherical combustion chamber
Compression ratio	...	9.9 to 1
Max. b.h.p. (nett)	...	108 at 6,700 r.p.m.
Max. b.m.e.p. (nett)	...	163 lb sq in at 4,500 c p.m.
Max. torque (nett)	...	104 lb ft at 4,500 r.p.m.
Carburettors	...	Twin 1¾in dia S.U. type H.6
Fuel pump	...	S.U. high pressure
Tank capacity	...	10 Imp. gallons (37.8 litres)
Sump capacity	...	12 pints max. (5.7 litres)
		7½ pints min. (3.6 litres)
Oil filter	...	Full flow
Cooling system	...	Pump, fan and thermostat
Battery	...	12 volt, 51 ampère hour

TRANSMISSION

Clutch	...	B and B. 8in dia single dry plate
Gear box	...	4 speeds and reverse, synchromesh on top, 3rd and 2nd. Central lever
Overall ratios	...	Top 4.30; 3rd 5.91; 2nd 9.52; 1st 15.65; reverse 20.47 to 1.
Final drive	...	Hypoid bevel, 4.3 to 1.

CHASSIS

Brakes	...	Dunlop disc. Hydraulic operation. Mechanical calipers for hand brake on rear wheels

Disc dia, pad width	...	10¾in outside dia (2½ x 1⅜in pads)
Suspension: front	...	Independent, coil springs and wishbones
rear		Live axle, half-elliptic leaf springs
Dampers: front	...	Armstrong in unit with wishbone pivots
rear		Armstrong lever arm, chassis-mounted
Wheels	...	Dunlop centre-lock steel disc type
Tyre size	...	5.90—15in Dunlop R.S.4
Steering	...	Rack and pinion
Steering wheel	...	16½in dia four spoke
Turns, lock to lock	...	2¼

DIMENSIONS

Wheelbase	...	7ft 10in (239 cm)
Track: front	...	3ft 11.9in (121 cm)
rear	...	4ft 0.87in (124 cm)
Overall length	...	13ft (396 cm)
Overall width	...	4ft 10in (147 cm)
Overall height	...	4ft 2in (127 cm)
Ground clearance	...	6in (15 cm)
Turning circle	...	31ft 4in (9.55 m)
Kerb weight	...	2,156 lb (19¼ cwt) (977 kg)

PERFORMANCE DATA

Top gear m.p.h. per 1,000 r.p.m.	...	17.3
Torque lb ft per cu in engine capacity		1.083
Brake surface area swept by linings	...	494.8 sq in
Weight distribution (dry)	...	F, 54.6 per cent
		R, 45.4 per cent

M.G. TWIN CAM MGA

WHEELBASE	7' 10"
FRONT TRACK	3' 11⅞"
REAR TRACK	4' 0⅞"
OVERALL LENGTH	13' 0"
OVERALL WIDTH	4' 10"
OVERALL HEIGHT	4' 2"

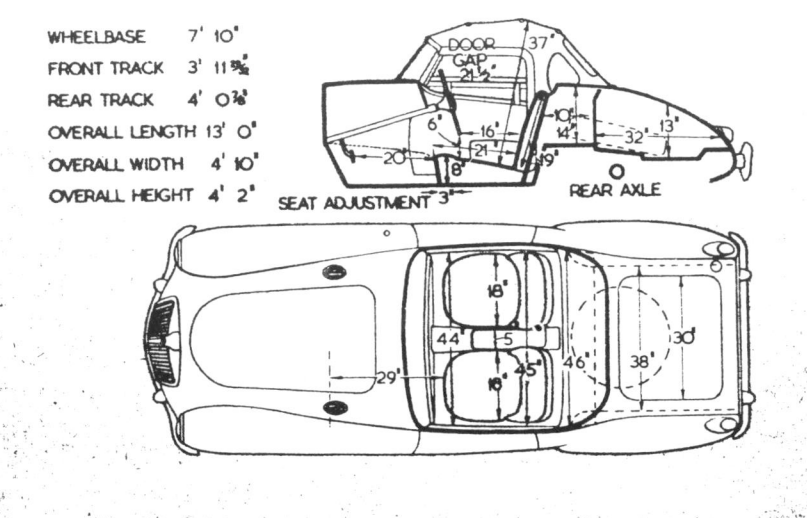

Scale ¼in to 1ft. Driving seat in central position. Cushions uncompressed

━━━ DATA ━━━

PRICE (basic), with two-seater body, £843.
British purchase tax, £422 17s.
Total (in Great Britain), **£1,265 17s.**

Extras:	£	s	d
Screen washer	3	0	0
Heater	18	7	6
Adjustable steering column	3	0	0
Oil cooler	13	10	0
Competition seats	9	18	9
Twin horns	2	1	3

ENGINE: Capacity, 1,588 c.c. (96.91 cu in).
Number of cylinders, 4.
Bore and stroke, 75.4 × 88.9 mm (2.97 × 3.5in).
Valve gear, twin overhead camshafts.
Compression ratio, 9.9 to 1.
B.H.P. 108 (nett) at 6,700 r.p.m. (B.H.P. per ton laden 96.5).
Torque, 104 lb ft at 4,500 r.p.m.
M.P.H. per 1,000 r.p.m. in top gear, 17.3

WEIGHT: (with 5 gals. fuel), 19¼ cwt (2,156 lb).
Distribution (per cent): F, 53.9; R, 46.1.
Laden as tested, 22½ cwt (2,506 lb).
Lb per c.c. (laden), 1.6.

BRAKES: Type, Dunlop disc.
Method of operation, hydraulic.
Disc diameter: F, 10½in; R, 10¾in.
Lining swept area: F, 247.4 sq in; R, 247.4 sq in.

TYRES: 5.90—15in.
Pressures (lb sq in); F, 18; R, 20 (normal).
F, 22; R, 24 (fast driving).

TANK CAPACITY: 10 Imperial gallons.
Oil sump, 12 pints.
Cooling system, 13⅝ pints (plus 1 pint if heater fitted).

STEERING: Turning circle, 32ft 6in.
Between kerbs, 31ft 4in.
Between walls, 33ft 5in.
Turns of steering wheel from lock to lock, 2¼.

DIMENSIONS: Wheelbase, 7ft 10in.
Track: F, 3ft 11⅞in; R, 4ft 0⅞in.
Length (overall), 13ft.
Height, 4ft 2in.
Width, 4ft 10in.
Ground clearance, 6in.
Frontal area, 13.8 sq ft (approximately).

ELECTRICAL SYSTEM: 12-volt; 51 ampère-hour battery.
Head lamps, Double dip; 50–40 watt bulbs.

SUSPENSION: Front, independent, coil spring and wishbones. Rear, half-elliptic leaf springs with live axle.

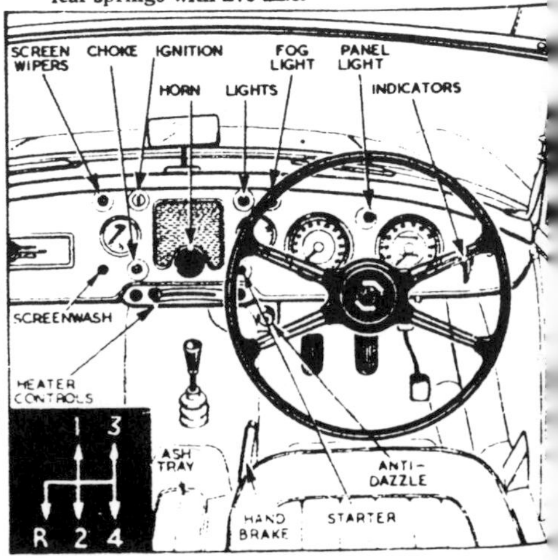

━━━ PERFORMANCE ━━━

ACCELERATION:
Speed Range, Gear Ratios and Time in sec.

	4.30	5.91	9.52	15.65
M.P.H.	to 1	to 1	to 1	to 1
10—30	—	—	4.5	3.3
20—40	11.0	7.1	4.5	—
30—50	10.2	7.4	4.9	—
40—60	10.5	7.5	—	—
50—70	11.7	7.6	—	—
60—80	11.7	8.9	—	—
70—90	13.6	—	—	—
80—100	18.7	—	—	—

From rest through gears to:

M.P.H.			sec.
30	..	..	4.3
40	..	..	6.9
50	..	..	9.4
60	..	..	13.3
70	..	..	17.3
80	..	..	22.5
90	..	..	30.0
100	..	..	41.1

Standing quarter mile, 18.6 sec.

MAXIMUM SPEEDS ON GEARS:

Gear		M.P.H.	K.P.H.
Top ..	(mean)	113.5	182.7
	(best)	114.0	183.5
3rd ..	..	86	138
2nd ..	..	53	85
1st ..	..	32	51

TRACTIVE EFFORT:

	Pull (lb per ton)	Equivalent Gradient
Top ..	..	232	1 in 9.6
Third ..	..	315	1 in 7.0
Second ..	..	486	1 in 4.5

SPEEDOMETER CORRECTION: M.P.H.

Car speedometer:	10	20	30	40	50	60	70	80	90	100	110	114
True speed:	11	20	28.5	38.5	48	58	69	80	91	101	112	114

BRAKES (at 30 m.p.h. in neutral)

Pedal load in lb	Retardation	Equivalent stopping distance in ft
25	0.45g	67.2
50	0.62g	48.7
75	0.81g	37.4
90	0.92g	32.8

FUEL CONSUMPTION:
M.P.G. at steady speeds

M.P.H.	Direct Top
30	42.4
40	40.0
50	35.6
60	31.7
70	27.4
80	23.6
90	20.2
100	18.1

Overall fuel consumption for 1,117 miles, 21.8 m.p.g. (12.9 litres per 100 km).

Approximate normal range 18–30 m.p.g. (15.7–9.4 litres per 100 km).

Fuel: Super premium.

TEST CONDITIONS: Weather: overcast, raining. Slight breeze. Acceleration and braking tests on dry surface.

Air temperature, 55–65 deg F.

Acceleration figures are the means of several runs in opposite directions.

Tractive effort obtained by Tapley meter.

Typically British, this new MGA will almost certainly be as popular in foreign markets as the previous models

IN the tradition of maintaining the breed, the new M.G. MGA 1600 is a direct successor to the MGA which, in its comparatively short existence, has become one of the most popular sports cars not only in England but also abroad. Indeed, as a dollar earner there are few cars which have done better. This new MGA is virtually identical except for an increase in engine capacity, the adoption of disc brakes at the front, and minor restyling attention to the body, including little 1600 motifs secured at either side near the bonnet louvres and on the boot lid.

With an engine capacity of 1,588 c.c. in place of 1,489 c.c., the gross power has been raised from 72 b.h.p. at 5,500 r.p.m. to 79.5 b.h.p. at 5,600 r.p.m. The effect of this increase is apparent as soon as one starts to drive the car, and there is no need of a stop-watch for evidence of the enhanced performance. Acceleration figures have improved over those of the previous model, and this is particularly noticeable in top gear at the higher cruising speeds. The figure for 50-70 m.p.h. in top gear has improved by almost 2sec, and the 60-80 m.p.h. figure by over 3sec. The car is capable of holding a genuine 100 m.p.h., but after several flat-out laps on a high-speed circuit it was noticed that the oil pressure was gradually dropping.

At 80 m.p.h., which appears very quickly on the quite accurate speedometer, the car moves happily at a natural and comfortable gait. There was a tendency for the engine of the test car to become rough and to vibrate at about 5,000 r.p.m., but if the throttle pedal was held down this disappeared as engine speed continued to mount. Members of the staff with experience of the previous MGA feel the more powerful engine to be rather more noisy and harsh. This is unlikely to deter the true sports car enthusiast; nor is the exhaust note. While not obtrusive at lower engine speeds, at 4,000 r.p.m. and above it is, perhaps, a little loud for town use, although the occupants of the car do not suffer from this so much as onlookers.

One of the greatest advantages of the new MGA is that the increased power has improved the flexibility of the engine, and where previously one had to use first and second while crawling in heavy traffic, one can now employ second and third gears quite comfortably. In fact, it was found that the car would pull away from under 10 m.p.h. in top gear, though, of course, it is unlikely that any driver of this type of car would do so.

One has to pay a price for these various benefits in a slightly greater fuel consumption—24 m.p.g. overall for the 1,590 miles of the test. A gentle touring consumption which involved keeping the speed below 60 m.p.h. and avoiding high engine speeds in the intermediate gears returned a figure better than 31 m.p.g. During the test the car used three pints of engine oil, and the radiator needed considerable topping-up on two occasions.

When the car was delivered, the gear box proved to be extremely stiff; quite often it was necessary to employ both hands to engage reverse gear, and more effort than expected was required to select the other gears. Towards the end of the test, however, the movement had freed itself quite considerably, and it was obvious that in a thousand miles or so this would be a pleasant box to manipulate. Ratios are the same as those on the 1500 MGA, and one gained the impression that this car could have coped adequately with a slightly higher final drive ratio. Smooth to operate, the hydraulically actuated clutch could contend comfortably with violent acceleration from a standstill with a minimum of slip.

While our previous experience of the MGA left us in

Increased in capacity by 82 c.c. and in power by 7.5 b.h.p., the 1600 MGA engine appears identical with its predecessor

Sleek, attractive lines of the MGA are not affected by the minor body alterations. Wire wheels and whitewall tyres are optional extras

slight doubt about the adequacy of the brakes relative to maximum performance, there is no doubt that the brakes of the 1600 are of a very high standard indeed. With Lockheed discs on the front and 10in drums on the rear, the car can be stopped repeatedly from its high cruising speeds very quickly without any trace of fade or loss of directional stability. For a maximum retardation stop a fair amount of pedal pressure is needed, but a mean efficiency of 98 per cent, without any tendency for the wheels to lock, is highly commendable. The comparatively high pedal loads arise because the braking system is not provided with servo assistance. The hand brake, of the fly-off type, is also powerful and held the car without trouble on a 1 in 3 gradient, from which incline the car moved away with plenty of power in hand.

By modern standards the suspension must be considered firm; on smooth roads this is, of course, no disadvantage, and the car could be really hurtled into corners, when it would go round with minimum fuss, sitting squarely on the road and feeling very safe and controllable during the whole performance. This did not apply on rougher surfaces, however, and a feeling that the wheels were hopping and jumping, accompanied by intermittent tyre squeal, indicated that the tyres were not maintaining full contact with the road. With standard tyre pressures there was some oversteer, but an increase in the rear pressures reduced this to a bare trace at the sacrifice of a little ride comfort. The steering—rack and pinion—had little self-centring action, but was commendably direct and precise. A degree of road shock was transmitted to the driver through the steering.

Body alterations centre round the restyling of the side, tail and turn indicator lights in order to bring them into conformity with new regulations in this country. The flasher lights on the front have been coloured amber, while at the rear the wing light units have been changed so that the turn indicators and rear lights are separate.

Side screens are now of the sliding panel type, and the manufacturers claim that these, with the hood up, give as much protection as a saloon car body. During the period that this car was on test the weather remained very fine and sunny, so that it was never possible to ascertain if rain would enter through the largish gap between the body and the leading lower edge of the side screen. A series of pastel shades of paintwork is available for the 1600; the test car was finished in an attractive beige called Alamo.

Since no alterations have been made to the interior, much of what had been said before still applies—the space provided inside is still cramped for a car of its dimensions. Well upholstered, leather-trimmed seats give moderately good support, and only for a very slim person is there any possibility of being insufficiently braced. A grab handle, incorporated in the windscreen mount, is provided for the passenger. An average-sized person found that he needed the driving seat in the fully back position to be comfortable, so that even with an adjustable steering wheel a tall person never seemed really at home in the driving position, his arms being bent considerably at the elbow. A fairly tall driver, however, has the advantage that his view of the nearside wing is unobscured by the centrally mounted driving mirror. Gear change lever and handbrake are conveniently placed, but the facia-mounted horn button—old M.G. practice—is not always found when needed suddenly. Also it is unusual today to find the ignition switch not incorporated with the starter control.

Mounted rather high, the dip switch needed a full stretch of the foot to operate, and the main beam warning light was obscured by the steering wheel. For normal cruising speeds the head lamps are entirely adequate, but if one were in a hurry more powerful beams would be desirable. The commodious door pockets are entirely adequate for all the odds and ends that normally find their way into motor cars, but it is a pity when manufacturers do not provide in an open car which cannot be locked up, a thief-proof facia compartment. On the M.G. this facia space was occupied by a radio; although pleasant at town speeds, the

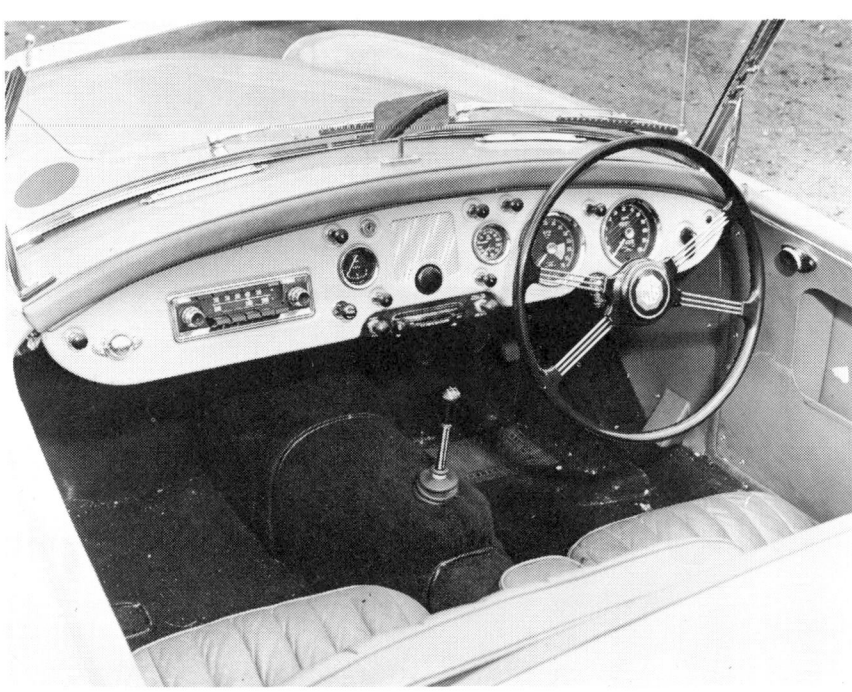

Instruments on the facia include speedometer, rev counter, water thermometer, oil pressure gauge and fuel gauge. On the extreme left there is a map-reading light

set became practically inaudible as one accelerated away from speed limits. Wind noise on this car was marked when in open form, but became an irritating roar with the hood up; in the latter trim, visibility was not greatly restricted.

One person can erect the hood, but it is much easier for two; even then it is wise to anticipate rain if one is not to get wet. With hood and sidescreens stowed behind the seats it was rather difficult to reach the boot catch. Much of the small boot capacity is taken up by the spare wheel and tool roll—a flattish suitcase and an air travel bag are about the limit for stowable baggage, and they would have to be taken out to get to the spare wheel.

A quick glance beneath the bonnet would not encourage the private owner to carry out minor adjustments himself, but in fact most of the components which might need servicing or adjustment are fairly accessible.

The M.G., with its powerful, responsive engine, combined with a moderately heavy but low-slung chassis, adequate steering and superlative brakes, and without any little vices or unpredictable traits in behaviour, maintains the traditional high standards of performance and safety of the marque.

M.G. MGA 1600

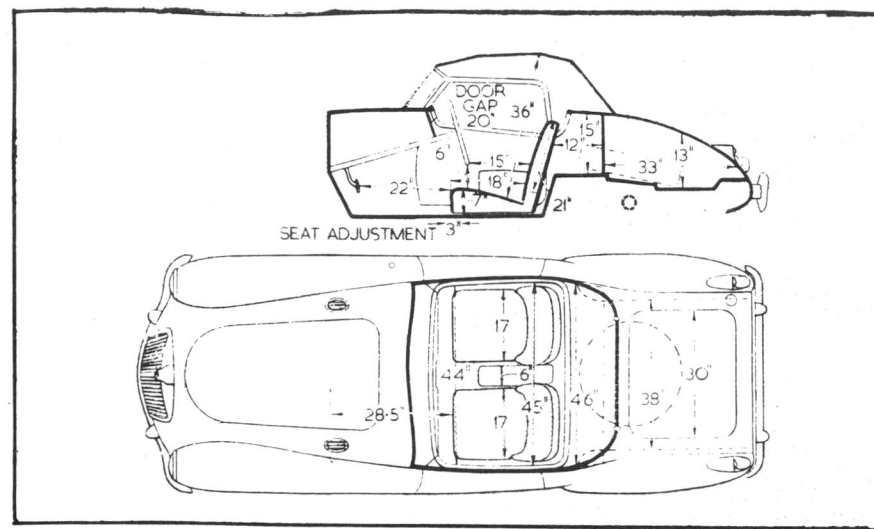

Scale ⅛in to 1ft. Driving seat in central position. Cushions uncompressed.

DATA

PRICE (basic), with two seater body and hood, **£663.**
British purchase tax, £277 7s 6d.
Total (in Great Britain), £940 7s 6d.
Extras: Radio £24 5s (£34 7s 1d with tax).
 Heater £12 5s (£17 7s 1d with tax).
 Windscreen washer £2 (£2 16s 8d with tax).

ENGINE: Capacity, 1,588 c.c. (96.9 cu in).
Number of cylinders, 4.
Bore and stroke, 75.39 × 88.9 mm (2.968 × 3.5in).
Valve gear, o.h.v. pushrods.
Compression ratio, 8.3 to 1.
B.h.p. 79.5 (gross) at 5,600 r.p.m. (b.h.p. per ton laden 75.3).
Torque, 87lb ft at 3,800 r.p.m.
M.p.h. per 1,000 r.p.m. in top gear, 17.16.

WEIGHT: (With 5 gals fuel), 18.12 cwt (2,030lb).
Weight distribution (per cent): F, 53, R, 47.
Laden as tested, 21.12 cwt (2,366 lb).
Lb per c.c. (laden), 1.49.

BRAKES: Type, Lockheed. F, Discs. R, Drums.
Method of operation, hydraulic.
Drum dimensions: 10in diameter; 1.75in wide.
Disc diameter, 11in.
Swept area: F, 240 sq in; R, 110 sq in.

TYRES: 5.60—15in.
Pressures (lb sq in): F, 17; R, 20 (normal).
F, 21; R, 24 (fast driving).

TANK CAPACITY: 10 Imp. gallons.
Oil sump, 8 pints (including filter).
Cooling system, 10 pints (plus 0.65 pint if heater fitted).

DIMENSIONS: Wheelbase, 7ft 10in.
Track: F, 3ft 11.5in; R, 4ft 0.75in.
Length (overall), 13ft.
Width, 4ft 10in.
Height, 4ft 2in.
Ground clearance, 6in.
Frontal area, 13.77 sq ft (approximately) (hood up).

ELECTRICAL SYSTEM: 12-volt: two 6-volt, 58 ampère-hour batteries.
Head lights: Double dip; 50—40 watt bulbs.

SUSPENSION: Front, coil springs.
Rear, semi-elliptic leaf springs.

PERFORMANCE

ACCELERATION (mean):

Speed range, Gear Ratios and Time in Sec.

m.p.h.	4.3 to 1	5.91 to 1	9.52 to 1	15.65 to 1
10—30	—	8.7	4.7	—
20—40	11.0	7.8	4.6	—
30—50	10.9	6.9	—	—
40—60	10.5	7.5	—	—
50—70	11.9	8.3	—	—
60—80	13.2	—	—	—
70—90	17.0	—	—	—

From rest through gears to:

30 m.p.h.	..	4.6 sec.
40 ,,	..	6.7 ,,
50 ,,	..	10.3 ,,
60 ,,	..	14.2 ,,
70 ,,	..	18.5 ,,
80 ,,	..	26.6 ,,
90 ,,	..	36.4 ,,

Standing quarter mile, 19.3 sec.

MAXIMUM SPEEDS ON GEARS:

Gear			m.p.h.	k.p.h.
Top	..	(mean)	100.9	162.4
		(best)	101.4	163.2
3rd	..	..	77.0	123.9
2nd	..	..	46.0	74.0
1st	..	..	27.0	43.4

TEST CONDITIONS: Weather: dry, overcast. 5-15 m.p.h. wind.
Air temperature: 69 deg. F.

BRAKES (at 30 m.p.h. in neutral):

Pedal load in lb	Retardation	Equivalent stopping distance in ft
25	0.22g	137
50	0.42g	70
75	0.74g	41
94	0.98g	30.8

FUEL CONSUMPTION:

Steady speeds in top

30 m.p.h.	40.0 m.p.g.
40 ,,	36.3 ,,
50 ,,	33.3 ,,
60 ,,	30.7 ,,
70 ,,	28.5 ,,
80 ,,	26.0 ,,
90 ,,	22.3 ,,

Overall fuel consumption for 1,590 miles, 24.1 m.p.g. (11.72 litres per 100 km).
Approximate normal range 24-31 m.p.g. (11.7-9.2 litres per 100 km).
Fuel: Premium grade.

TRACTIVE EFFORT (by Tapley meter):

			Pull (lb per ton)	Equivalent Gradient
Top	..	..	245	1 in 9.1
Third	..	..	345	1 in 6.4
Second	..	..	550	1 in 3.9

STEERING: Turning circle.
Between kerbs, L, 31ft 2¾in, R, 31ft 5in.
Between walls, L, 32ft 8in, R, 33ft.
Turns of steering wheel, lock to lock, 2¾.

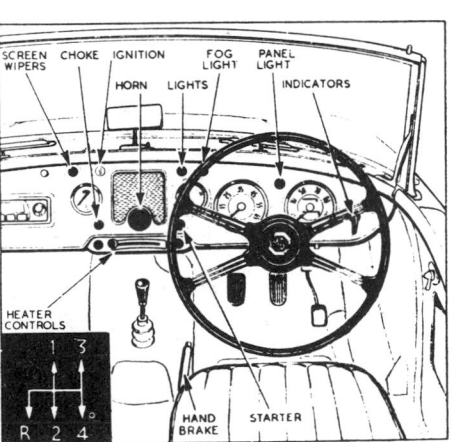

SPEEDOMETER CORRECTION: M.P.H.

Car speedometer:	10	20	30	40	50	60	70	80	90	100
True speed:	11	20	30	39	49	59	68	77	87	97

Published *The Autocar,* 18 August 1961

The Autocar road tests

M.G. MIDGET

An M.G. badge is incorporated in the radiator grille, and there is a central chromed flash on the bonnet

SINCE the new M.G. Midget was introduced at the end of June, the Chancellor's tax adjustments have increased the U.K. total price by some £20; yet it remains within the £700 bracket. At this price it is still good value as a thoroughly well-planned and soundly constructed little car, and promises to regain the popularity won by its pre-war predecessors. It is no secret that the car is in effect a luxury version of the Austin-Healey Sprite II, and is thus £30 dearer with tax.

Mechanical dissimilarities are few, and the differences in performance between the Midget and the Sprite II (which we tested on 2 June) must be attributed to variations of tune, and mileage run since new by the test cars. Throughout the speed range, the Midget accelerated slightly faster in any given gear, and showed a saving of 3sec, for example, from 60 to 80 m.p.h. in top. In acceleration from rest, some of this advantage was lost by a clutch which was not ideal

for rapid take-offs. It took up the drive rather abruptly over a small part of the long and largely ineffective pedal travel, pulling engine revs below the point of maximum torque. Attempts to slip the clutch during rapid getaways resulted in clutch spin, which also prevented the car from restarting on a 1-in-3 test gradient.

Starting was always immediate, and there was no need for the choke in mild weather. After the car has stood for more than half-an-hour or so, the engine is often a little reluctant to pull straight away; this hesitance disappears rapidly as the engine warms up in the first few hundred yards, and acceleration is then crisp and responsive.

One is immediately impressed by the smoothness of the Midget's power unit. Normally the rev counter needle is held between 2,000 and 4,000 r.p.m. on the open road, but 5,000 r.p.m. may be used without roughness or excess noise from the engine. A noticeable surge of power is felt at 2,500 r.p.m. There was a noticeable engine period between 5,000 and 5,500 r.p.m., it became smooth again up to the valve bounce speed of 6,500 r.p.m. At this speed the unit remained sweet and smooth, so that a watchful eye had to be kept on the rev counter, which is standard equipment. On this an orange warning band starts at 5,500 r.p.m. and changes to red at 6,000 r.p.m.; the calibration extends to 7,000 r.p.m.

An intelligent choice of gear ratios enables full advantage to be taken of the wide span of engine power. When making a fast getaway there is a logical progression through the gears, and after reaching peak revs in bottom and second a useful range of acceleration remains in the subsequent gear. Second is particularly useful up to 45 m.p.h. for spurting past slow-moving traffic, and allows up to 50 m.p.h. Yet the docile behaviour of the engine at low revs enables the car to pull away from a walking pace in second gear.

In third gear the most practical range extends from about 25 m.p.h. to 60 m.p.h., with a 70 m.p.h. maximum in reserve. Complementing these excellent gear ratios are the

Under-bonnet accessibility is fair, although the compartment is unusually crowded on the Midget. The dipstick is below the sparking plug leads

Large amber winking indicators blend neatly with the stop and tail lamps. The rear side-screen panel is slipped forward to give access to the interior as there are no outside handles

ease and speed with which changes can be made, for the lever can be snatched from one position to the next almost as quickly as the hand can move. For fast upward changes the synchromesh cannot always quite cope, especially if the lever is pulled smartly from bottom to second. Distinctive but unobtrusive gear whine is audible in all the indirects. The gear lever is placed conveniently only a few inches from the driver's left hand on the steering wheel, and its knob is of hard plastic, insulated with rubber.

Bearing in mind the engine's willingness to rev, top gear gives just the right combination of liveliness with high-speed cruising, the road speed being just over 60 m.p.h. at 4,000 r.p.m. The fastest speed reached with the Midget was 86 m.p.h. at 5,600 r.p.m., when the engine is nowhere near the point of "running out of revs." The theoretical maximum, based on the engine's safe rev limit, would be just short of 100 m.p.h.

Factors tending to dissuade one from taking full advantage of the car's abilities were a marked increase in noise above 70 m.p.h., accompanied on this example by vibration, apparently from the transmission. The most comfortable and restful cruising rate is around 60 m.p.h., and the fuel consumption figures at constant speeds show that 60 m.p.h. is relatively economical, for at a steady 70 m.p.h. 10 miles fewer are averaged per gallon. If faster speeds are sustained, as when the car was held at 80 m.p.h. and above for long periods on M1, the oil pressure drops rapidly from its normal 60 p.s.i. maximum to nearer 40 p.s.i. Three pints of oil were consumed in 1,037 test miles, equivalent to nearly 3,000 m.p.g. At the higher speeds also, slight final drive whine was heard.

As for fuel consumption, the best figure obtained was 48·5 m.p.g. on a main road run with restrained use of the performance, but this figure dropped to 34·1 m.p.g. when the same 20-mile stretch of road was covered as fast as the car would go. In city traffic and at sustained high speeds consumption naturally increases, giving the overall figure of 33·4 m.p.g. for the entire test, but any owner in search of economy will have no difficulty in exceeding 40 m.p.g. with the Midget.

The 948 c.c. engine has a compression ratio of 9-to-1, and needs to be run on super premium grades of fuel. The lower compression ratio of 8·3-to-1 is optional to suit normal premium grades of petrol, and any increase in consumption resulting from this would probably be recovered in reduced petrol costs; performance, naturally, would be a little lower. The fuel tank holds only six gallons, so that frequent refuelling is necessary when the car is driven hard.

Directional stability of the Midget at speed is much affected by cross winds, and frequent correction is necessary to maintain a straight course. This characteristic is made less troublesome than it would be otherwise by the excellent precision of the rack-and-pinion steering. The control is completely free from lost movement, and with 2¼ turns of the wheel between the extremes of acceptably wide steering locks, it requires only small or even imperceptible move-

A padded roll runs along the top of the facia. Roomy pockets for maps and oddments are fitted to the inside of both doors. Right: Both seats tilt forward to give access to the rear compartment in which a seat cushion is an optional extra. An ashtray is also available at 7s 9d extra

M.G. Midget

With the hood in place instead of the hardtop the Midget uses the same sidescreens as are fitted to the Austin-Healey Sprite, but the car is still identifiable in this view by the full-length rubbing strip and "MG Midget" motifs on the luggage locker lid

ments of the wheel to control the car on a straight road.

When cornering the basic characteristic of the car is to oversteer, as a result of the rear wheel steering effect of the back axle, which is suspended on quarter-elliptic leaf springs. A newcomer to the car may find at first that the Midget corners unexpectedly sharply, but the handling is never vicious, and in a short time he is able to throw the Midget round corners taking full advantage of the responsive steering to correct any tendency for the tail of the car to move outwards. On winding country lanes and cross-country routes this little M.G. is really at home.

During the test some increase in travel of the brake pedal was noticed, and there was always a rather dead feel to the brakes. However, they do have a good reserve of stopping power, and fade does not occur in normal use. Pedal pressures required are fairly high, but although there is room for improvement in this respect, the driver is soon reassured that if he presses hard on the pedal the car will stop rapidly. The handbrake is controlled by a chromed pull-up lever to the left of the transmission tunnel and held the car without difficulty on the 1-in-3 test hill. The pedals are well-placed and allow easy simultaneous use of the brake and throttle.

Acceptably Soft Suspension

Extremely good bump absorption is provided by the suspension, which is softer than its layout would suggest. On secondary or badly surfaced city roads the car sits down well and does not jolt its occupants. On rough *pavé* the limited vertical wheel travel begins to tell, and the rear suspension bottoms violently on bump stops which seem to be too small.

Severe humps in the road naturally result in some firm upward movement, and when tall drivers were at the wheel they found their heads were near enough to the hardtop for them to hit it as the car bounced.

The stylish and well-made, glass-fibre hardtop with plastic interior linings may be fitted or removed single-handed in a matter of minutes. However, with the hardtop, side-screens different from those supplied with the standard hood are necessary. As the total cost of the hardtop and side-screens is some £73, including purchase tax, when they are ordered with the new car, most owners will probably be content with the basic p.v.c. hood as all-the-year-round weather protection. Purchase tax on the hardtop kit is not payable if it is ordered after delivery of the car, and the price is then £50.

The draught-sealing with the hood in place is about as satisfactory as one may ever hope for in a car with detachable sidescreens, and a particularly good seal is made by the rubber surrounds. The sidescreens have light alloy frames with double sliding Perspex windows allowing opening for ventilation at both front and rear. The hood fit is also good, and a metal bar sewn into the leading edge ensures a perfect overlap joint at the top of the windscreen, while the strut springs can be locked, and then released

The toolkit comprises a side-lifting jack, a wheelbrace, and a socket spanner for the sparking plugs. Storage bags are provided for the hood

when the hood is in position. When not in use the struts separate like tent poles at the centre and fold away into a bag for stowage in the luggage locker. At above 70 m.p.h. wind pressure causes the leading edge of the sidescreens to bow out.

A generously large luggage locker is provided with an exterior lockable handle—an important point since the car doors do not lock. Although the spare wheel lies flat in the centre of the boot floor there is ample room around it for carefully packed luggage. At the forward end of the compartment some space is lost when the folded hood is stowed in the bag provided. The boot is held open by a swivelling prop which proved annoyingly clumsy.

Visibility is particularly good, and the driver sits high enough to see over the steering wheel and scuttle without difficulty, and with both front wings and the bonnet in sight. The windscreen pillars are slender and offer little or no obstruction to visibility even when the car is closed. To the rear of the windscreens with the hood in place, vision is better than when the hardtop is fitted, as rear quarter windows are incorporated in the hood.

Self-parking wipers have blades as long as allowed by the depth of the windscreen, but a large portion is left unswept at both ends. The interior mirror is mounted too low and vibrates; for safety's sake we added a suction-fitting interior mirror to the screen of the test car.

Well-upholstered seats are adjustable fore-and-aft, and covered in black p.v.c. with a red-painted car. The cushion is comfortable and the backrest provides good lateral support, but it is too firm at the top, and tends to make the occupants slump forward; more support is needed in the small of the back. The occasional rear seat fitted to the test car costs £4 5s, and is adequate for two children if the adults have their seats well forward to provide rear legroom. The floor and gearbox housing are covered with dark moulded rubber flecked with red. Carpet is used behind the seats and, for protection, on the lower portions of the folding seat backrests. Both front floor mats are readily removable.

A plain but functional instrument layout is provided, with the main rev counter and speedometer on either side of the steering column. A fuel gauge is on the right, and a combined oil pressure gauge and coolant thermometer is fitted on the left, where it is partly masked by the driver's left hand on the steering wheel. Provision of a trip mileometer in the speedometer is particularly welcome. The steering wheel and column surround adjoining the facia are of yellowy

plastic material somewhat out of keeping with the character of the rest of the car.

Tumbler switches are used for the wipers and for the lamps, which are the latest sealed-reflector and filament pattern. They give ample main beam illumination for the speed potential of the Midget, and have a generously long reach on dipped beam without dazzling oncoming drivers. A switch similar to that for the lamps is mounted centrally on the facia to control the winking indicators. They are not self-cancelling, but a bright warning lamp is fitted above the steering wheel boss.

Twin windtone horns fitted to the test car are a specially desirable extra, priced at £1 12s 1d including tax. A fresh-air heater is another practically essential optional fitting, and costs £17 10s with tax. This was also among the £116 worth of accessories on the Midget tested, and gave a good flow of air through inlets with cut-off flaps to either side of the engine bulkhead. An overriding air control is fitted on the facia, and a tap on the engine allows the hot water supply to be turned off for the summer. There is no provision for a reversing lamp to be fitted. Twelve grease points require attention every 1,000 miles.

This new M.G. is an endearing little car with a remarkable capacity for nipping about among heavy traffic. It is easy and safe to drive, and certainly is approaching the ideal for the market which it is intended to serve.

M.G. MIDGET

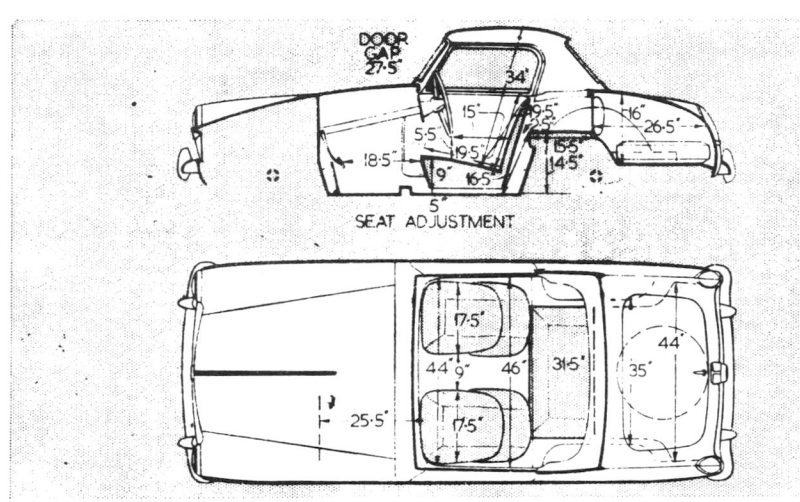

Scale ⅛in. to 1ft. Driving seat in central position. Cushions uncompressed.

---------------- PERFORMANCE ----------------

ACCELERATION TIMES (mean):

Speed range, Gear Ratios and Time in Sec.

m.p.h.	4·22 to 1	5·73 to 1	8·09 to 1	13·5 to 1
10—30	—	10·1	6·3	—
20—40	13·3	8·6	6·2	—
30—50	14·1	9·5	7·1	—
40—60	15·7	11·2	—	—
50—70	17·9	16·5	—	—
60—80	28·6	—	—	—

From rest through gears to:

30 m.p.h.	..	6·3 sec.
40 ,,	..	9·4 ,,
50 ,,	..	14·4 ,,
60 ,,	..	20·2 ,,
70 ,,	..	32·8 ,,
80 ,,	..	56·8 ,,

Standing quarter mile 21·9 sec.

MAXIMUM SPEEDS ON GEARS:

Gear			m.p.h.	k.p.h.
Top	..	(mean)	84·7	136
		(best)	86	138·4
3rd	..	..	70	112
2nd	..	..	50	81
1st	..	..	30	48

TRACTIVE EFFORT (by Tapley meter):

		Pull (lb per ton)	Equivalent gradient
Top	..	180	1 in 12·4
Third	..	240	1 in 10·8
Second	..	350	1 in 15·8

BRAKES (at 30 m.p.h. in neutral):

Pedal load in lb	Retardation	Equiv. stopping distance in ft
25	0·16g	187
50	0·39g	77
75	0·92g	32·8

FUEL CONSUMPTION (at steady speeds in top gear):

30 m.p.h.		51·6 m.p.g.
40 ,,		54·8 ,,
50 ,,		47·2 ,,
60 ,,		43·0 ,,
70 ,,		33·8 ,,

Overall fuel consumption for 1,037 miles, 33·4 m.p.g. (8·4 litres per 100 km.).
Approximate normal range 32-34 m.p.g. (8·8-5·9 litres per 100 km.).
Fuel: Super Premium.

TEST CONDITIONS: Weather: dry; sunny intervals, 10 m.p.h. wind gusting to 25 m.p.h.
Air temperature, 68 deg. F.

STEERING: Turning circle:
Between kerbs, L, 30ft 0in. R, 30ft 3in.
Between walls, L, 31ft 5in. R, 31ft 8in.
Turns of steering wheel from lock to lock, 2.25.

SPEEDOMETER CORRECTION: m.p.h.

Car speedometer	..	..	..	10	20	30	40	50	60	70	80
True speed	..	..	..	10	19	29	40	50	60	70	80

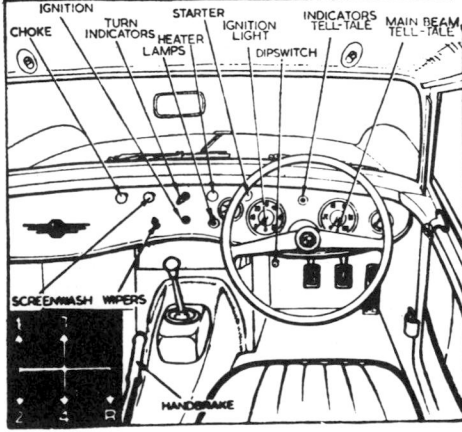

Published *Autocar*, 26 October 1962

M.G. MGB 1800 1,798 c.c.

WHATEVER the diehard enthusiast may say to the contrary, and however hard the traditionalist may cling to a superseded model, there is no doubt that the new M.G. MGB 1800 is a much superior car to its predecessor, the MGA in all its forms. One cannot think of any aspect of this new sports car which does not show appreciable advantage in comparison with the previous model.

In terms of performance, ever important in this class of car, the gains are particularly marked. The standing quarter-mile time is some half a second quicker, at 18·7sec, and acceleration from rest to 90 m.p.h. takes 32·6sec compared with 36·1sec obtained in our last test of the MGA. Throughout the range, all performance figures are progressively faster with the new car.

Both models weigh almost exactly the same, and the improved performance is largely what one would expect to be achieved as a result of the increase in engine capacity from 1,622 to 1,798 c.c. It is significant that the new engine has lost the harshness but none of the low-speed traction of

its predecessor, while at the upper end of the range the engine has much more freedom to rev. Previously, 6,000 r.p.m. was regarded as a maximum safe limit, but now the engine may be taken up to 6,800 r.p.m. This allows 34, 55 and 91 m.p.h. respectively to be reached in the three indirect ratios, but it also permits an easy 70 m.p.h. in third gear, which is a very useful ratio for fast overtaking and main road cornering. A pink segment marked on the rev. counter from 5,500 r.p.m. changes to red at 6,000, and this should be regarded as a normal safety limit for the owner. Within this range, the engine remains relatively quiet, and runs through no vibration periods. An easy 100 m.p.h. is available with the MGB, and cruising at 5,000 r.p.m. allows 90 m.p.h. to be sustained without evidence of stress. The one-way maximum of 105 m.p.h. is 3 m.p.h. more than with the MGA. For overseas markets an oil cooler is standard, and is an optional extra in the U.K., recommended for those who habitually drive fast. Fitted to the test car, it prevented any reduction in oil pressure from the normal figure of 65 p.s.i. even after sustained high speeds.

Only a moment's use of the choke is necessary for the first start of the day, after which the engine pulls strongly and without hesitation. It seemed that the mixture on the car tested was set fairly rich for highest performance, with the result that the tickover when hot was rather lumpy, with a tendency to stall unless a touch of throttle was used to speed up the idling rate.

The overall fuel consumption of 21·4 m.p.g. is within 1 m.p.g. of the figure (22·3 m.p.g.) obtained with the MGA Mk. II, while all the fuel consumptions measured at constant speeds were more economical with the new car. The overall figure, of course, reflects performance testing, hard driving and considerable high-speed work, but it would be folly to think that anyone will buy the MGB simply to dawdle; and accordingly consumption in the region of 22-24 m.p.g. is to be regarded as normal.

Fuel tank capacity is 10 gallons, and normally less than

PRICES							
2-door sports	..	..	..	..	£690		
Purchase tax	..	..	..	..	£259 15s		3d
			Total (in G.B.)		**£949 15s**		**3d**
Extras (including tax)							
Heater	..	..	..	..	..	£16 16s	11d
Wire wheels	..	..	..	..	..	£34 7s	6d
Folding hood	..	..	..	..	..	£5 10s	0d
Full-length tonneau cover		..	..	..	..	£11 0s	0d
Anti-roll bar	..	..	..	..	..	£2 15s	0d
Ashtray	..	..	..	..	..	£1 7s	6d
Luggage grid	..	..	..	..	..	£14 15s	0d
Oil cooler	..	..	..	..	..	£8 18s	9d
Twin horns	..	..	..	..	..	£1 17s	10d

Make · M.G.   Type · MGB 1800

Manufacturer : The M.G. Car Co. Ltd., Abingdon-on-Thames, Berks.

Test Conditions

Weather ... Mist, brightening later,
with 0-5 m.p.h. wind
Temperature ... 13 deg. C. (56 deg. F.). Barometer
29·9in. Hg.
Dry concrete and asphalt surfaces.

Weight

Kerb weight (with oil, water and half-full fuel
tank) 18·5cwt (2,072lb-972kg)
Front-rear distribution, per cent F, 52·4; R, 47·6
Laden as tested .... 21·5cwt (2,408lb-1,092kg)

Turning Circles

Between kerbs .... L, 32ft 0in.; R, 32ft 10in.
Between walls .... L, 33ft 4in.; R, 34ft 2in.
Turns of steering wheel lock to lock .... 2·9

Performance Data

Top gear m.p.h. per 1,000 r.p.m. .... 17·9
Mean piston speed at max. power ... 3,150ft/min.
Engine speed at mean max. speed ...... 5,770 r.p.m.
B.h.p. per ton laden .... 88·3

FUEL AND OIL CONSUMPTION

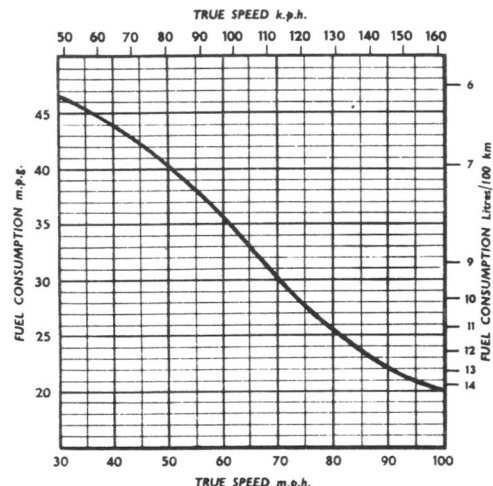

FUEL ....Premium Grade
(97 octane RM)
Test Distance .... 1,144 miles
Overall Consumption .... 21·4 m.p.g.
(13.3 lit/100 km.)
Normal Range ....20-29 m.p.g.
(14.3—9.8 lit/100 km.)
OIL: S.A.E. 30 ... Consumption: 4,500 m.p.g.

HILL CLIMBING AT STEADY SPEEDS

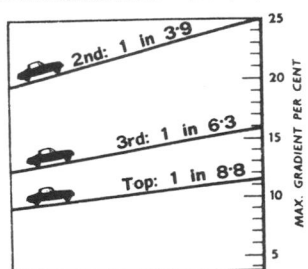

GEAR	Top	3rd	2nd
PULL	255	350	550
(lb per ton)	1 in 8·7	1 in 6·3	1 in 3·9
Speed range (m.p.h.)	48-52	42-46	34-38

MAXIMUM SPEEDS AND ACCELERATION (mean) TIMES

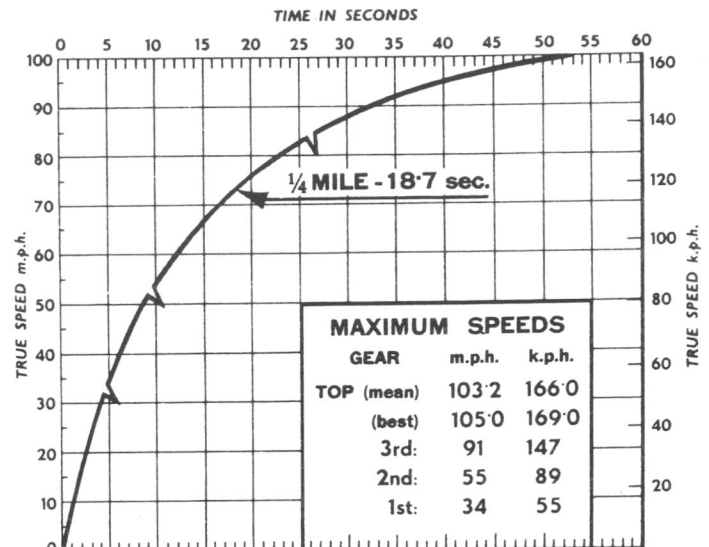

¼ MILE - 18·7 sec.

MAXIMUM SPEEDS		
GEAR	m.p.h.	k.p.h.
TOP (mean)	103·2	166·0
(best)	105·0	169·0
3rd:	91	147
2nd:	55	89
1st:	34	55

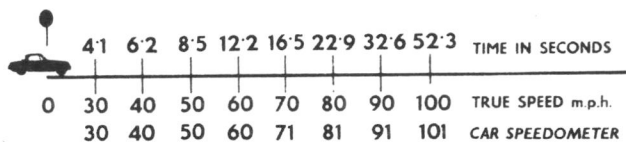

	4·1	6·2	8·5	12·2	16·5	22·9	32·6	52·3	TIME IN SECONDS
0	30	40	50	60	70	80	90	100	TRUE SPEED m.p.h.
	30	40	50	60	71	81	91	101	CAR SPEEDOMETER

Speed range and time in seconds

m.p.h.	Top	3rd	2nd	1st
10—30	—	8·1	4·3	3·3
20—40	11·4	6·9	4·4	—
30—50	9·7	6·1	4·9	—
40—60	8·7	7·0	—	—
50—70	10·4	8·1	—	—
60—80	12·0	10·2	—	—
70—90	15·7	18·0	—	—
80—100	29·8	—	—	—

BRAKES	Pedal Load	Retardation	Equiv. distance
(from 30 m.p.h.	25lb	0·20g	152ft
in neutral)	50lb	0·42g	72ft
	75lb	0·75g	40ft
	100lb	1·0g	30·2ft
Handbrake		0·40g	75ft

CLUTCH   Pedal load and travel—40lb and 4·5in.

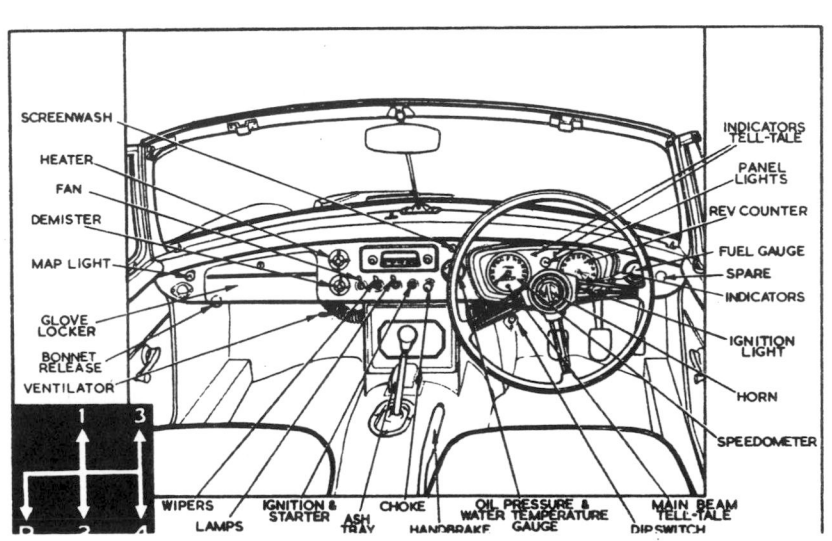

A map light on the left of the facia may be turned on when the exterior lamps are in use. The ashtray on the transmission hump is an optional extra. A padded roll above the facia is extended along the top edge of each door

200 miles are covered between refuelling stops, which may be considered only just adequate. For the standard high compression engine fitted to the MGB (8·75 to 1), fuel of at least 98 octane is recommended; but in fact the engine did not pink and only occasionally ran on with the normal premium grades of fuel (97 octane) which were used throughout the test.

Clutch take-up is delightfully smooth, and the pedal operating load is relatively light; the car had no difficulty in restarting on the 1 in 3 test hill.

A higher ratio final drive compensates for the smaller wheels fitted (14in. instead of 15in. as on the MGA), and top gear speed per 1,000 r.p.m. is almost the same at 17·9 m.p.h. (previously 17·7 m.p.h). Bottom gear is slightly lower than before, but a higher second gear ratio would be appreciated, though there is the advantage with the present gearing that the car will start from rest smoothly in second without judder. There is thus no need to engage the unsynchronized bottom gear when on the move in traffic, and when bottom gear is reluctant to engage at rest—which does happen occasionally—there is no difficulty in moving away in the next higher gear. The gear change itself is both precise and rigid, and a joy to use. Synchromesh on the three upper ratios was never beaten, even in the snatched gear changes of performance testing. Reverse is easily engaged if the lever is knocked to the left, instead of attempting to lift and push it against the safety spring.

Rack-and-pinion steering is retained, and by incorporating a universal joint in the steering column a "straight-on" wheel angle has been obtained. Some drivers found that the steering wheel was a little too large and mounted rather high, so that the top of the rim interfered with forward vision, but all were agreed that the steering itself is above criticism. It combines the virtues of lightness at low speeds, and a turning circle of only 32ft between kerbs, with a superb degree of accuracy. No lost movement is present, and hairline steering corrections control the course of the car at speed; cross wind effects are scarcely, if ever, noticed. A popular complaint against rack-and-pinion steering—wheel shock and tremor over rough surfaces—does not apply with the MGB.

A fine compromise between the needs for sports car firmness and the superior comfort to be expected from this much improved car has been achieved in the design of the

suspension. Small, firm, vertical movement of the car is felt in most conditions, particularly at speed on an indifferent surface; yet there is remarkably good insulation from the larger irregularities of road surface, and the way in which the car rode over a typical badly neglected secondary road at 70 m.p.h. was outstanding. Again, on very rough going, such as irregular *pavé* taken at 50 m.p.h. (which is decidedly fast for such conditions), the occupants are aware of the work being done by the suspension, but still are not shaken about. Aeon rubber buffers at the rear absorb the shock of severe spring deflection without trans-

Whether with hood raised or with the optional full length tonneau cover fitted, the car looks impressively neat and well-finished. Both doors may be locked with the key; the passenger door has a locking catch

Apart from the distributor, which is obscured by the pipes to the oil cooler, all components are commendably accessible. The oil cooler, which is optional on home market cars, is visible ahead of the radiator

An inconvenient prop has to be fixed in position to hold the boot lid open. Luggage space is severely restricted by the positioning of the spare wheel

M.G. MGB 1800 . . .

mitting any severe bottoming to the back of the car over the roughest tracks. This car would certainly be at home for high-speed cruising on fast but ill-surfaced roads of the Continent.

For owners of the MGA, one of the greatest joys of the model has always been the tidy, surefooted and easily controllable handling characteristics; and the new MGB is even better. There is slight understeer until the limit of adhesion is approached, when the rear wheels begin gently to break away. The response to steering correction is immediate, and at speed on twisting country roads the M.G. is most satisfying to handle.

Allied to the responsive nature of the car is its feeling of tautness. There is no scuttle shake, and the whole car feels immensely sturdy and rigid. The same is true with the hood in place, when there is still freedom from rattles.

Lockheed brakes are fitted, with discs at the front. There

is no servo assistance, yet reassuring response is available without need for excessively heavy pedal effort. It is certainly creditable that like the last B.M.C. sports car road tested—the Austin-Healey 3000 Mk. II Convertible—the MGB's brakes returned a deceleration figure of 1g (the theoretical maximum) at 30 m.p.h. with 100lb pedal pressure. Higher pedal pressures resulted in a tendency to wheel lock, and slight slewing towards the left, but without any marked loss of efficiency. On the road they are superb brakes for fast driving with safety.

Just to the left of the driving seat is the handbrake lever, ideally placed for convenient use. It held the car securely on the 1 in 3 test hill.

It is obvious that a great deal of work has gone into the design of the bad weather equipment for this more refined model. A choice of hoods is available, the standard version being entirely detachable and stowed in the luggage compartment. On the test car, the optional version was fitted, which costs £5 10s extra including tax. When lowered, it lies in the well behind the driving seat, while when raised it makes a thoroughly neat and weatherproof finish to the car. It could not be said that raising and lowering the hood were simply the "work of a moment," as with some true convertibles. On each side there are three press studs, four Lift-the-Dot fasteners, two slides and one over-centre windscreen clip to be operated; and if the driver is alone he is involved in quite a battle, and a succession of trips from one side to the other, to convert the car from the open or closed condition. With practice, times can be reduced.

A Valued Extra

A short tonneau cover is provided as standard equipment and there is also available a full-length tonneau cover with detachable rail, which makes a smart finish to the MGB when open. This is virtually essential for the effort saved by not having to erect the hood, in case of rain, every time the car is parked. It is well tailored, covering the lowered side windows, and including zip-up slots for use with safety belts.

More attention is needed to draught-sealing when the hood is raised, at the point where the side window nestles against the hood flap; but in other respects the car is very cosy when closed. The hood seal along the top of the windscreen is first class, and is tightly secured by the two over-centre clips mentioned earlier. With the hood lowered, the cockpit seems to enclose a pocket of fairly still air, and the occupants are not buffeted or exposed to severe draughts. The side windows wind smoothly and easily.

On the test car the efficiency of the optional extra heater was impaired because its fan was not working, and the usual low-temperature thermostat fitted to B.M.C. cars left the coolant too cold to be of much use in the heater. However, air delivery by ram effect above the scuttle is good, and is governed by rotary controls on the facia; and with better temperature maintenance the heater would be amply effective. A small trap door on each side of the heater console allows the supply of hot air to be cut off absolutely in warm weather, and for use when it is very hot there is a cold air vent with two-position control beneath the facia. This had the rare distinction of admitting air which was really cold.

Ahead of the heater console is a large loudspeaker mounting which serves a second duty by assisting in the commendable scuttle rigidity. On the test car the Smiths all-transistor Radiomobile receiver provided good tone quality and a wide range of undistorted volume. Speech from the radio is clearly audible even at 100 m.p.h. with the hood down. This also emphasizes the low level of wind noise.

A windscreen tie rod securing the upper rail is also used as the mounting for the rear mirror, with the useful feature that the mirror can be adjusted to the correct height for maximum rearward vision, to suit the individual driver. Although the screen is shallow and fairly far forward, visibility is good, and the quarter windows are not unduly obstructive. Comfortable and softly padded seats, upholstered in leather, are appreciated, and give good support in the small of the back and right under the thighs, as well as holding the occupant securely in fast cornering. They have ample range of fore-and-aft adjustment to suit all drivers, and the angle of rake of the squab may also be reset. A sturdy hook at the bottom of each backrest prevents it from tilting forward, but if, as we found, it is preferred to be able to tilt the seats forward to give easy access to the rear "trench" for luggage, these may be unbolted and reversed.

For some drivers the pendant pedals are mounted too high, as also is the foot-operated dipswitch. Heel-and-toe operation of brake and accelerator is not practicable; the side of the foot has to be used, which is possible, but awkward.

Instrumentation is excellent, and it is worthy of special note that the speedometer was accurate within 1 m.p.h. right up to maximum speed. Ignition and headlamp main beam warning lights are incorporated in the rev counter and speedometer, and there is variable brightness control for the instrument illumination. The oil pressure gauge and coolant thermometer are in a combined dial to the left of the speedometer. A singularly vague and inaccurate fuel gauge indicated anything between full and empty according to whether the car was accelerating or braking.

Three identical tumbler switches to the left of the ignition-starter keyhole control the heater blower, wipers and lights. As a result of the layout, it is difficult to find the switch for the lights quickly—a specially bad point as a headlamp flasher which such a car certainly should have is not fitted. The wipers work quite vigorously, at one speed, and clear a good area of the windscreen. A direct-pressure windscreen washer is fitted, and is convenient to use. A finger-tip control beneath the steering wheel operates the winking indicators, which are self-cancelling and have well-placed repeater lights ahead of the driver—valuable advances over the MGA time switch arrangement.

Ample illumination for the top performance to be used at night is provided by the sealed filament headlamps, although these were set too high on the test car. Twin horns, sounded by the steering wheel boss button (with MG octagon), are optional at £1 17s 10d extra.

Considerable improvement has been made in the provision of luggage accommodation, both behind the seats, and in the lockable boot. The spare wheel occupies much of the boot space, but there is still room for a fair amount of well-stowed luggage; a self-fixing stay would be preferable to the prop provided. A different key from that for the ignition and door locks is used for the boot, and for the diminutive facia locker. The passenger door is locked from the inside by turning a catch. Neither door, when locked, can be opened by its interior handle—a wise provision to discourage theft when the car is left with the tonneau cover fitted.

There was much desirable optional equipment on the car tested—to a total value of some £83 which would have increased the tax-paid cost of the car to £1,032. But in standard form, this MGB is still an altogether superior car to its predecessor.

Specification

ENGINE

Cylinders ...	...	4
Bore ...	...	80·3mm (3·16in.)
Stroke ...	...	89·0mm (3·5in.)
Displacement ...	...	1,798 c.c. (109·6 cu. in.)
Valve gear ...	...	Overhead, pushrods and rockers
Compression ratio	...	8·8 to 1
Carburettors ...	...	Twin S.U. HS4 semi-downdraught
Fuel pump ...	...	S.U. HP electric
Oil filter ...	...	Tecalemit full flow
Max. power ...	...	95 b.h.p. (net) at 5,400 r.p.m.
Max. torque ...	...	110 lb. ft. at 3,000 r.p.m.

TRANSMISSION

Clutch ...	...	Borg and Beck, 8in. dia. single dry plate, diaphragm spring type
Gearbox ...	...	Four-speed synchromesh on 2nd, 3rd and top, central floor change
Overall ratios ...	...	Top 3·91, 3rd 5·37, 2nd 8·66, 1st 14·21, Reverse 18·59
Final drive ...	...	Hypoid bevel, 3·91 to 1

CHASSIS

Construction ...	...	Integral with steel body

SUSPENSION

Front ...	...	Independent, coil springs and wishbones; Armstrong lever-type dampers forming top link.
Rear ...	...	Live axle; semi-elliptic leaf springs; Armstrong lever-type dampers
Steering ...	...	Rack and pinion. Wheel dia., 16·5in.

BRAKES

Type ...	...	Lockheed, hydraulic, disc front, drum rear; no servo
Dimensions ...	...	F. 10·75 in. dia. discs; R. 10in. dia. drums, 1·75in. wide shoes.
Swept area ...	...	F. 203 sq. in; R. 107 sq. in. Total: 310 sq. in (335 sq. in. per ton laden)

WHEELS

Type ...	...	Pressed steel disc, 4 studs; centre-lock wire wheels extra
Tyres ...	...	5·60-14in. Dunlop RS5

EQUIPMENT

Battery ...	...	12-volt 58-amp. hr (2 × 6-volt)
Headlamps ...	...	Lucas sealed-filament 50–40-watt
Reversing lamp	...	None
Electric fuses	...	2
Screen wipers ...	...	Single speed, self-parking
Screen washer ...	...	Standard, manual plunger
Interior heater ...	...	Extra, Smith's fresh air with electric booster
Safety belts ...	...	Extra, anchorages provided
Interior trim ...	...	Leather on wearing surfaces
Floor covering ...	...	Pvc mats; carpet over transmission tunnel
Starting handle	...	Standard
Jack ...	...	Side lifting, rotary handle
Jacking points ...	...	1 below each door
Other bodies ...	...	None

MAINTENANCE

Fuel tank ...	...	10 Imp. gallons
Cooling system ...	...	9·5 pints (plus 0·5 pints in heater)
Engine sump ...	...	7·5 pints. Change oil every 3,000 miles; change filter element every 6,000 miles
Gearbox ...	...	4·5 pints SAE30. Change oil ever 6,000 miles
Final drive ...	...	2·25 pints SAE90. Change oil every 6,000 miles
Grease ...	...	8 points every 3,000 miles
Tyre pressures ...	...	F. 17; R. 20 p.s.i. (normal driving). F. 23; R. 26 p.s.i. (fast driving). F. 20; R. 24 p.s.i. (full load)

Scale : 0·3in. to 1ft.

Cushions uncompressed.

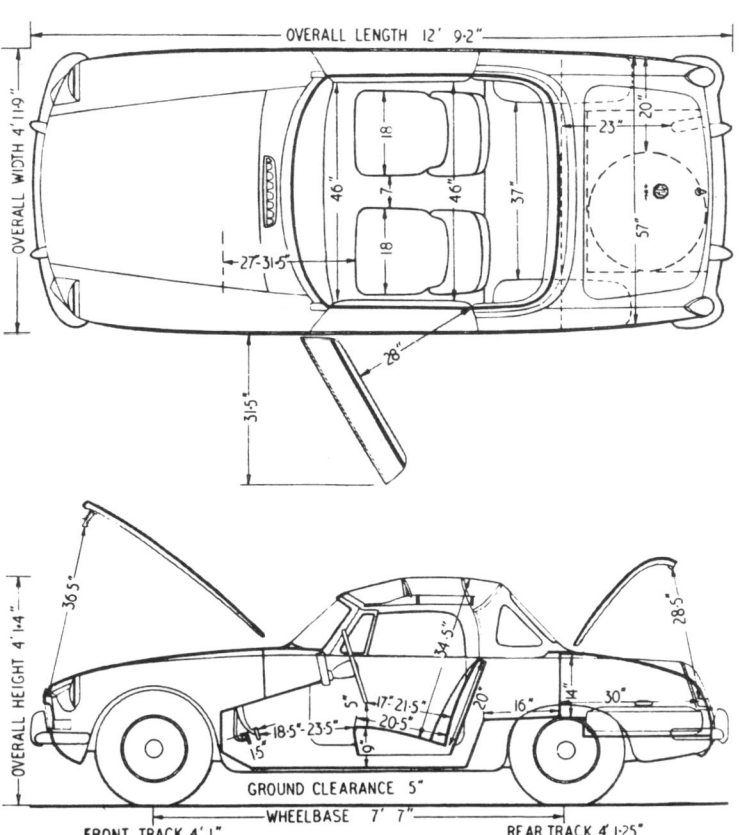

OVERALL LENGTH 12' 9·2"

OVERALL WIDTH 4' 1·9"

OVERALL HEIGHT 4' 1·4"

GROUND CLEARANCE 5"

WHEELBASE 7' 7"

FRONT TRACK 4' 1"

REAR TRACK 4' 1·25"

Autocar ROAD TEST NUMBER 2159

M.G. MGC 2,912 c.c.

AT A GLANCE. New derivative of MGB with six-cylinder engine. Lack of low speed torque and engine reluctant to rev. Very noisy fan. New all synchromesh gearbox works well, but has odd choice of ratios with overdrive. Heavy fuel consumption. Light brakes, with some fade. Good ride; strong understeer; steering low geared. Lots of legroom. Heater extra. Good finish.

MANUFACTURER
MG Car Co. Ltd., MG Division, British Motor Corporation, Abingdon-on-Thames, Berkshire.

PRICES

Basic	..	..	..	£895	0s 0d
Purchase Tax	..	..		£206	16s 6d
Seat belts (pair)		..		£6	0s 0d
Total (in GB)	..	..		£1,111	16s 6d

EXTRAS (inc. P.T.)

Overdrive	..	..	£61	9s 2d
Wire wheels	..	..	£30	14s 7d
Heater	..	..	£15	1s 2d
Radio	..	..	£20	0s 0d

PERFORMANCE SUMMARY

Mean maximum speed	120 mph
Standing start ¼-mile..	17·7 sec
0-60 mph	10·0 sec
30-70 mph (through gears)	9·8 sec
Fuel consumption ..	19 mpg
Miles per tankful ..	228

THERE has been talk of a new big sports car from BMC now for a couple of years. Rumours of a new big Austin-Healey with this or that kind of new engine, and of various coupés from the Abingdon stable have all been doing the rounds. After all these exciting stories, the new MGC must have come as a disappointment to many, because it looks just like the MGB and only a keen car spotter would notice the bulging bonnet hiding the six-cylinder engine. Inside there have been a few changes; all these also apply to the four-cylinder "B". Squeezing the bigger engine into the MGB shell has called for quite a number of engineering changes, so what in effect is much more than just the engine option it seems, adds £154 to the total price.

For the moment the Austin-Healey 3000 continues as a parallel model priced at £24 more than the MGC. In effect it shares the same engine, although that in the "C" has three extra main bearings and a revised cylinder block. Our issue of the 19 October described the new car in some detail, so we will run over only the essential statistics again here.

Basically the 3-litre engine has not changed its layout; it still uses push-rods and rockers for its valve gear, but the block has been redesigned to make it shorter and a little lighter. Somewhere along the line a few horsepower have been lost (either in extra bearing friction or as windage losses from the reduced crank web clearances) and the MGC engine develops 145 bhp net compared with the Healey's 150. Maximum torque is about the same with 170 lb. ft. at 3,500 rpm.

To match the revised engine the gearbox has been brought up to date by adding synchromesh to first, and without overdrive the ratios are much the same as those of the MGB, with an appropriate raising of the final drive ratio from 3·91 to 3·07 to 1. With overdrive a 3·307 axle is used, and for a reason BMC have not explained to us, a much higher first gear is fitted as well, with only slightly raised other indirects. Our test car had the latter arrangement, and while the long-legged, easy cruising at 27 mph per 1,000 rpm in overdrive top was appreciated on the continent, the gap between second and third spoilt an otherwise excellent set of ratios. Even without overdrive the MGC revs at only 4,200 rpm at 100 mph, so

Autocar road test number 2159

Make: M.G.
Type: MGC 2,912 c.c.

TEST CONDITIONS
Weather: Sunny. Wind: 8 mph
Temperature: 11 deg. C. (53 deg. F.)
Barometer: 29·3in. Hg.
Humidity: 55 per cent
Surfaces: Dry concrete and asphalt

Figures taken at 2,900 miles by our own staff at the Motor Industry Research
Association proving ground at Nuneaton.

WEIGHT
Kerb weight 22·1 cwt (2,477lb–1,125kg)
(with oil, water and half-full fuel tank)
Distribution, per cent: F, 55·7; R, 44·3
Laden as tested: 25·5 cwt (2,853lb–1,294kg)

MAXIMUM SPEEDS

Gear	mph	kph	rpm
OD Top (mean)	120	193	4,450
(best)	121	195	4,490
Top	120	193	5,450
OD 3rd	115	185	5,550
3rd	97	156	5,750
2nd	62	101	5,750
1st	44	71	5,750

Standing ¼-Mile 17.7 sec 79 mph
Standing Kilometre 32 sec 103 mph

FUEL CONSUMPTION

(At constant speeds—mpg)

	OD Top	Top
30 mph	33·1	29·4
40	35·1	29·2
50	32·0	27·0
60	30·8	24·5
70	26·8	22·9
80	24·4	21·4
90	22·2	19·2
100	19·7	17·3

Typical mpg 19 (14.9 litres/100km)
Calculated (DIN) mpg 20.8 (13.6 litres/100km)
Overall mpg 17.5 (16.1 litres/100km)
Grade of fuel, Premium, 4-star (min 97RM)

OIL CONSUMPTION
Miles per pint (SAE 20W/40) .. 1,000

TIME IN SECONDS	4·0	5·6	7·6	10·0	13·8	18·0	23·1	29·3	40·9	
TRUE SPEED MPH	30	40	50	60	70	80	90	100	110	120
INDICATED SPEED	31	42	51	62	71	82	92	101	111	121

Mileage recorder 0·9 per cent over-reading.   Test distance 1,031 miles.

Speed range, gear ratios and time in seconds

mph	OD Top (2·68)	Top (3·31)	OD 3rd (3·54)	3rd (4·32)	2nd (6·82)	1st (9·86)
10— 30	—	11·1	10·4	7·6	4·5	3·4
20— 40	13·2	9·6	9·0	6·3	4·4	3·3
30— 50	11·4	9·1	8·5	7·0	4·0	—
40— 60	11·5	10·0	9·1	6·8	4·3	—
50— 70	14·2	10·7	9·3	7·3	—	—
60— 80	16·9	11·1	10·1	8·5	—	—
70— 90	13·8	12·8	11·9	9·0	—	—
80—100	25·3	15·4	13·9	—	—	—
90—110	33·6	18·3	19·0	—	—	—

BRAKES (from 30 mph in neutral)

Load	g	Distance
25 lb	0·25	100 ft
50 „	0·58	52 „
75 „	0·98	30·7 „
100 „	1·03	29·2 „
Handbrake	0·36	84 „

Max. Gradient, 1 in 3
Clutch Pedal: 35lb and 5in.

TURNING CIRCLES
Between kerbs L, 35ft 9in.; R, 35ft 9in.
Between walls L, 36ft 9in.; R, 36ft 9in.
Steering wheel turns, lock to lock .. 3·5

HOW THE CAR COMPARES:

MAXIMUM SPEED (mean) MPH

100	110	120	130

MG MGC
Austin-Healey 3000 Mk III
MG MGB
Reliant Scimitar 3-litre
Triumph GT6

0-60 MPH (sec)

30	20	10

MG MGC
Austin-Healey 3000 Mk III
MG MGB
Reliant Scimitar 3-litre
Triumph GT6

STANDING START ¼-MILE (sec)

30	20	10

MG MGC
Austin-Healey 3000 Mk III
MG MGB
Reliant Scimitar 3-litre
Triumph GT6

MPG OVERALL

10	20	30

MG MGC
Austin-Healey 3000 Mk III
MG MGB
Reliant Scimitar 3-litre
Triumph GT6

PRICES

MG MGC	£1,102
Austin-Healey 3000 Mk III	£1,126
MG MGB	£948
Reliant Scimitar 3-litre	£1,516
Triumph GT 6	£985

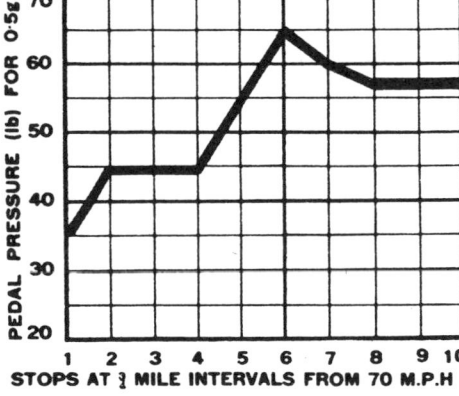

LAMPS
HEATER
FAN
DEMISTER
MAP LIGHT
GLOVE LOCKER
BONNET RELEASE
VENTILATOR

INDICATORS TELL-TALE
PANEL LIGHTS
REV COUNTER
FUEL GAUGE
OVERDRIVE
INDICATORS
IGNITION LIGHT
HORN
SPEEDOMETER

WIPERS
SCREENWASH
IGNITION & STARTER
ASH TRAY
CHOKE
HANDBRAKE
OIL PRESSURE & WATER TEMPERATURE GAUGE
MAIN BEAM TELL-TALE
DIPSWITCH

PEDAL PRESSURE (lb) FOR 0·5g
STOPS AT ¼ MILE INTERVALS FROM 70 M.P.H

R 1 2 3 4

M.G. MGC . . .

it is hard to see why this option is listed. For the first time there is the alternative of Borg-Warner automatic transmission.

The engine is something of an enigma. It is smooth and flexible, but completely lacking in sporty characteristics. Whilst it pulls evenly from very low revs (below 500 rpm in top), there is very little low speed torque *and* the engine seems reluctant to rev or develop much top end power. This impression is borne out by the top gear acceleration figures, which are less quick than those of MGB for every 20 mph increment up to 70 mph (20-40 mph : 8·6 sec MGB, 9·6 sec MGC; 30-50 mph : 8·7 sec MGB, 9·1 sec MGC; 40-60 mph : 9·1 sec MGB, 10·0 sec MGC). Overall through the gears, however, the new car is appreciably quicker with a 0 to 60 mph time of 10·0 sec (MGB: 12·9), and a fast standing quarter-mile in 17·7 sec (MGB: 18·9).

Usually the engine is sweet and docile, but once or twice we experienced slight plug fouling after fairly long spells in heavy traffic. For the first few minutes after a cold start it was particularly difficult to keep the engine from dying, and when accelerating hard oil surge caused clouds of blue smoke from the exhaust. A new moulded plastic cooling fan in a metal cowl whines and whirrs all the time very loudly, and at high revs the driver hears a loud noise like a supercharged vacuum cleaner. To avoid the fuss and bother of making the engine rev, one never goes much above 3,000 rpm for everyday driving, except for the occasional burn-up away from the lights.

Getting the car away from rest quickly was hampered by clutch slip when we tried over 3,500 rpm for take-offs, and by a definite lack of torque below these revs. Even so, a 0 to 100 mph time of under 30 sec is pretty brisk, and might even be faster on the non-overdrive car with better gearbox ratios. Our in-the-gears maxima of 44, 62 and 97 mph at an indicated 5,500 rpm (5,750 actual) show up the odd spacing mentioned earlier. Overdrive third takes the car on to 115 mph, and in both direct top and overdrive top we recorded mean maxima of 120 mph. The Laycock overdrive is operated by a little cranked toggle switch on the facia under the wheel rim on the right; it engaged and disengaged very smoothly, but with a definite delay on the upward shift.

The gearbox has a firm and robust-feeling remote control with a nice large ball-shaped knob rather spoilt by a sharp-edged nut underneath it. Movements are very positive and the powerful synchromesh stood up perfectly to all the punishment we could

The 6-cyl. engine fills all the available space, but everything needing routine attention is easily reached, especially the oil filter, on the left of the block

give it during acceleration runs. The gate is very narrow and there is spring loading towards the first and second gear plane; this makes it harder to be sure one is in neutral, and initially the change up from second to third feels strange. All the indirect gears are very quiet, except for a slight whine on the over-run.

For maximum speed runs we took the MGC to Belgium and found it cruised very well at 100 mph with arrow-like stability. Wind roar round the hood drowns out all conversation and the radio, and anyone preferring to tour over long distances rather than have the option of fresh air would be better off with the alternative GT version.

Compared with the Austin-Healey 3000, the new MG is slightly slower in both top speed (121 mph for the Healey) and acceleration (0 to 100 mph : 25·7 sec for the Healey). Fuel consumption is also not as good as that of the Healey and much heavier than the MGB's. Overall we man-

aged only 17·5 mpg with the MGC, although at a steady 70 mph, for example, it covers nearly 23 mpg in direct top and 26·8 mpg in overdrive; overall figures for comparison are 22·0 mpg for the MGB (with overdrive) and 20·3 mpg for the Healey (again with overdrive).

Of course, the new car is not as heavy as the Healey, but it weighs a full 350 lb more than the MGB. The six-cylinder engine is 210 lb heavier than the B-series unit, and the new gearbox is larger. Considering all this amounts to 16·4 per cent extra on the weight of the MGB, it must have been very hard for the manufacturers to keep the weight distribution reasonably balanced. The front-end weight is up from 52·6 to only 55·7 per cent of the total, and a corresponding increase in the recommended tyre pressure differential (from equal front and rear to a 4 psi front bias) restores handling. To lighten the steering load a lower geared rack is used and the king-pins have been de-castored.

The boot holds a remarkable amount of soft luggage, but there is no trimming. With the hood down the cover and irons take up a good deal of room. A strut has to be used to hold the lid open

KOV 259F

Left: The facia layout is identical to the MGB's. The standards of fit and finish are very high, with leather on the seats and rubber floor mats. Right: There is a vast amount of adjustment on the seats. The flap type door handles are very neat and easy to use

Even so, the steering is heavy and it is by no means a delicate car to drive. For a start the steering wheel feels huge (it has a 16·5in. dia.) and there are now 3·5 turns needed for a 35ft 9in. turning circle instead of 2·9 turns for a 32ft 4in. one. It was no help that our car pulled strongly to the left and the steering wheel was not straight on its splines. It now has a stitched on leather glove over its rim.

Apart from the low-geared steering there is strong understeer which makes the front end slow to respond. In the low gears there is enough torque to help the back round, but on wet surfaces we found it very hard indeed to catch the tail if it got out of line, so we settled for a slow-in, fast-out (once it was straight) technique. The MGC lacks the "chuckability" of both the MGB and the Austin-Healey 3000; it is better suited to *Routes Nationales* than mountain *cols*.

MGC wheels are an inch bigger in diameter and an inch wider than those of the MGB, and Dunlop SP 41 radial-ply tyres are standard. Grip is good and it is virtually impossible to spin the rear wheels on wet roads. Once or twice, however, we locked a front wheel when braking hard. There is little thump from the tyres on ridges and catseyes, but they are prone to squeal during hard cornering, even in the wet.

To get the new engine in the MGB frame the front cross-member has been discarded, and to transfer the suspension loads back to the stiff scuttle area, longitudinal torsion bars replace the coil springs used on the "B". For a sports car the ride is quite soft and almost in the saloon car class for comfort. Firm damping retains something of the traditional taut feel, and there is no pitch and very little roll at any time. Only on very rough roads does the vertical motion become harsh, but even then there is surprisingly little body shake

and no scuttle flexing.

Braking has been revised to suit the new weight distribution and there is a vacuum servo. Pedal loads are light and progressive up to a maximum of over 1·0g at 80lb. Surprisingly for a sports car we measured a lot of fade during ten stops from 70 mph at ¾-mile intervals, and the front discs got very hot and smoked. The handbrake is powerful and held the car on a 1-in-3 facing either way; the cranked brake lever, fitted in between the driving seat and the tunnel, is convenient to use and well placed.

Unlike most two-seater sports cars, the MG is built for big people. Even our 6ft testers did not need the seat right back; there is an abundance of legroom and enough foot room in spite of the wider tunnel. On the other hand, our shorter staff found that they sat too low in the car and therefore had difficulty in seeing enough of the bonnet to locate themselves on the road. By the latest

standards, the windscreen seems shallow, especially on a dark, wet night, and the wiper blades park on the screen obscuring some of the driver's view of the left-hand kerb. At last the wipers have two speeds.

Some features of the revised interior have been dictated by the new American safety requirements. The flush interior door handles are neat and practical, but the rubber knobs on the window winders repeatedly came off. The glove locker lid can be held shut only by locking it with its key, which also locks the boot. There is another key for the ignition and doors.

The heater is a £15 extra, and it is controlled by two rotary knobs on the left of the facia. The top one works a simple water valve, which seems to have no intermediate temperature between hot and cold, and the lower one directs the air to screen or footwells. There is no ram effect at all, so the single-speed fan must be used all the time heat or demisting is

Reversing lamps are built into the tail panel. From the rear, only the small MGC sign above the octagon badge shows which model this is

required. A separate cold-air intake is worked by a lever under the left of the facia.

The hood is still one of those detachable pvc and tubular frame affairs which must be taken off and folded up before stowing it in the boot, or in settled climates leaving it at home. Putting it up in a hurry is quite quick, but experience helps a lot in reducing the frequent trips from side to side when doing this alone. Sealing round the doors is not completely storm-proof.

We were amazed to find the boot has no self-propping strut for its lid, and this is a real nuisance when loading or unloading an armful of odds and ends. With the optional wire wheels one really needs several soft bags for luggage as the hub of the spare pokes up in the way of a normal suitcase.

Probably our impressions of the MGC would have been more favourable if we had taken it for a holiday to the south of Spain and back. As it is, we were able to use it only around England and for a brief day trip to the Jabekke road in Belgium. The MGC is the latest example from a very famous factory which has regularly produced classic sports cars in the past; somewhere in the large BMC complex it has lost the "Abingdon touch."

SPECIFICATION : M.G. MGC (FRONT ENGINE, REAR-WHEEL DRIVE)

ENGINE
Cylinders	..	6, in line
Cooling system	..	Water; pump, fan and thermostat
Bore	..	83·4mm (3·28in.)
Stroke	..	88·9mm (3·50in.)
Displacement	..	2,912 c.c. (177·7 cu. in.)
Valve gear	..	Overhead; pushrods and rockers
Compression ratio		9-to-1: Min. octane rating: 98 RM
Carburettors	..	2 SU HS6
Fuel pump	..	SU electric
Oil filter	..	Full flow, renewable element
Max. power	..	145 bhp (net) at 5,250 rpm
Max torque	..	170 lb. ft. (net) at 3,400 rpm

TRANSMISSION
Clutch	..	Borg and Beck diaphragm spring, 9in. dia.
Gearbox	..	Four-speed, all synchromesh; overdrive on Third and Top.
Gear ratios	..	Top 1·0; OD Top 0·82 OD Third 1·07; Third 1·31; Second 2·06; First 2·98; Reverse 2·67
Final drive	..	Hypoid bevel, 3·31-to-1

CHASSIS and BODY
Construction	..	Integral with steel body

SUSPENSION
Front	..	Independent, torsion bars, wishbones, telescopic dampers, anti-roll bar
Rear	..	Live axle, half-elliptic leaf springs, lever arm dampers

STEERING
	..	Rack and pinion Wheel dia. 16·5in.

BRAKES
Make and type	..	Girling discs front, drums rear
Servo	..	Girling vacuum type
Dimensions	..	F, 11·06in. dia.; R, 9in. dia. 2·5in. wide shoes
Swept area	..	F, 226·2 sq. in.; R, 127·2 sq. in Total 353·4 sq. in. (277·3 sq. in./ton laden)

WHEELS
Type	..	Pressed steel disc standard—optional 72-spoke wire wheels on test car, 5in. wide rim
Tyres —make	..	Dunlop
—type	..	SP41 radial-ply tubed
—size	..	165—15 mm.

EQUIPMENT
Battery	..	12-volt 58-amp. hr. (2 × 6-volt)
Alternator	..	Lucas 16AC 33-amp
Headlamps	..	Lucas sealed filament 100-180-watt (total)
Reversing lamp	..	2 standard
Electric fuses	..	2
Screen wipers	..	2-speed, self-parking
Screen washer	..	Standard, manual plunger
Interior heater	..	Extra, water valve type
Heated backlight		Not applicable on roadster

Safety belts	..	Extra, anchorages built in
Interior trim	..	Leather and pvc seats
Floor covering	..	Carpet and rubber mats
Starting handle	..	No provision
Jack	..	Screw pillar
Jacking points	..	One each side under sills
Windscreen	..	Laminated
Underbody protection	..	Phosphate treatment prior to painting

MAINTENANCE
Fuel tank	..	12 Imp. gallons (no reserve) (54·8 litres)
Cooling system	..	18·5 pints (including heater) (10·5 litres)
Engine sump	..	12·8 pints (7·2 litres) SAE 20W/40. Change oil every 6,000 miles; Change filter element every 6,000 miles
Gearbox and overdrive	..	14·5 pints SAE 20W/40. Change oil every 6,000 miles
Final drive	..	1·75 pints SAE 90EP. No oil change needed, check level every 6,000 miles
Grease	..	4 points every 3,000 miles
Tyre pressures	..	F, 26; R, 22 p.s.i. (normal driving). F, 28; R, 32 p.s.i. (fast driving)

PERFORMANCE DATA
Top gear mph per 1,000 rpm	22·12
Overdrive top mph per 1,000 rpm	26·95
Mean piston speed at max power	3,060ft/min
Bhp per ton laden	113·7

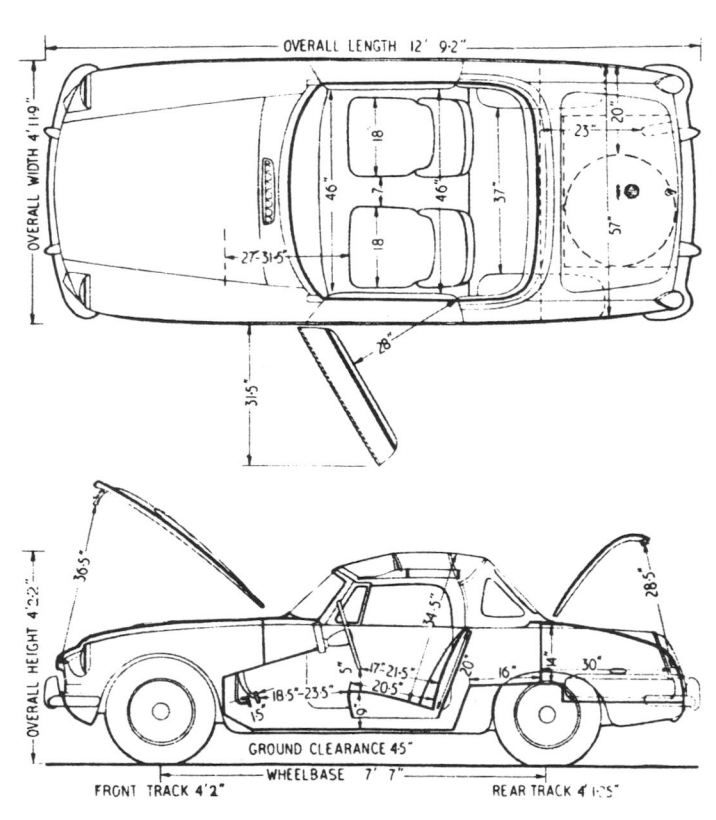

AUTO TEST

MG Midget 1500

1,493 c.c.

Smallest British Leyland sports car given much more punch by bigger engine. Quick, accurate steering but handling throttle-sensitive and inclined to oversteer. Harsh ride, excessive wind noise with hood up. Undergeared. Limited range

The Midget rolls considerably when cornered hard and the outside front wheel becomes heavily loaded as seen here. If at this point the steering wheel is held steady the car increasingly oversteers as the corner continues; lifting off the accelerator causes the tail to twitch sharply outwards

THERE was an outburst of lamentation from MG enthusiasts when the Midget 1500 was announced, apparently because the A-series engine had been replaced by a Triumph-designed unit. From an engineering point of view the change was almost inevitable. The Midget needed a bigger engine to counteract the effect of safety and antipollution equipment in America, where it sells in its greatest numbers; and at 1,275 c.c., the A-series unit was at the end of its "stretch potential". The answer was to instal the Triumph engine which, while of similar design and vintage, had long ago been given a longer stroke to bring its capacity to 1,493 c.c., its first application being the now-defunct front-drive Triumph 1500.

The purists may decry the move, but Triumph is a name long respected in the sports car business and there is no reason to suppose the Spitfire engine should be unsuitable for the Midget. It might be more in order to complain that a considerable increase in swept volume has resulted in a negligible increase in quoted power, from 64 bhp (net) to 66 bhp (DIN). On the other hand torque, a more important part of a sports car's character, than most people realize, is increased by a greater margin. Against all this has to be balanced the greater weight of the new car, with a kerb weight (our measurement) of 15·3cwt compared with the 13·8cwt of the last 1,275 c.c. Midget we tested.

Performance and economy

The proof of the Midget 1500 is in the stopwatch, and there is no doubt it is substantially quicker than the late-series 1,275 c.c. car. Comparisons are valid because the final drive ratio remains unchanged at 3·9 to 1; the adoption of the single-rail "corporate" gearbox has meant some change in internal ratios, which are wider than before. Tyre size likewise remains the same.

The Midget 1500 is a genuine 100 mph car, and this represents a great advance on the 1275 which managed only 94 mph mean when tested in 1971. Unfortunately maximum speed takes the car over the red line on its rev counter, which over-read by a modest 100 rpm at maximum speed; clearly, therefore the Midget is substantially undergeared to make best use of its peak power, which falls at 5,500 rpm. Higher gearing would not only improve economy, but also permit higher speeds in the intermediate gears.

Although we ran the Midget beyond the 6,000 rpm red line to attain its ultimate maximum speed, we stuck to the limit in the lower gears with the result that first gear would not quite take the car to 30 mph, and third stopped just short of 70 mph. Our figures point up the considerable gap between second (47 mph maximum) and third, which is felt on the road to some extent but is disguised by the spread of useful torque.

Open sports cars always suffer in performance at the top end when they are run with the hood down, and the Midget was no exception. Lowering the hood took the maximum speed down to 94 mph – apart from making life very uncomfortable at that speed. We took no acceleration figures with the hood down, but there is no doubt they would be inferior to those obtained with the hood in place.

AUTOTEST — MG Midget 1500

All the Midget 1500 acceleration figures are far superior to those of the 1275, whether from a standing start or in any particular gear. Standing starts are best accomplished without a surfeit of revs and sudden engagement of the clutch, which tends to produce strong and uncomfortable axle tramp. A more gentle procedure, feeding in the clutch fairly fast from a 2,000 rpm starting point, trims half a second off the 1275 time to 30 mph, giving a respectable 3·7sec to this speed. The 1500 proceeds to 60 mph in 12·3sec (a 1·8sec improvement), and to 90 mph in 35·3sec. In !ike fashion, the standing quarter-mile now takes 18·5sec compared with 19·6 before.

In the gears, every single feature claimed by the 1275 is bettered by a substantial margin. Not only is the torque curve flatter; the 1500 does not run out of breath so quickly at the top end, while flexibility is improved to the extent of being able to pull away from 10 mph in top, which the 1275 would not tolerate.

Comparisons

MAXIMUM SPEED MPH
MG Midget 1500	(£1,560)	101
Ford Escort 1600 Sport	(£1,860)	100
Triumph Spitfire 1500	(£1,689)	100
Fiat 128SL 1300	(£1,791)	99
Renault 15TL	(£1,969)	94

0-60 MPH, SEC
Ford Escort 1600 Sport	10·3
MG Midget 1500	12·3
Fiat 128SL 1300	13·1
Triumph Spitfire 1500	13·2
Renault 15TL	13·6

STANDING ¼-MILE, SEC
Ford Escort 1600 Sport	17·9
MG Midget 1500	18·5
Fiat 128SL 1300	18·8
Triumph Spitfire 1500	19·1
Renault 15TL	19·3

OVERALL MPG
Renault 15TL	31·8
Triumph Spitfire 1500	29·1
Fiat 128SL 1300	28·5
MG Midget 1500	27·9
Ford Escort 1600 Sport	27·5

Performance

ACCELERATION SECONDS

True speed mph	Time in Secs	Car Speedo mph
30	3·7	30
40	5·8	40
50	8·5	50
60	12·3	61
70	17·0	71
80	24·0	82
90	35·3	92
100	—	102

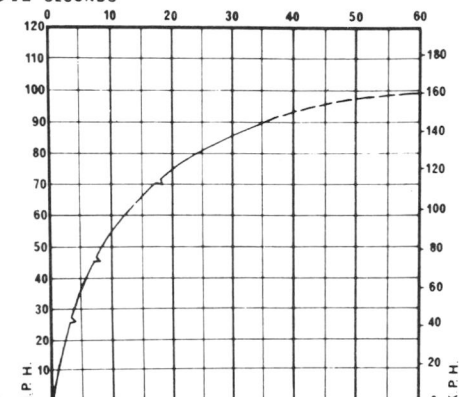

Standing ¼-mile
18·5sec 72 mph

Standing kilometre
34·9sec 90 mph

Mileage recorder: accurate

GEAR RATIOS AND TIME IN SEC
mph	Top (3·90)	3rd (5·58)	2nd (8·23)
10–30	9·8	6·2	3·9
20–40	9·2	5·8	4·0
30–50	8·7	5·8	—
40–60	9·6	6·7	—
50–70	10·2	7·9	—
60–80	12·5	—	—
70–90	19·3	—	—

GEARING
(with 145–13in. tyres)
Top	16·44 mph per 1,000 rpm
3rd	11·50 mph per 1,000 rpm
2nd	7·79 mph per 1,000 rpm
1st	4·82 mph per 1,000 rpm

MAXIMUM SPEEDS
Gear	mph	khp	rpm
Top (mean)	101	163	6,140*
(best)	102	164	6,200*
3rd	69	111	6 000
2nd	47	76	6,000
1st	29	47	6,000

*See text

BRAKES
FADE (from 70 mph in neutral)
Pedal load for 0·5g stops in lb
1	35		6	45–65
2	40–45		7	50–65
3	40–60		8	50–65
4	45–65		9	50–65
5	45–55		10	50–60

RESPONSE (from 30 mph in neutral)
Load	g	Distance
20lb	0·22	137ft
40lb	0·46	65ft
60lb	0·70	43ft
80lb	0·96	31ft
Handbrake	0·33	91ft
Max Gradient	1 in 3	

CLUTCH
Pedal 42lb and 4¾in.

Consumption

FUEL
(At constant speed – mpg)
30 mph	48·8
40 mph	44·5
50 mph	39·2
60 mph	34·2
70 mph	29·8
80 mph	26·2
90 mph	22·1
100 mph	17·6

Typical mpg 30 (9·4 litres/100km)
Calculated (DIN) mpg 32·5
(8·7 litres/100km)
Overall mpg 27·9 (10·1 litres/100km)
Grade of fuel Premium, 4-star (min 97RM)

OIL
Consumption (SAE 20W/50) 1,000 mpp

TEST CONDITIONS:
Weather: Fine
Wind: 0·3 mph
Temperature: 15deg C (58deg F)
Barometer: 29·95in. Hg
Humidity: 65 per cent
Surface: Dry concrete and asphalt
Test distance 883 miles

Figures taken by our own staff at the Motor Industry Research Association proving ground at Nuneaton.

Dimensions

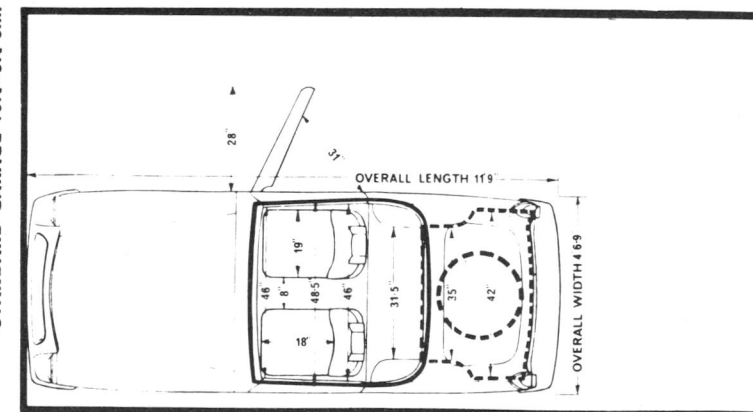

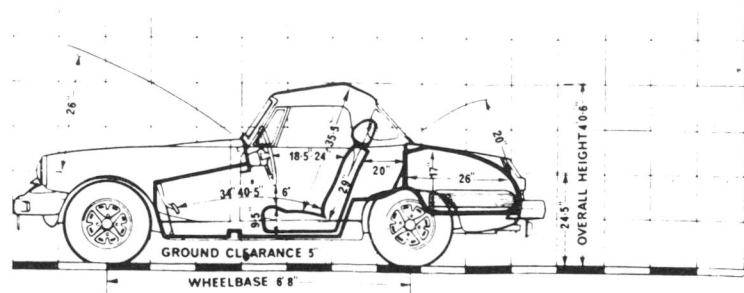

STANDARD GARAGE 16ft x 8ft 6in.

OVERALL LENGTH 11'9"
OVERALL WIDTH 4'6"
OVERALL HEIGHT 4'0·6"
GROUND CLEARANCE 5"
WHEELBASE 6'8"
FRONT TRACK 3'10·3"
REAR TRACK 3'8·75"

TURNING CIRCLES:
Between kerbs
L, 30ft 10in.; R, 31ft 11in.
Between walls
L, 32ft 2in.; R, 33ft 3in.
Steering wheel turns, lock to lock 2¾

WEIGHT:
Kerb Weight 15·4cwt (1,720lb–780kg) (with oil, water and half full fuel tank)
Distribution, per cent F, 53·7; R, 46·3
Laden as tested: 18·0cwt (2,020lb–917kg)

Where economy is concerned, one might expect the 1500 to be less economical because of its larger engine. On the other hand its economy should at least be comparable, because the car remains the same size and there is no reason why any more power should be needed to push it along. Two factors upset this tidy calculation. One is that the Midget in its new form is a good deal heavier; the other is its extra performance, which is used some if not all of the time. As a result, our overall fuel consumption emerged as 27·9 mpg compared with 29·6 mpg for the smaller-engined car. This is not a particularly good figure – worse than the Spitfire 1500 for instance, but then the Spitfire has higher gearing and, for our test, overdrive as well. It was noticeable, though, that the Midget's consumption stayed almost constant whoever the driver and whatever the journey, and at no time did it record a brim-to-brim figure of better than 30 mpg.

This is not to say that 30 mpg is unattainable. Our steady-speed figures show that cruising at a constant 60 mph (with the hood up!) enables the driver to better that figure with ease. If this limit were observed and fierce acceleration avoided, the Midget would prove quite economical; but it is not inherently so, still less the way it is likely to be driven.

Handling and brakes
The Midget sticks to its simple suspension arrangement with double wishbones at the front

Specification   MG Midget 1500

FRONT ENGINE, REAR-WHEEL DRIVE

Final drive	Hypoid bevel, ratio 3·90 to 1
Mph at 1,000 rpm in top gear	16·44

CHASSIS AND BODY
Construction	Integral, with steel body

SUSPENSION
Front	Independent: double wishbones, lever arm dampers, anti-roll bar
Rear	Live axle, semi-elliptic leaf springs, lever-arm dampers

STEERING
Type	Rack and pinion
Wheel dia	15½in.

BRAKES
Type	Disc front, drum rear
Dimensions	F 8·25in. dia R, 7·0in. dia, 1·25in. wide shoes
Swept area	F, 135 sq. in., R, 55 sq. in. Total 190 sq. in. (211 sq. in./ton laden)

WHEELS
Type	Pressed steel Rostyle, 4-stud fixing, 4in. wide rim
Tyres – make	Pirelli Cinturato (on test car)
– type	Radial ply tubeless
– size	145–13in.

EQUIPMENT
Battery	12 volt 40 Ah.
Alternator	28 amp a.c.
Headlamps	Sealed beam, 120/90 watt (total)
Reversing lamp	Standard

ENGINE
Cylinders	4, in line
Main bearings	3
Cooling system	Water; pump, fan and thermostat
Bore	73·7mm (2·90in.)
Stroke	87·5mm (3·44in.)
Displacement	1,493 c.c. (91·1 cu. in.)
Valve gear	Overhead: pushrods and rockers
Compression ratio	9·0 to 1. Min octane rating: 97RM
Carburettors	2 SU HS4
Fuel pump	SU mechanical
Oil filter	Full-flow, replaceable cartridge
Max power	66 bhp (DIN) at 5,500 rpm
Max torque	77 lb. ft. (DIN) at 3,000 rpm

TRANSMISSION
Clutch	Diaphragm-spring, 7·25in. diameter
Gearbox	4-speed, all-synchromesh
Gear ratios	Top 1·0
	Third 1·43
	Second 2·11
	First 3·41
	Reverse 3·75

Electric fuses	4
Screen wipers	Single-speed
Screen washer	Standard, manual plunger
Interior heater	Standard, water valve type
Heated backlight	Not available
Safety belts	Static type
Interior trim	Pvc seats
Floor covering	Carpet
Jack	Screw pillar type
Jacking points	One each side
Windscreen	Toughened
Underbody protection	Phosphate treatment under paint

MAINTENANCE
Fuel tank	7 Imp gallons (32 litres)
Cooling system	7½ pints (inc heater)
Engine sump	8 pints (4·5 litres) SAE 20W–50. Change oil every 6,000 miles. Change filter every 6,000 miles
Gearbox	1·5 pints. SAE 90EP. Check every 6,000 miles
Final drive	1·75 pints. SAE 90EP. Check every 6,000 miles.
Grease	8 points every 6,000 miles
Valve clearance	Inlet 0·010in. (cold) Exhaust 0·010in. (cold)
Contact breaker	0·015in. gap.
Ignition timing	10deg BTDC (stroboscopic at 650 rpm)
Spark plug	Type: Champion N9Y. Gap 0·025in.
Tyre pressures	F 22; R 24 psi (normal driving) F 26; R 28 psi (high speed) F 22; R 26 psi (full load)
Max payload	420lb (190kg)

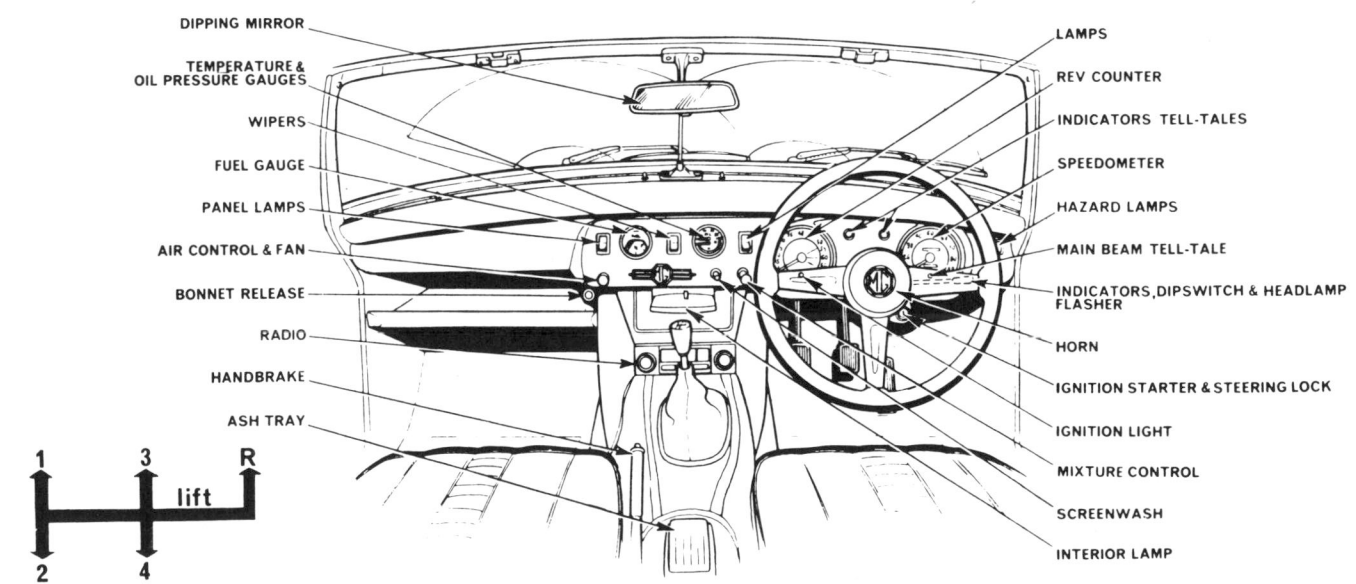

DIPPING MIRROR
TEMPERATURE & OIL PRESSURE GAUGES
WIPERS
FUEL GAUGE
PANEL LAMPS
AIR CONTROL & FAN
BONNET RELEASE
RADIO
HANDBRAKE
ASH TRAY

LAMPS
REV COUNTER
INDICATORS TELL-TALES
SPEEDOMETER
HAZARD LAMPS
MAIN BEAM TELL-TALE
INDICATORS, DIPSWITCH & HEADLAMP FLASHER
HORN
IGNITION STARTER & STEERING LOCK
IGNITION LIGHT
MIXTURE CONTROL
SCREENWASH
INTERIOR LAMP

Servicing   6,000 miles

Time Allowed (hours)	3·5
Cost at £4.30 per hour	£15.05
Engine oil	£2.50
Oil Filter	£2.15
Air Filter	£1.08
Contact Breaker Points	£0.52
Sparking Plugs *	£1.48
Total Cost:	**£22.78**

*when required

Routine Replacements:	Time hours	Labour	Spares	TOTAL
Brake Pads – Front (2 wheels)	1·00	£4.30	£3.80	£8.10
Brake Shoes – Rear (2 wheels)	1·35	£5.80	£3.80	£9.60
Exhaust System	0·85	£3.65	£19.50	£23.15
Clutch (centre + driven plate)	8·00	£34.40	£12.83	£47.23
Dampers – Front (pair)	1·55	£6.65	£28.88	£35.53
Dampers – Rear (pair)	1·00	£4.30	£25.52	£29.82
Replace Half Shaft	0·55	£2.35	£13.80	£16.15
Replace Alternator	0·70	£3.00	£27.00	£30.00
Replace Starter	1·60	£6.90	£15.86	£22.76

and a live rear axle located by semi-elliptic leaf springs with no other form of assistance. It worked well enough in the past, given the Midget's very limited wheel travel, but there are signs that the latest car needs something more sophisticated to cope with its greater torque and performance.

Part of the trouble lies in the fact that the Midget, like the MGB, has been given increased ride height at the back to compensate for the greater weight of its "5 mph" bumpers and associated structure. As a result, roll stiffness at the back end has been reduced and there is much more tendency to oversteer. This is despite the heavier engine which means the front wheels bear a greater part of the total weight.

The best feature of the Midget, as always, is its very quick and accurate steering. With less than three turns of the wheel between extremes of an average 32ft turning circle, the driver never has to tie his arms in knots to turn a corner or rescue a situation. Inevitably, there is some kick-back on rough surfaces, but this is by no means the most tiring feature of the car.

Straight-line stability is no better than average, except on ultra-smooth surfaces. Normally, the Midget feels willing enough to keep to a straight course but if the wheel is released for a moment it soon reveals its willingness to wander off-line. The feeling of stability is actually due to the driver

Massive front bumper makes the whole car look bigger than before; inset lights are well protected by lipped extensions. Door mirrors are part of standard equipment. Headlamps are sealed-beam units, not halogen

Standard number plate is mounted beneath the new "5 mph" bumper, rather than below the boot lid as in previous Midgets. Reversing lights are standard and boot lid can be left unlocked if the driver wishes

being barely conscious of the tiny but constant corrections he is applying.

The handling, as we have already said, holds the promise of oversteer. It is not evident at first, for in gentle driving the Midget stays very close to neutral. When driven harder into a corner, if the driver holds the wheel and accelerator steady, the tail will come out steadily until some of the lock has to be paid off before the car gets too sideways. In itself this is no bad thing, for it enables the Midget to be driven in distinctly sporting fashion by someone who knows what he is doing. At the same time it holds the seeds of danger for anyone less clever.

The real snag to the Midget's handling in 1500 form lies in its sensitivity to the throttle. Given the previous situation where the car has been wound hard into a long, tight bend, any sudden re-

lease of the accelerator will bring the tail out very smartly, calling for opposite lock to pin it down. Again, this is a situation beloved of some drivers but it means the Midget is much less predictable, and certainly calls for more skill, than many small saloons of equal performance *and* cornering ability. The drawback is compounded by limited roadholding, which can leave the car well-balanced fore and aft, but skittering sideways onto a wider line than desired. Despite the increased weight and torque, the tyre section remains the same at 145–13in., and it is difficult to avoid the conclusion that the 1500 is somewhat under-tyred.

In the wet, the roadholding is considerably reduced and the Midget tends to skate around on smooth-surfaced corners. In this case, however, it is much more forgiving and the quick

steering really comes into its own.

The brakes need moderate effort and generally work well, giving a well-controlled ultimate stop of 0·95g for a pedal effort of 80lb – well within reasonable limits. The brakes have good "feel", with no sign of sponginess, and no tendency to snatch when cold. Their fade performance is less reassuring with a near-doubling of effort for a 0·5g stop during our ten-stop test, and some smell of linings towards the end; but even then there is no increase in pedal travel.

The handbrake works well, our test car recording a 0·33g stop when the handbrake was used alone on the level. It also held the car well facing either way on the 1-in-3 test hill, on which a restart was easily achieved thanks to the low first gear – but not without a smell of clutch lining.

Comfort and convenience

The Midget could hardly be described as anything but cramped, with difficult entry and exit. It has always been so, and buyers have accepted it. But the statistics tell us that Britons are getting bigger – not to say Americans – and we are surely approaching the point where it may be too small for its own good. In fact our largest staff members (the largest of all scaling 16½ stone and 6ft 2in.) found the interior space just sufficient with the driver's seat moved to its back stop, but complained of their inability to shift position to relieve numb spots. More serious were the contortions involved in getting in and out, even with the hood down.

The seats do not look especially inviting, reminding one of the shapeless BMC equipment of a few years ago. This is doing them less than justice. Together with the generally tight confines of the interior they locate driver and passenger well, and they do their best to damp out the effects of the generally mediocre ride. The ride itself will not disappoint Midget enthusiasts and could only be described, euphemistically, as "good for the liver". The limited wheel travel and high spring rates give the Midget no chance of offering a comfortable ride and the result is misery when the car is driven quickly on any uneven surface, let alone a really rough one. On the credit side it is very rare for the suspension actually to bottom, and the 1500 is notably free of the crashes and bangs which afflicted some earlier Midgets, especially when their dampers were past the first flush of youth. Nor is the handling very much affected by suspension movement, so a driver fit enough to withstand the battering can make rapid progress along almost any British road.

Bigger Triumph 1500TC engine does not look unduly large under Midget bonnet, with plenty of length to spare and room for the massive heater trunking. Access to some items is good, but others (such as battery behind heater blower unit) are difficult to reach

Above: Black crackle-finished facia panel gives slightly vintage air to the interior. Rev counter and speedometer are widely separated but can still be seen inside rim of large steering wheel. Minor dials are less easily read

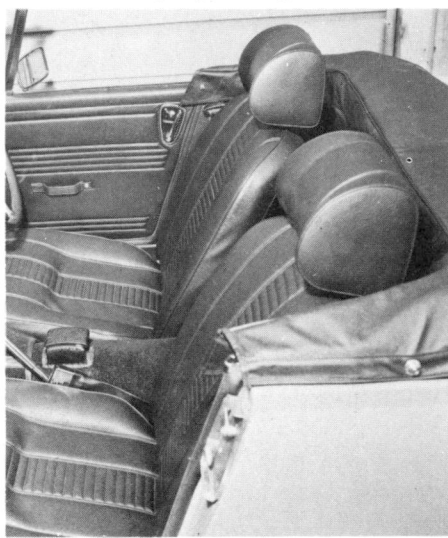

Left: Midget seats look rather stylized but not very well shaped; in fact they are quite comfortable, damping out the worst effects of the ride, while the small size of the interior ensures good location. Note the awkwardly-placed door handle by the occupant's shoulder

Boot lid is supported by a single self-locking strut. Capacity is strictly limited and there is a low sill over which luggage must be lifted. Spare wheel and fuel tank lie flat on the boot floor and beneath it respectively

The controls are not well laid out, but at least they are easy to understand and are clearly labelled. There are signs of penny-pinching in the single (too slow) speed wipers, the manual-plunger washer, the primitive heater control. Of the major controls, the steering wheel is larger than one might expect and close to the chest by modern standards; the pedals are understandably close together in their narrow tunnel. Clutch effort is high but pedal movement limited, though the clutch takes up sweetly enough. In the test car, however, the accelerator linkage was rather "sudden" and no help to gentle driving. The gearchange is precise but not as quick as some of its rivals.

A major drawback of the Midget is its high interior noise level. For the most part it is made up of wind noise, which drowns the other components to the extent where one is unsure how much contribution the engine is making until one switches off and coasts at high speed. The wind noise itself comes from the hood, and while this may seem inevitable there are other soft-top cars which do not suffer in the same way (or at least, not to the same extent). In the Midget's case it is noticeable that the car is much quieter with the hood down, and the radio easier to hear, at speeds as high as 70 mph. Indeed, with the hood up the radio is almost inaudible above this speed. The

engine actually makes a lot of noise at higher speeds – it simply can't compete with the wind roar. Induction and exhaust noise is high when the car is accelerating hard, at anything over 5,000 rpm; but when the car is driven more gently the 1500 unit is quiet and refined. Noisy or not, it is very smooth right up to the red line and beyond, in a way that may surprise MG diehards.

Even with the hood up, visibility is not bad. At first sight the windscreen is shallow but it seems to provide sufficient view for short and tall drivers; the hinged quarter-lights obstruct the front-quarter view a little, but the "over-the-shoulder" blind spot is cleared by two extra windows let into the hood. Two door mirrors are standard, but on the test car they continually flopped down to a useless position. The wipers clear only a small area of screen and are too slow to cope with heavy rain. Sealed-beam headlights give good illumination at night but the driver's low eyeline prevents him making the most of it. Reversing lights are standard.

The heater is a primitive affair with a single push-pull control for temperature, and a single-speed fan which can only be switched on when full heat is selected. There is no means of selecting airflow to screen or floor, the output being shared arbitrarily. However, the fan is quiet and the heater clears the screen quickly even in humid conditions. There is no direct-flow ventilation other than via the quarter-lights.

Living with the Midget 1500
By comparison with Midget hoods of a few years ago that of the 1500 is easy to contend with. It is not yet a simple one-handed operation either to stow or erect it, though, and in particular it is much easier to fit its leading edge to the windscreen rail if four hands are available. With the hood down one does not get too battered by the airflow, even at high speed, but one driver found that when driving open in light rain the inside of the windscreen soon became covered in droplets and the occupants of the car dampened.

A basic appeal of the Midget is its simplicity, and this is still so with the 1500 which is no more difficult to work on than its predecessors. The most awkward servicing point is the need

to reach the battery at the very rear of the engine compartment under the hinge line of the bonnet; the dipstick is not easy to find, especially in the dark. A link with tradition is the need to attend to eight grease points during the 6,000-mile service – but there are no intermediate service intervals, so an average car requires only twice-a-year attention.

A main drawback of the car is its small (7-gallon) tank, which gives a safe range of less than 200 miles. It is filled via a simple cap in the rear panel, and unlike many modern tanks can be filled quickly to the brim with no danger of blow-back.

There are few accessories to be added to the Midget from the MG option list. A hardtop is expensive but might prove an investment in terms of reduced wind noise and long-journey comfort; wire wheels are available for those who can face the chore of cleaning them; and head restraints may be specified. There is no overdrive option, far less an automatic. Static seat belts are standard – apparently there is no room for inertia-reel units.

In conclusion
There is no doubt that the performance of the Midget has been greatly improved by its change of engine, and there is now a spread of torque which allows the car to be driven sportingly or to be lugged along all the way in top gear by a lazy or tired driver. At the same time the handling has suffered in some respects and the car is no longer as predictable or forgiving as it was.

People are bound to differ on how badly cramped they find the interior (though few will argue with the infuriating difficulty of reaching the interior door handles), but few would quarrel with the conclusion that the ride is harsh and the noise level over-high.

Now that the Midget and the Spitfire share the same engine, the question of their joint survival must arise. For our money – and there is scant price difference between the two – the Spitfire is much more practical and civilized. There will always be those who will scorn it for precisely those reasons, but if further rationalization comes to pass it will be difficult to make out a case for the Midget *vis-à-vis* its stablemate. □

MANUFACTURER:
British Leyland UK Ltd., Austin-Morris Division, Longbridge, Birmingham

PRICES		Insurance	Group 5
Basic	£1,333.00		
Special Car Tax	£111.08	**EXTRAS (inc VAT)**	
VAT	£115.53	Wire wheels	£56.12
Total (in GB)	**£1,559.61**	Hard top	£112.09
Seat Belts, static type	(standard)	Head restraints *	£18.27
Licence	£40.00	*Fitted to test car*	
Delivery charge (London)	£15.00		
Number plates	£6.60		
Total on the Road (exc		**TOTAL AS TESTED ON**	
Insurance)	**£1,621.21**	**THE ROAD**	**£1,639.48**

*The first of the really modern MG sports cars, the MGA is
now a collectors item*

MG Record Breakers: pictures 1 and 2 show Ex 135, in which Goldie Gardner broke so many records; 3, 4 and the main picture show the tear-shaped Ex 181, driven by Stirling Moss

1

2

3

4

Fastest of the current MGs, the B GT V8, with 3½ litres of Rover engine

You can do it in an MG

ALAN COREN recalls his first sports car.

THE first car I ever owned was an MG PA Midget, five years my senior; which no doubt entitled it to the mastery over me it always showed. Its sturdy little doors were bound to its sturdy little body with piano wire (since what it conspicuously lacked were sturdy little hinges), and when you hit the brakes, the speedometer fell in your lap. In wet weather, it was fitted with a passenger, this being the only method of holding the roof on, and the combined roar of engine, exhaust, tappets, rear-axle whine and wind was a feature that has left me with a permanent shout: even today, gliding along on the silken purr of some modern seven-bearing crank-shaft, I have difficulty in talking below a shriek.

Now, some of you may feel that, as far as sales pitches go, they have come across more seductive examples. You are, with respect, wrong: when I bought the above item in 1959, it was twenty-five years old, had passed through almost as many hands, had been caned across some

two hundred thousand miles of rough road, yet it remained not only an object of joy and love, but would also have gone up the North Face of the Eiger in third, if one had managed to get a decent run at it.

It cost twelve quid; and even granted that inflation has accelerated at a rate that would leave any sports car at the post, that was still not exactly a king's ransom in 1959. And yet, in terms of the mystique it conferred and the delight it afforded, its true value was incalculable.

Even stationary, the Midget did all I ever asked of it, viz. snatch girls' eyes from less worthy occupations and draw their attention to an object which might otherwise have passed as unnoticed as any other pimply duffle. After which, it was then up to me to capitalise upon it; and it is fair to say that to MG must go the credit for much of my character-development, required as I was to live up to the image of a dashing adventurer, a heroic hedonist, a bit of a dog, yet a mature and capable man withal, a bloke

with the enviable gift of twitching something volatile out of the wet on a dodgy corner.

That is one of the great strengths of the sports car; it can be all things to all men, conferring maturity on youth, and youth on middle-age – I now recognise that there is no better rejuvenator for both the ego and the image than some-thing low, snorty and mutli-carburetted. It is far less painful than having your follicles transplanted, and far less ridiculous than forcing your welling gut into a pair of flared hipsters.

All of this ego-boosting may well apply to women, too: I am constantly being told that girls are unconcerned with the panache bestowed by this motor car or that, but having seen a number of them hacking a roaring piece of pastel-painted metal away from the lights, giant sunglasses shoved with careful abandon into their coiffes and the dainty left hand twinkling over the gearstick for all the world like something attached to a busty Fittipaldi, I beg leave to entertain my doubts.

I thought long about the wisdom of saying what I finally decided to say next; I have spent large chunks of my writing life in attacking advertisements of one kind or another, usually on the basis of their nonsensical claims or the pre-posterous life-style they promote, and nothing sets my molars grinding more than a palpable lie tarted up to pass for truth. I naturally worried, therefore, whether I ought to bring this chat about sports cars in general down to the specific object of this advertisement by saying that the name MG is virtually synony-mous with the words sports car.

What persuaded me to say that it was is the fact that it is true, and there is no denying it is true, and it is as good a way as any of moving from the general to the particular, since everything I have said about sports cars applies emphatically to the MG. It is an evocative and a haunting name, girt with romance and nostalgia, calling up another era. In a modern MG, one not only slips into the role of present hero, one picks up the accumulated heroics of all the blokes who ever sat behind that thrilling wheel-boss and its poetic enamelling.

In short, it is nice to think that there are still MGs around to drive.

153

MGB GT

1877 1977

**Cheerful facelift for Leyland's veteran sports car.
Suspension modifications restore its enjoyable handling.
New seats and facia cannot disguise the MG's age.
Outperformed in almost every respect by newer designs,
it is fading quietly away in a shrinking corner of the market**

NOF 480R

TO DESCRIBE the MGB as an "evergreen" is surely one of motoring's great understatements. Introduced in 1962, it has been an old favourite, or an evergreen, for going on 10 years.

In many ways it symbolises all that is best and worst about British cars. This classic sports car design is one which has sold tremendously well world wide; a credit to its designers. But, on the other hand, it has remained largely unchanged save for cosmetic or safety modifications during its life. Critics have written themselves to distraction pointing out its inadequacies, a monument to that dubious philosophy "If it sells, why bother to improve it"

At least, that seemed to be the case until last year, when much to everyone's surprise a revised MGB appeared with almost all the detailed points of criticism improved. As we said in our news headline at the time: "Facelift for MGB — at last". The 14-years-on improvements were a restyled facia, new heater controls, fabric seats, modified pedal layout, and a variety of minor mechanical changes.

These latter were mainly aimed at improving the handling and roadholding which had suffered when the B's ride height was raised to accommodate the American specification bumpers a year previously. Though the ride height remained unaltered, the open car was given a front anti-roll bar, having previously not had one, while the GT's was increased to the same thickness. Both models also gained a rear anti-roll bar for the first time. At the same time the steering wheel size was reduced to 15in. and the rack ratio increased from three to three-and-a-half turns from lock to lock.

Despite its rarely changing specification and performance that is bettered by more family saloons each year, the MGB goes on, selling in numbers that surprise even some Leyland executives. The detail changes give us reason to re-examine the MGB GT, a model that we last "re-examined" in 1971.

Like Wimbledon, the MGB seems to have becomes part of the British summertime sporting tradition and it too has compromised only a little to meet changing demands. The massive, rubber faced Federal safety bumpers are viturally the only exterior styling change to the GT

Performance

The weight increase caused by the massive American bumpers has not helped performance, but, more significantly, during the MGB's lifetime the whole concept of what is acceptable performance has changed. The GT's acceleration must now rate as slow, even by family car standards; yet when it first appeared, back in 1965, this sort of performance was quite acceptable.

Maximum speed in direct top corresponds closely with the 5,500 rpm power peak at 99 mph, the best leg of the MIRA banking giving 101 mph. Overdrive is available on both top and third gears, gearing up top by some 20 per cent. But the car is not keen to pull the higher gearing and the overdrive maximum is very wind-dependent. With the wind slightly in its favour, the GT's one-leg best was 104 mph, but the mean was still just 99 mph.

Straight line acceleration is really very modest. The B manages 60 mph in 14 seconds, which is a second slower than the GT we tested six years ago. Power output has not changed significantly over the years, so the main reason for the lower acceleration must be that kerb weight is up from 21.2 to 21.6 cwt.

Power output is currently 84 bhp at 5,500 rpm, and maximum torque 105 lb. ft. at 2,500 rpm. The quoted figures have varied slightly during the past few years as the B-series engine has been modified for emission control regulations, and these regulations have also been responsible for the loss of some of the unit's former character.

Never noted for its free-revving liveliness, the B-series engine was always a solid, durable unit with a broad spread of power and a complete absence of fussiness. Unfortunately, the emission-inspired changes have seen the delightful low speed torque replaced by a succession of flat spots. Our test engine was also seriously guilty of running on, a not uncommon B-series problem, and pinked under load — fairly familiar problems with some emission modified engines.

The B's gearchange is one of its most characteristic features, and one which has not been spoiled by the advancing years. It is the true sports car shift; a short, gaitered lever, ready to hand and offering notchy, firm, yet very precise movements through its accurate gate. Overdrive is, of course, standard, and one of the improvements on the latest car has been to re-locate the operating switch away from the facia and onto the gear-lever knob. For the first time, an MGB driver can now change gear and operate the overdrive without taking both hands off the wheel!

Gear ratios are unchanged and so the rather low second gear remains

More dramatic changes inside where the scattered dashboard has been re-fashioned and the seats given a new deckchair striped cloth facing

The rear bench is really a nominal plus-two, being flat and hard with very limited head and legroom for all but the smallest children

MGB GT

— even holding on to 6,000 rpm only gives a maximum of 50 mph. On the other hand, overdrive third, allowing up to 95 mph, is a superb ratio and the car can be driven over give-and-take routes for miles, flicking between third and overdrive third.

Economy
The B-series engine is inherently an economical unit, and even in MGB tune it returns impressive consumption figures. Of course, overdrive is a great asset in the pursuit of good fuel consumption. Our steady-speed fuel consumption figures show what sort of difference it makes — around 14 per cent at 70 and 80 mph, the sort of speeds at which it is most likely to be used. Indeed, overdrive makes 30 mpg motorway cruising a ready possibility, as the figures show, and our own journeys confirmed this. While our overall consumption dropped to 25.7 mpg, journeys with a large element of motorway all hovered near the 30 mpg mark.

Handling
The 1½ in. increase in ride height needed to meet American bumper regulations had quite disastrous effects on the handling and roadholding of the B which was formerly a well-balanced, emminently driveable sports car. Instead, the open version which we tested shortly after the change was found to have heavy roll oversteer and a very twitchy response.

Thankfully, the anti-roll bar modifications have now largely cleared up the problem — though it must remain a mystery why Leyland did not provide them from the start. With the changes, the car has now reverted a good way back to its original levels of handling and roadholding.

The B has never been the sort of sports car to set standards in roadholding; its crude lever arm dampers and basic, leaf-spring rear axle see to that. Rather the pleasure of driving it has come from its taut and predictable reactions. An initial modest understeer gives way, as cornering speeds build up, to readily controllable oversteer. Ultimate levels of roadholding are not high, but the car's controllability makes it fun to drive.

The lower-geared rack has made the steering significantly lighter, its heaviness being a noticeable feature of past MGs. Though the steering wheel is a little smaller, it is still too large for some tastes, and certainly its rim is too thin.

Brakes are first class, with servo assistance allowing near 1g stops with only 60lb pedal effort. The 10-stop fade test showed up no problems.

Ride and noise
Once again, the B has been overtaken by later designs in the handling/ride compromise. Newer cars have managed to combine good handling with a higher all-round level

of ride comfort than the MG's. Its ride is quite firm — hard if compared with saloons of similar performance — and would once have been thought typically sports car-ish if more recent cars had not proved otherwise. The harshness is especially noticeable on rougher roads, when the lever arm dampers and leaf springs get caught out from time to time over successions of bumps.

However, worst aspect of overall driving comfort is the noise level inside the GT. The door window sealing is very poor and at any speed above 60 mph the roar of wind completely drowns conversation or radio. It is a long-standing problem, yet appears to have received no attention. The engine is also surprisingly noisy; despite now having an electric fan it still suffers from just the sort of noise one would expect from a big, belt-driven fan.

Behind the wheel
The MG has the sort of cockpit that marks it out as a sports car of the traditional school; seats are set close to the floor and legs stretch out horizontally along the sides of the large central tunnel. The facia and steering wheel dominate the small cabin.

The new facia is certainly a pleasant change, even if it has been a long time coming. The dashboard shape is unchanged, as is the material, but its black crackle finish has been toned down to a more restrained grey. It is the instrumen-

The new facia is a considerable improvement, though the new shape steering wheel masks the smaller dials and the piano key switches can be confusing. Speedometer and rev counter face the driver with a fuel gauge between and oil pressure, water temperature to the left and right. The left stalk operates wipers/washers and the right lights and indicators, while a small flip switch by this is the lights master control. The ignition key is hidden awkwardly forward and below these. Below the central piano key switches for heated rear screen, map light, fan and hazard flashers are the manual choke, map light and rotary heater controls

ENGINE
	Front; rear drive
Cylinders	4-in-line
Main bearings	5
Cooling	water
Fan	Electric
Bore, mm (in.)	80.26 (3.16)
Stroke, mm (in.)	88.90 (3.50)
Capacity, c.c. (in³)	1,798 c.c. (109.7)
Valve gear	Ohv
Camshaft drive	Chain
Compression ratio	9.0-to-1
Octane rating	97 RM
Carburettors	Twin SU HIF4
Max power	84 bhp (DIN) at 5,500 rpm
Max torque	105 lb.ft. at 2,500 rpm

TRANSMISSION
Type four-speed, all synchromesh, o/drive on 3rd and 4th

Gear	Ratio	mph/1000rpm
O/d Top	0.820	21.83
Top	1.000	17.90
O/d 3rd	1.133	15.81
3rd	1.382	12.96
2nd	2.167	8.26
1st	3.036	5.20
Final drive gear	Hypoid bevel	
Ratio	3.909-to-1	

SUSPENSION
Front—location	Double wishbones
—springs	Coil
—dampers	Lever
—anti-roll bar	Yes
Rear—location	Live axle
—springs	Leaf
—dampers	Lever
—anti-roll bar	Yes

STEERING
Type	Rack and pinion
Power assistance	No
Wheel diameter	15.0 in.

BRAKES
Front	10.75 in. dia disc
Rear	10.00 in. dia drum
Servo	Yes

WHEELS
Type	Steel
Rim width	5J
Tyres—make	Pirelli Cinturato
—type	Radial ply
—size	165SR14

EQUIPMENT
Battery	12 volt 66 Ah
Alternator	45 amp 18 ACR
Headlamps	55-55 watt halogen
Reversing lamp	Standard
Hazard warning	Standard
Screen wipers	Two-speed and flick wipe
Screen washer	Electric
Interior heater	Water valve
Interior trim	Fabric seats, pvc headlining
Floor covering	Carpet
Jack	Pillar
Jacking points	4
Windscreen	Laminated
Underbody protection	Bitumastic

MAINTENANCE
Fuel tank	11 Imp gal (50 litres)
Cooling system	12 pints (inc heater)
Engine sump	6 pints SAE 20w/50
Gearbox	6 pints SAE 20w/50
Final drive	1½ pints SAE 90
Grease	7 points
Valve clearance	Inlet 0.013 in. (hot) Exhaust 0.013 in. (hot)
Contact breaker	0.014-0.016 in. gap
Ignition timing	10 deg BTDC (stroboscopic at 1,000 rpm)
Spark plug —type	Champion N9Y
—gap	0.025 in.
Tyre pressures	F21; R24 psi (normal driving)
Max payload	394 lb (179 kg)

Maximum Speeds

Gear	mph	kph	rpm
O/d Top (mean)	99	159	4,520
(best)	104	167	4,750
Top	99	159	5,500
O/d 3rd	95	153	6,000
3rd	78	125	6,000
2nd	.50	80	6,000
1st	31	50	6,000

Acceleration

True mph	Time (sec)	Speedo mph
30	4.8	31
40	7.0	40
50	9.3	50
60	14.0	60
70	19.1	70
80	28.5	80
90	35.7	90

Standing ¼-mile:
19.1 sec, 70 mph
Kilometre:
36.4 sec, 91 mph

mph	O/d Top	Top	O/d 3rd	3rd	2nd
10-30	—	12.5	—	7.6	4.4
20-40	17.1	11.5	9.1	6.8	4.3
30-50	16.3	9.9	8.3	6.8	5.0
40-60	16.8	10.9	10.2	7.7	—
50-70	16.7	16.9	14.1	9.3	—
60-80	21.8	22.2	16.4	11.7	—
70-90	—	32.0	22.0	—	

Consumption

Fuel
Overall mpg: **25.7**
(10.99 litres / 100km)
Calculated (DIN) mpg: 27.1
(10.42 litres / 100km)

Constant speed:

mph	mpg	O/d Top
30	48.0	55.6
40	41.3	50.5
50	37.2	44.2
60	34.2	36.7
70	29.8	33.7
80	25.6	29.2
90	22.9	25.1

Autocar formula
Hard driving, difficult conditions
23.1 mpg
Average driving, average conditions
28.3 mpg
Gentle driving, easy conditions
33.4 mpg
Grade of fuel: Premium, four star
(97 RM)
Mileage recorder: 1.8 per cent
over-reading

Oil
Consumption negligible

Brakes

Fade (from 70 mph in neutral)
Pedal load for 0.5g stops (lb)

	start/end		start/end
1	30/30	6	30/35
2	35/35	7	30/35
3	30/35	8	30/35
4	30/35	9	30/35
5	30/35	10	30/35

Response (from 30 mph in neutral)

Load (lb)	g	Distance (ft)
20	0.25	120
40	0.65	46
60	0.95	31.7
Handbrake	0.35	86
Max gradient: 1 in 3		

Clutch Pedal 25lb and 5½ in

Test Conditions

Wind: 5-20 mph
Temperature: 12 deg C (54 deg F)
Barometer: 29.6 in. Hg
Humidity: 100 per cent
Surface: wet Ashphalt and concrete
Test distance 1,224 miles

Figures taken at 9,500 miles by our
own staff at the Motor Industry
Research Association proving ground at
Nuneaton.

All Autocar test results are subject to
world copyright and may not be
reproduced in whole or part without the
Editor's written permission

Regular Service

Interval (miles)

Change	3,000	6,000	12,000
Engine oil	Check	Yes	Yes
Oil filter	—	Yes	Yes
Gearbox oil	Check	Check	Check
Spark plugs	—	Clean	Yes
Air cleaner	—	—	Yes
C/breaker	—	—	Yes

| Total cost | £7.15 | £23.24 | £31.85 |

(Assuming labour at £5 50/hour)

Parts Cost

(including VAT)

Brake pads (2 wheels)—front	£14.04
Brake shoes (2 wheels)—rear	£8.86
Silencer(s)	£38.34
Tyre—each (typical advertised)	£29.50
Windscreen	£22.95
Headlamp unit	£4.86
Front wing	£52.38
Rear bumper	£27.81

Warranty Period
12 months / unlimited mileage

Weight

Kerb, 21.8 cwt / 2,442lb /
1,108 kg
(Distribution F/R, 52/48)
As tested, 25.0 cwt / 2,800lb /
1,271 kg

Boot capacity: 9.6 cu.ft.

Turning circles:
Between kerbs L, 33ft. 11in. R,
35ft. 1 in.
Between walls L, 34ft. 2in. R,
35ft. 4 in.
Turns, lock-to-lock: 3.5

OVERALL LENGTH 13' 2·25"
OVERALL WIDTH 5' 1·75"
OVERALL HEIGHT 4' 3"
GROUND CLEARANCE 5"
WHEELBASE 7' 7"
FRONT TRACK 4' 1"
REAR TRACK 4' 1·25"

Test Scorecard

(Average of scoring by
Autocar Road Test team)

Ratings: 6 Excellent
5 Good
4 Above average
3 Below average
2 Poor
1 Bad

PERFORMANCE	3.16
STEERING AND HANDLING	3.83
BRAKES	4.20
COMFORT IN FRONT	3.00
DRIVERS AIDS	3.37
(instruments, lights, wipers, visibility, etc)	
CONTROLS	3.50
NOISE	2.83
STOWAGE	3.33
ROUTINE SERVICE	3.90
(under-bonnet access dipstick, etc)	
EASE OF DRIVING	4.00
OVERALL RATING	**3.52**

Comparisons

Car	Price (£)	Max mph	0-60 (sec)	Overall mpg	Capacity (c.c.)	Power (bhp)	Wheelbase (in.)	Length (in.)	Width (in.)	Kerb wt lb	Fuel (gal)	Tyre size
MGB GT	**3,576**	**99**	**14.0**	**25.7**	**1,798**	**84**	**91.0**	**158.3**	**61.8**	**2,442**	**11.0**	**165x14**
Colt Celeste 2000GT	3,349	104	11.2	24.9	1,995	98	92.1	162.0	63.0	2,190	9.9	165x13
Toyota Celica Liftback ST	3,413	102	12.7	27.6	1,968	96	98.2	166.9	63.8	2,356	12.8	165x14
Triumph TR7	3,371	109	9.1	26.4	1,998	105	85.0	160.0	66.3	2,206	12.0	175/70x13
Fiat X1/9	3,298	99	12.7	30.7	1,290	73	86.8	150.8	61.8	2,016	10.5	165/70x13
Ford Capri 2000S	3,522	106	10.4	24.0	1,993	99	101.0	171.0	67.0	2,273	12.7	165x13

tation and switchgear that has been most thoroughly revised and improved.

Speedometer and rev counter still sit in front of the driver, viewed through the steering wheel, with its new four-spoke design, but the oil pressure and water temperature gauges are now separated and lie to the outside of the main dials. The fuel gauge sits in the centre, between the two main instruments. Though the dials are crisply numbered and easily read, unfortunately the oil and water gauges are hidden by the driver's hands.

The formerly chaotic muddle of switches has also been rationalized into a tidy row under the central pair of fresh-air vents, operating heated rear screen, map light, heater fan, and hazard flashers. The piano-key switches are all clearly labelled but pose the problem common to this sort of layout, in that it is easy to flip the wrong one until touch-familiar with their location. Stalk controls operate wipers and indicators together with light dipping and flashing. The lights master switch sits to the right of the steering wheel at the base of the column. Near it is the ignition switch, which is fiddly and awkward to use, buried deep in the column and having a tiny tab to release the key from the lock.

The map light is now a small, rotateable affair, mounted on top of the centre console between the cigarette lighter and choke lever. Below is space for the optional radio and ranged below that again are the heater controls, with a clock set between them. The heater is the same old water-valve unit, which means that the temperature is awkward to regulate accurately. But the controls have been usefully improved and now comprise two clearly-marked circular knobs, for attempted temperature regulation and distribution. The two fresh-air vents give a good airflow, but extraction is improved by opening a rear-quarter window.

A very visible improvement to the MGB is the new seating material, a vivid deckchair-striped nylon cloth that faces the wearing surfaces. Our test car was trimmed in discreet shades of grey, but there are other, much more lurid trim colours available. The material looks very chic, just the sort of thing for the market the car is aimed at, and is certainly a lot more comfortable than the old vinyl.

The seats are unchanged in design and are as comfortable as ever, with plenty of lateral support around the thigh and back. They can be partially reclined, but by awkward-to-use levers mounted on the backrests. Adjustable headrests are also fitted. The straight-legged seating position allows drivers of most heights to find a comfortable position behind the wheel. Revised pedal positions allow heeling-and-toeing — 14 years after we complained in our road test of the then new car that this was impossible.

Behind the front seats is a candy-stripe bench which is really

Familiar B-series engine has lost some of its sparkle through emission tuning, which has also cluttered the engine bay with pipework

The modest boot extends usefully in size when the rear seat back is folded and loading is easy through the deep tailgate. Below: Spare wheel and jack stow under the floor

only suitable for small children, leg and headroom being much too restricted to carry anyone larger except perhaps a single adult sitting crosswise. The bench is crude and flat, held in place just by "lift-the-dot" style fasteners, so that it can be easily removed for access to the battery. The seat back can be unclipped and folded down on it to extend the luggage area.

The MG is, of course, much more of a pure sports car than most of its newer two-plus-two rivals, and, in consequence, its boot space is fairly modest. It does extend usefully, however, if the rear seat is folded flat. The wheel arches, which have the large inertia reels of the seat belts mounted awkwardly on top of them, do intrude to some extent, and the spare wheel is stowed along with the jack under the boot floor.

Access to the boot is easy through the full-depth tailgate, but the latter's remarkably strong springs send it slamming down hard at the slightest provocation. Aside from the boot, stowage space is very restricted; just the glovebox, a map bin in front of the passenger's door, and a small box under the central armrest. But, at last, the glovebox can be opened without a key (though it is still lockable) so saving the owner the irritation of having to stop and remove the ignition keys to read a map.

In service

The MGB is a straightforward, uncomplicated car, as easy to service and maintain as it is to drive. Starting is straightforward, using the manual choke, but the car does not run happily from cold, being rather jerky and fluffy.

Under the bonnet, the once-so-simple B-series engine is how heavily disguised by emission plumbing. But it is still essentially a straightforward engine to service. The distributor and spark plugs are accessible, the rocker box easily removed for tappet adjustment, and items like the coil and fluid reservoirs are all to hand.

The fuel tank holds 11 gallons and fills through an unobstructed neck that has a twist-off cap. Reversing lamps, two exterior mirrors, a laminated screen, and

halogen headlamps are all now fitted as standard. Service interval is 6,000 miles, with an optional 3,000 mile check, and the Supercover warranty can be extended to two years for a modest charge.

Where it fits in

Now that the V8 GT has been discontinued, there are two versions of the MGB — the open sports and the GT. The latter is considerably more expensive, at £3,576, compared with the open car which costs £2,854.

There are now a number of other sporting two-plus-twos, some more obviously sporting than others. The Ford Capri is perhaps the most attractive, the 2000S at £3,522 being a close price rival for the MGB GT.

The Japanese also have recent rivals to offer; from Colt, the 2-litre Celeste at £3,349, and from Toyota the 2000ST liftback at £3,413. The VW Scirocco at £4,161 is perhaps a little expensive for comparison, but there are a number of other coupés that do not have hatchbacks which come into the price range — the Opel Manta 1.9SR, Lancia Beta 1600, and even the Ford Escort RS2000.

Conclusion

The MGB is now so aged and out-paced as to be strictly a minority taste; it is easily outsold by Leyland's newer sports car, the TR7. Certainly the modifications improve it, but it is incredible to think that one has had to wait 14 years for little things like the glovebox lock alteration.

The facia is tidier and the seating material very smart, but they are reminiscent of the facelift on an ageing film star — they cannot hide all the cracks. Presumably the MGB is now in that sort of ageing car's limbo where its sales generate enough profit to keep it in production, but not sufficient to encourage the sort of substantial re-design it needs.

As it is, it remains a pleasant to drive, easy to service and maintain GT car, with classically sporting lines and predictable handling, yet very modest performance.

MANUFACTURER:	
Leyland Cars	
Grosvenor House	
Redditch, Worcestershire	
PRICES	
Basic	£3,056.00
Special Car Tax	£254.67
VAT	£264.85
Total (in GB)	**£3,575.52**
Seat belts	Standard
Licence	£50.00
Delivery charge (London)	£47.50
Number plates	£7.50
Total on the Road	**£3,680.82**
(exc insurance)	
Insurance	Group 6
EXTRAS (inc VAT)	
Wire wheels	£80.84
TOTAL AS TESTED	
ON THE ROAD	**£3,680.82**

INDEX